SECRET GARDENS OF THE CITY OF LONDON

First Published in 2020.

ISBN 9798675300686

Front Cover Art and Design by Stephen Liddell

Dedication

This book is dedicated to Tash Leventis, who is as beautiful and spiritual as any garden here but a whole lot nosier and giver of epic hugs.

And also to someone who loves exploring the alleys and lanes of old London town as much as I do; my friend and one of the best guides in London, Kevin Pearman.

Sir, if you wish to have a just notion of the magnitude of this city, you must not be satisfied with seeing its great streets and squares, but must survey the innumerable little lanes and courts. **- Dr Samuel Johnson**

Table of Contents

Page

Preface

I've been creating and running unique walking tours in London for almost 7 years now with my company Ye Olde England Tours. I've always enjoyed exploring; it doesn't matter if it is a desert, a forest or London.

Without including neighbouring and adjoining satellite towns, Greater London itself is 611 square miles or 1,572 square kilometres. It is composed of dozens of once tiny villages and settlements that have grown together over 2,000 years to create the great city that we live, work and travel in.

There is London and then there is the City of London, or Londinium as the Romans called it. The oldest part of the city; the City or Square Mile. Full of the buildings and institutions that have shaped our lives and not just our world, but the world.

Greater London itself has just been declared the world's first National Park City with 50% of it being in some way green or indeed blue; gardens, footpaths and bridleways of course, canals, rivers, woods and parks. Many of them are known well beyond our shores, Hyde Park, Richmond Park, Wimbledon Common, Hampstead Heath to name but a few. Like many of the most famous districts, streets and buildings, they are not really in London but in places such as Westminster or Chelsea.

The real London, the City of London, is something of a mystery to many, even those who work here every day, decade after decade. It has none of the wide streets of the West End or the mile upon mile of well-to-do housing of Notting Hill or Kensington. And maybe that is why it remains a mystery. Between St Paul's Cathedral and the Tower of London is largely a hidden world all shaped by geography, Romans, Vikings, Saxons and the dynasties that came after the Norman invasions, the Great and not so great fires, the plagues and other natural disasters and all those wars.

Several of my tourists from neurological professions have told me that it is medically proven that those few people who know London like the back of their hand end up with such a specially wired brain that they have a higher inbuilt resistance to diseases such as Alzheimer's, London being such an unfathomable maze. An epic, senseless mess of a place until one learns every road, every alley, every wild goose chase of a short cut and dead end… then it makes perfect sense.

I still remember the day when the first steps towards writing this book took place. It was a freezing cold, muddy December day in 2017. I was out exploring so many of the multitude of lanes and courts that Dr Johnson himself would have been proud of me. There came a point towards the end of the day when I realised my shoes were muddy. Not dirty from the odd puddle or the natural winter grime of a big city but caked in mud. I realised that in all my life I had been to London to work, to study, to live, to shop, to eat, to enjoy culture, to date even but never before had my shoes got so muddy that I might as well have trudged miles through the Lake District.

It piqued my curiosity, all those little green spaces I vaguely knew of and no doubt countless more I was blissfully unaware of. Every one of these gardens or squares had a reason for being. They were all different and largely overlooked even by workers passing the nearest busy road, often just feet away.

I didn't think anyone else would be interested in my hare-brained line of thought. Of all the things to see in London, who would want to literally get away from it all? As it turned out tourists, like myself, were in awe that we could be standing in the middle of perhaps the most powerful and epic city of all time and yet be totally alone save for flowers, bushes, trees, butterflies, birds, mammals and more. Weekdays would see us barely meet anyone; weekends would see us meeting fewer still. I remember Boxing Day in 2018 and the 2nd of January 2020, when we didn't see a single person in the entire City of London.

Everyone who had been round with me had enjoyed it so much that it convinced me that these little secret and often sacred gardens should garner a little bit more publicity. Not too much of course, that would be a disaster! So I decided to write this book, a catalogue and guide to these pocket parks. Little did I know how many there would be. How many could there be within the Square Mile? 40? 50 perhaps. I can't have been thinking straight as I knew 70 or 80 off the top of my head but if I had known there were 124 gardens in the City of London then I might never have even started writing.

I've tried to make this as exhaustive as possible. I've walked down every road, lane and alley I could find and have been doing so for years. I've played hunches, and looked at old books and maps and the latest satellite imagery too. London is always changing, that's one of its great and sometimes annoying qualities. Several parks each year are renovated, new buildings spring up and even in the last year or two new developments have brought us gleaming new parks and open spaces in the City of London.

All the information and maps are as accurate as possible at the time of publication but if you spot something that needs updating or even a new garden that appears then do let me know and I'll credit you in any future edition.

This book doesn't claim to be in any way a garden encyclopaedia, it is just a guide to hopefully encourage more people to get the train or tube into the City of London and go off and explore this great old city that is so well visited and yet unexplored. Go out and find your own favourite garden, bench, tree or statue. I would say how badly could you get lost in a square mile? The answer is not only 'very' but also 'totally and utterly'.

If this book is anything then it is an act of love; I hope you'll forgive me this act of indulgence.

25 Cannon Street

At A Glance: Almost uniquely it seems in the City of London, these gardens don't seem to have an official name despite their prestigious location just across the road from St Paul's Cathedral.

Site location: New Change/Cannon Street
Postcode: EC4R 2YA
Grid ref: TQ325808
Type of site: Public Gardens
Date(s): 2000
Designer(s) Robert Myers Associates
Site ownership: Pembroke
Site management: Pembroke
Open to public?: Yes
Opening times: 24/7
Public transport - Tube Station: St Paul's (Central); Mansion House (District, Circle)   Contains OS data © Crown copyright and database rights 2020

History

This garden rather resembles a garden square one might find west of the city with a large oval lawn, surrounded by dense planting and a multitude of benches to sit and admire the garden or the fine view of the dome of St Paul's.

24 Cannon Street

It's a very pleasant place to spend some time, and the use of Portland stone walls and steps goes well with the adjoining Neo-classical building. Step out to the north and you might find a bust of Admiral Arthur Phillip which commemorates the discovery and fixing of the site of Sydney, Australia on 23rd January 1788. A few days later, on the 26th January, the ship's officers formally founded the modern nation of Australia. There are also two bronze plaques which show HMS Supply arriving in the bay, and the formal founding of the city by the officers on board.

The bust was not originally placed here but was relocated from St Mildred's church having been rescued from the destroyed church during WWII.

In May 2020 it was announced that the garden would be redeveloped and include a reflection pool with views of St Paul's.

Nearby you have One New Change which offers a birds-eye view of St Paul's but if you take a wander down Watling Street and turn right down Bow Lane not only do you get to experience a very pleasant neighbourhood but you end up at St Mary Aldermary.

Abchurch Yard

At a glance: Just off busy Cannon Street and a few minutes' walk from The Monument, Abchurch Yard is the former churchyard of St Mary Abchurch. The first references to a church on this site can be found in the 12th century and there are still a few remains of the churchyard from the early years of the 13th century that are visible south of the church.

Site location: Abchurch Lane

Postcode: EC4N 7BA

Grid ref: TQ327809

Size in hectares: 0.0325

Type of site: Square

Date(s): 12th and 14th century, 1681-6; 1877

Designer(s): Edward I'Anson was responsible for the paving of the churchyard.

Listed structures: St Mary Abchurch

Site ownership: Diocese of London

Site management: City of London Corporation

Open to public? Yes

Opening times: The square is always open. The Church: Mon-Thur 10.30am-3pm; Fri 10.30am-12noon

Public transport - Tube Stations: Monument (District, Circle)/Bank (Central, DLR, Northern, Waterloo & City); Cannon Street (District, Circle) and National Rail.

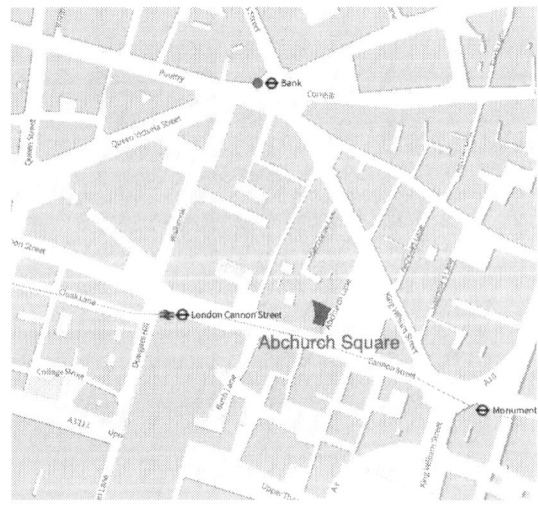

Contains OS data © Crown copyright and database rights 2019

History: The etymology of St Mary Abchurch has various origins and could possibly have been named after a benefactor called Abbe or Abbo, or it could be a corruption of Upchurch with it standing on comparatively high ground.

A daughter chapel of what is now Southwark Cathedral (St Mary Overie), the first reference to the church is in the 12th century to 'Robert, the priest of Habechirck'.

A 14th-century vaulted chamber was discovered beneath the churchyard after the bombings of WWII, which is believed to likely be the undercroft of a chapel.

St Mary Abchurch was badly damaged in the Great Fire and rebuilt by Sir Christopher Wren between 1681 and1686, and he might have moved the tower from south-west to its north-west position.

Back then the yard was an enclosed burial area and it remained that way through most of the 19th century until the Bishop of London sanctioned it to be opened up and paved over as a public space.

The church suffered bomb damage and was restored in 1945-57 with further restoration works occurring more recently.

The 1877 paving design by Edward l'Anson is still here with circular patterns in decorative paving stones and cobbles with seats by the wall of the church. Venture inside the church, and you can admire the splendid painting in the dome by William Snow with a representation of the Name of God in Hebrew.

Aldermanbury Square

At a glance: A lovely quiet spot not far from the old Roman barracks, where a century or two after the Romans left it is thought that the Anglo-Saxon Kings lived until Edward the Confessor established the Palace of Westminster.

Following substantial damage from the Blitz, Aldermanbury Square was drawn up in 1962 as part of the 1955 London Wall Plan. In 2006 it was again remodelled and it is now a traffic-free square complete with trees, public lighting, seats and even a water feature.

Site location: Aldermanbury Square
Postcode: EC2V 7HR
Grid ref: TQ324815
Size in hectares: 0.0306
Type of site: Square
Date(s): 1962 and 2000
Designer(s): Eric Parry Architects (2006)
Listed structures: None
Site ownership: City of London Corporation
Site management: Open Spaces Department
Open to public? Yes
Opening times: 24/7
Public transport - Tube Stations: Moorgate (Hammersmith & City, Circle, Northern, Metropolitan). **National Rail:** Moorgate

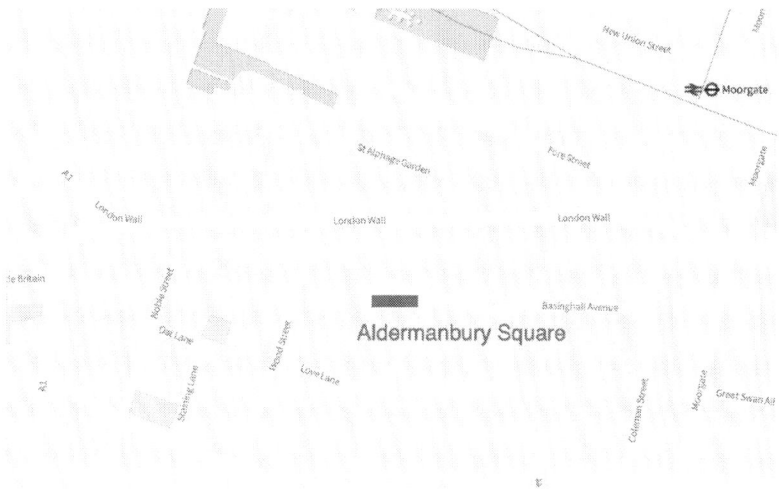

Aldermanbury Square

Contains OS data © Crown copyright and database rights 2019

History

Despite its long history, the real origins of Aldermanbury Square today are from the 1960s. It was laid out in 1962 and is bordered on the north side by the Brewers' Company Hall which has been here since around 1408 AD though rebuilt in 1958-60 after the earlier Hall, itself rebuilt after the Fire of London of 1666, was destroyed by bombing in 1940.

The layout of the new square came out of the post war London Wall Plan to reimagine a 28-acre area that had been so damaged during WWII, and it led to the creation of several of the open spaces in this guide and many made uses of the old Roman city walls.

Happily the plan had provision for gardens and open spaces such as Aldermanbury Square and several others in this guide, a number of these gardens featuring remains of the old Roman city walls such as the garden at St Alphage's Church.

Aldermanbury Square enjoyed a facelift for the Millennium. One of the additions was a bench which has been inscribed with some of the historical highlights of the site. 'Near this space stood the Augustinian Priory of Elsing Spital, 1329-1536 and since c1400 Brewers' Hall which was destroyed in the Great Fire of 1666 and Blitz of 1940 and rebuilt 1960'.

To celebrate the dawn of the second millennium, sculpture was put in places that includes the last words said by the mother of St Augustine; "Nothing is Distant from God" and as part of an ongoing 21st-century scheme, the square was made traffic free.

High quality natural stone has been used which is set off well by the 20 trees, soft landscaping, seats and the attractive water feature.

Aldgate Square

At a glance: Just two years ago there was no Aldgate Square but following years of construction in the area, we now have at the time of writing perhaps the newest public space at street level in the City and the largest new gardens in over 100 years.

Site location: Aldgate High Street
Postcode: EC3N 1AF
Grid ref: TQ335808
Size in hectares: 0.32 estimated
Type of site: Public Gardens
Date(s): 2018
Designer(s): Gillespies | Make Architects
Listed structures: None
Site ownership: City of London Corporation
Site management: Open Spaces Department
Open to public? Yes
Opening times: 24/7
Public transport - Tube Stations: Aldgate (Metropolitan and Circle) and Aldgate East (District and Hammersmith and City) **National Rail:** Fenchurch Street   Contains OS data © Crown copyright and database rights 2019

History

The £25m redevelopment of Aldgate Public Realm for The City of London Corporation took over seven years to complete and involved the rerouting of the existing gyratory to create one of the largest open spaces in the Square Mile.

It is located between Sir John Cass's Foundation Primary School and St Botolph Without Aldgate Church just west of Aldgate underground station.

The main square includes a central lawn area flanked by generous raised planters which provide informal seating. A majestic curve of pleached hornbeams provides cover and shade to the southern boundary. A water feature of parabolic jets is fascinating to watch and for play.

The social enterprise café, Kahaila, in Portsoken Pavilion, serves decadent cakes, artisan coffee and a variety of hot and cold breakfasts and lunches and, keeping the planet in mind, drinking fountains are also to be found in the square.

The square is centred round a new pavilion and comprises a large lawn with seating and a water feature.

The churchyard gardens have been enlarged to sensitively realign the setting of the church, bringing the focus back to the historic building and re-establishing its presence within Portsoken. The gardens are lush and include over 70 trees.

The new Aldgate Square looking west towards the City and The Scalpel building.

The completion of the square has significantly improved not only the appearance of the area but also the air quality within this part of London, signalling the importance of investing in high-quality public spaces.

Aldgate was one of the ancient gates into the City on the Roman Wall. The wall has gone (actually buried inside an old subway), but this is a great enhancement to this part of the City. Whilst you're here walk a few minutes towards the City and visit Mitre Square and St Katherine Cree.

All Hallows-by-the-Tower Churchyard

At a glance: Bordering the busy Byward Street, All Hallows was already ancient when the Tower of London was built.

Founded in 675 AD on land owned by the Abbey of Barking, this is the oldest surviving church in the City of London. Beneath this one time Saxon church there is even a section of 2nd-century Roman pavement and many other treasures including some great American history. Sadly much of the old church, which survived the Fire of London, was destroyed in WWII though grandly rebuilt. The churchyard was once larger but closed for burials in the 1850s and soon it was being used as public open space. The remaining garden area lies at the east end of the church, with areas of grass, trees and shrubs with some tombs and gravestones and a pleasant café.

Site location: Byward Street/Great Tower Street
Postcode: EC3R 5BJ
Grid ref: TQ333806
Size in hectares: 0.0705
Type of site: Churchyard
Date(s): 675 AD; 19th and 20th centuries
Designer(s): Unknown
Listed structures: All Hallows Church, railings and walls
Site ownership: Diocese of London
Site management: City of London Corporation Open Spaces Department and Friends of All Hallows
Open to public?: Yes

Opening times: 24/7 - Church open Mon-Fri 8am-6pm, Sat/Sun 10am-5pm except during services. Closed Bank Holidays
Public transport - Tube Stations: Tower Hill (Circle and District)
National Rail: Fenchurch Street

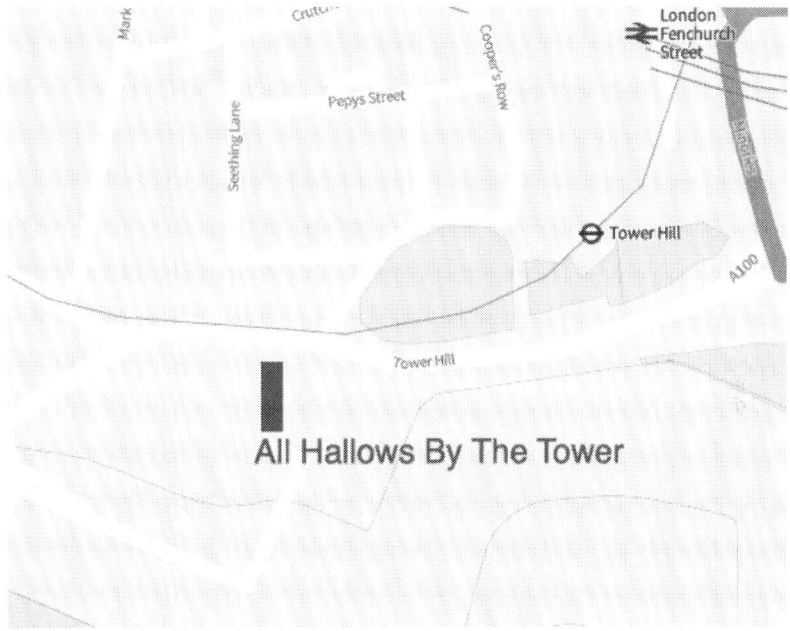

Contains OS data © Crown copyright and database rights 2019

History

All Hallows was founded in AD 675 around 400 years before the Tower of London was built. Saxon coffins have been found here and the WWII bombing revealed the oldest archway in London, once covered for centuries. In fact the undercroft of the church is a veritable treasure trove of not just ancient London but artefacts from across the Roman Empire and beyond.

Thanks to the orders of Admiral Sir William Penn of the nearby Navy Office who had the houses between the fire and the church and Navy Office demolished to prevent the spread of the fire, All Hallows escaped the Great Fire of London. However it was not so fortunate during 1940 when bomb damage reduced the old building to its tower, north and south walls and part of the east end.

Reconstruction works commenced in 1948, and the new church was dedicated by the Bishop of London on 23 July 1957. With the nearby St Dunstan-in-the-East also destroyed by bombing though not rebuilt, the parish was amalgamated with that of All Hallows.

All Hallows is associated with numerous well known historical figures including Samuel Pepys, who watched the Great Fire of London from the church tower. William Penn, son of Admiral Sir William Penn and later founder of Pennsylvania, was baptised here in 1644 whilst John Quincy-Adams, later the 6th President of the USA, was married here in 1797.

It is sometimes joked that the coffins here are the shortest in London given the amount of beheaded figures that were laid to rest here.

Partial remains of the churchyard garden can be found to the east of the church and consist of two grassy areas with tombs and gravestones. The Vestry Restaurant was added in the 1990s and the

All Hallows By The Tower with the Tower of London & Tower Bridge in the background.

remaining garden was opened up and then became more accessible to those with disabilities.

Befitting such a remarkable old church it is home to various traditions, none more interesting than the medieval tradition of Beating the Bounds each year on Ascension Day. The custom goes back to when parishes reaffirmed their boundaries by processing round them at Rogation Tide. They beat each boundary marker with wands and pray for protection and blessings for the land in the parish. I recently saw the Knollys Rose ceremony here too.

Whilst you're here why not walk up Seething Lane and visit Seething Lane Gardens and St Olave's.

All Hallows On The Wall

At a glance: Not the most tranquil garden but interesting nonetheless, this is really all that remains of the former churchyard to the medieval All Hallows Church on the wall with the church dating from around 1130 AD.

Uniquely, the north wall of the church sits on the Roman foundations of London Wall with the vestry on foundations of a Roman bastion. Part of the medieval remains of London Wall form one boundary of the churchyard west of the church.

There is now a small raised public garden that is home to a few trees, bushes and flowerbeds as well as some benches.

Site location: London Wall
Postcode: EC2M 5ND
Grid ref: TQ330814
Size in hectares: 0.0299
Type of site: Public Gardens

Date(s): 1348; 1765-7 and 19th century.

Listed structures: All Hallows Church and section of London Wall bounding churchyard

Site ownership: Diocese of London

Site management: City of London Corporation Open Spaces Department

Open to public?: Yes

Opening times: 24/7 - Church: Wed 4.30-7.30pm; Fri 11am-3pm except last Fri in month 12.30-2pm

Public transport - Tube Stations: Liverpool Street (Central, Metropolitan, Circle, Hammersmith & City Lines) **National Rail:** Liverpool Street

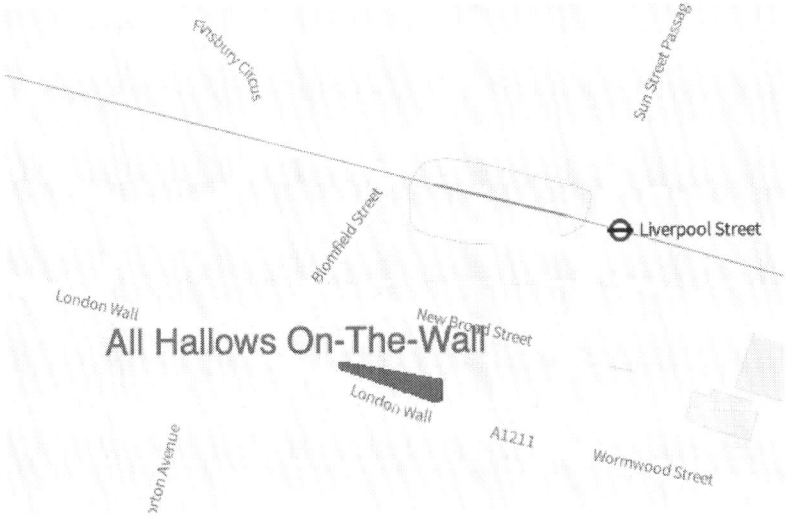

Contains OS data © Crown copyright and database rights 2019

History

A church has existed on this site since the first decades of the 12th century with an associated churchyard created alongside.

The medieval church of All Hallows was replaced in 1765-7 by the present building, the first church to be designed by George Dance the Younger, when he was aged just 24. Escaping relatively lightly from WWII, the building was later restored in the 1960s.

In 1993 an IRA bomb damaged the church but it was sympathetically restored by 1995. Rather plain looking on the outside, inside it is light and airy and since 2006 often home to art exhibitions.

Some of the north wall of this church actually rests on the foundations of the Roman city wall and the vestry sits on the remains of a Roman bastion whilst one of the boundaries of the garden that was once a churchyard is flanked by sections of the city wall that date back to medieval times. The front, however, is marked off from the pavement by a distinctly non-medieval hedge.

There is some lovely old York paving here, and benches are set into niches in the wall and in the summer the raised flowerbeds make it a good place to stop for a while. There are also trees, bushes and roses though these lessen as the garden narrows towards the west.

Amen Court

At a glance: Tucked away out of sight, Amen Court dates from the 17th century when houses were built for the canons of St Paul's Cathedral with a further terrace of houses built two centuries later. Ave Maria Lane gained its name from being a processional route of the clergy to the Cathedral.

Site location: Ave Maria Lane
Postcode: EC4
Grid ref: TQ318812
Size in hectares: Unknown
Type of site: Private Garden
Date(s): 1670 AD
Listed structures: London Wall Section and other structures
Site ownership: Private
Site management: Unknown
Open to public?: No
Opening times: None
Public transport - Tube Stations: St Paul's (Central Line) **National Rail:** City Thameslink

History

Amen Court is now the only wholly residential street in the City of London. As originally intended, all of the original buildings at Amen Court remain in residential use for the clergy of St Paul's Cathedral and consist of the range of three houses built in the 1670s and six

Queen Anne revival houses from the 1870s. There are groups of trees within the private garden, which has a tasteful ragstone and flint wall at its southern edge.

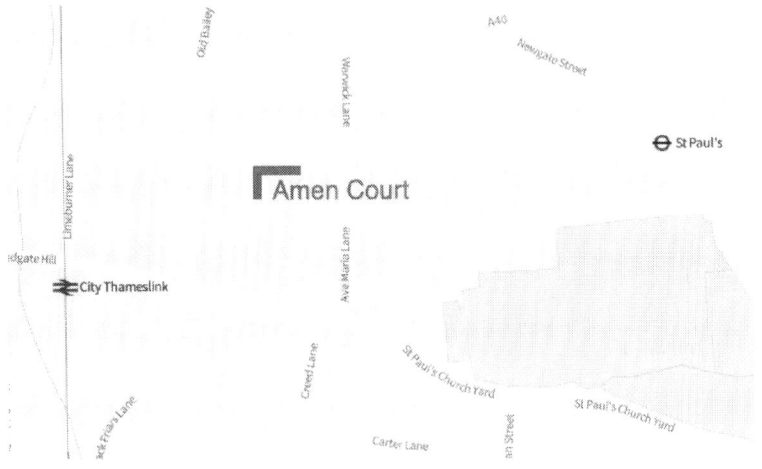

Contains OS data © Crown copyright and database rights 2019

A few minutes' walk up the road takes you to Christchurch Greyfriars.

Apothecaries' Hall

At a glance: A garden that requires just a little bit of planning to visit, but it's well worth the effort to enjoy this historic courtyard garden.

Site location: Blackfriars Lane
Postcode: EC4V 6EJ

Grid ref: TQ317810

Size in hectares: 0.019

Type of site: Square

Date(s): 17th and 18th centuries.

Listed structures: Apothecaries' Hall

Site ownership: The Worshipful Society of Apothecaries

Site management: The Worshipful Society of Apothecaries

Open to public?: By Appointment Only

Opening times: Open weekdays 10am-5pm, apart from public holidays and summer recess last 2 weeks August, first week September (Visits: call 020 7236 1189) Also has opened for the Open House events.

Public transport - Tube Stations: Blackfriars (District Line)

National Rail: City Thameslink and Blackfriars

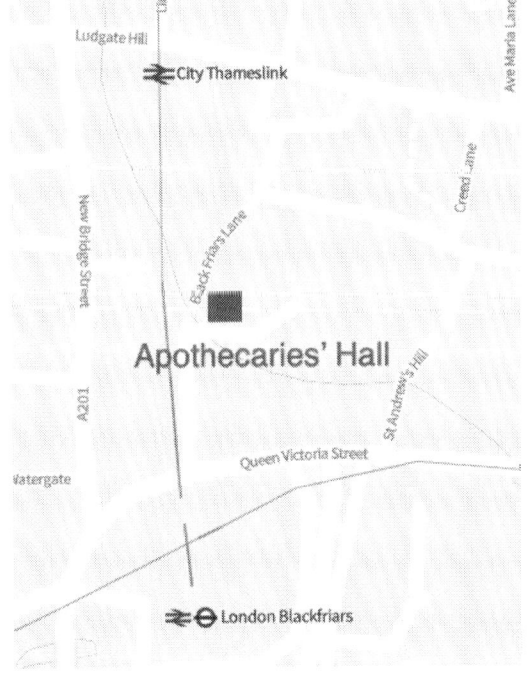

History

The Society of Apothecaries was long a member of the Grocers' Society until finally obtaining its own charter in1617 when it was recognised by James I. However it took another 15 years before they bought the home of Lord Cobham to have as their hall. For centuries this site had been on the lands held by the Dominican Priory of the Black Friars, dissolved in 1538 before it passed to Lord Cobham.

Sadly all of this burnt down in the Great Fire in 1666 and a new Hall was built from 1668-73 when an internal colonnaded courtyard was also added. The Apothecaries' Society supplied the Navy and many others with drugs. In 1671 a pharmaceutical laboratory was established at the ground floor of the Great Hall, just to the east of the courtyard and is notable for being the first large-scale manufacturing production of drugs.

The Society founded the famous Chelsea Physic Garden in 1673 which it ran until 1899. Restoration of the property was undertaken in the 1780s as the pharmaceutical business continued to grow.

A pharmacy operated on the north of the courtyard and it had a separate entrance on the street but in 1922 the Hall sold its pharmaceutical business, leaving the steps and railings in place.

The courtyard was worked upon in the latter decades of the 20th century with a number of plaques on display, including one which commemorates the 350th anniversary of the Apothecaries' Charter of 1967 when repaving of the courtyard was undertaken 'through the generosity of the Honourable Freemen and Members of the Livery and Yeomanry'.

Bank of England Garden Court

At a glance: Located in the centre of old Roman London and the heart of the financial district. In fact it's actually right in the heart of the Bank of England which makes this small private garden and courtyard difficult to catch a glimpse of.

Site location: Threadneedle Street
Postcode: EC2R 8AH
Grid ref: TQ327812
Size in hectares: 0.0732
Type of site: Private Garden
Date(s): 1781 and 1939
Listed structures: Bank of England
Site ownership: Bank of England
Site management: Bank of England Property Services
Open to public?: Very occasionally
Opening times: Best chance of entry is through the Open House London event.
Public transport - Tube Station: Bank (Central, DLR, Northern, Waterloo & City)/Monument (Circle, District)

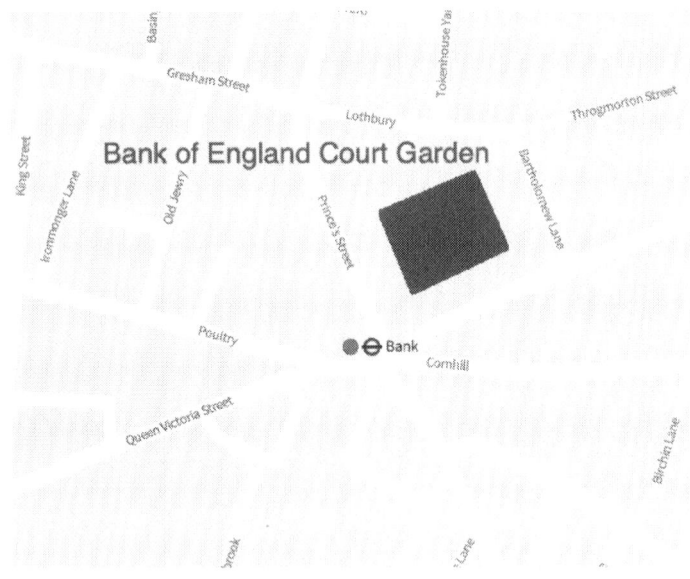

Contains OS data © Crown copyright and database rights 2019

History

Originally the church of St Christopher-le-Stocks stood here from the 13th or 14th centuries, and by the time of the Great Fire in 1666 there was a cloister around the north churchyard that was mostly destroyed and rebuilt by Sir Christopher Wren.

Though the Bank of England dates from 1694, it did not have its own building until 1724. The Garden Court came into being in 1781 as the fast expanding bank had the Church of St Christopher-le-Stocks demolished to allow for further buildings and repurposing the churchyard as a garden.

This made the church of St Christopher-le-Stocks to be the first church to be demolished since the destruction of many City of London churches in the Great Fire. It was to be far from the last, however, and during the Victorian era as the population moved out of the City to the growing suburbs a rationalisation of church parishes took place resulting in the loss of many.

The Bank of England buildings have expanded at least twice since that time and after WWI the garden was moved to the present location complete with a bronze war memorial. Entirely enclosed by the bank, the garden is home to trees, flowerbeds and lawns.

Easier to find across the road are the gardens of the Royal Exchange.

Barber-Surgeons' Hall Gardens

At a glance: There is so much to see around Barber-Surgeons' Hall Gardens which are on the site of Hadrian's fort, which dates from 122 AD with remains of a bastion from 300 AD. The Worshipful Company of Barbers was founded in 1308 and their hall was created here shortly thereafter.

Until 1987 the site of the present garden was still a derelict bomb site but now has both formal and informal areas, and looks out over water and beyond to St Giles Church, whose churchyard once reached this way.

Site location: Wood Street/London Wall

Postcode: EC2   **Grid ref:** TQ322816

Size in hectares: 0.3554   **Type of site:** Public Gardens

Date(s): 15th century onwards to the 1980s.

Listed structures: London Wall

Site ownership: City of London Corporation/Worshipful Company of Barbers

Site management: City of London Corporation/Worshipful Company of Barbers

Open to public?: Yes   **Opening times:** 24/7

Public transport - Tube Station: St Paul's (Central), Barbican (Hammersmith & City, Circle, Metropolitan)

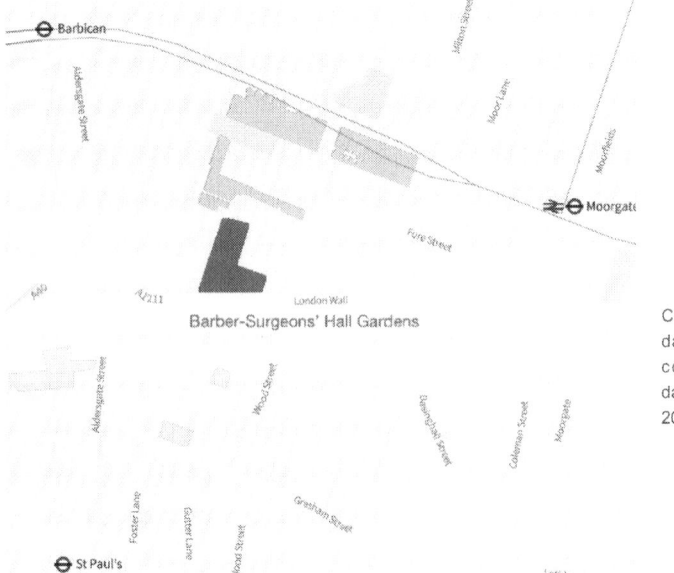

Barber-Surgeons' Hall Gardens

Contains OS data © Crown copyright and database rights 2019

History

The Barber-Surgeons' Hall Garden is one of 10 Livery Company gardens remaining in the City of London and there has been a garden here for almost 500 years, possibly longer.

The Hall was rebuilt after the Great Fire and then again in the 1960s following its destruction in the Blitz.

Dating from 1987, the present garden comprises of a formal planted area to the south of the Hall, whereas to the north is a considerably larger and more informal garden with trees and grass that looks out over water and beyond to St Giles Church, whose churchyard once reached this way.

The Worshipful Company of Barbers' Herb Garden has 45 smaller areas spread amongst four areas. In one area are plants relating to surgery, dentistry, wounds and burns whilst in another one can find plants that dyes can be made from as well as other uses. There is a medieval planting area and another which contain specimens that are the basis of modern medicines or in which modern medicines have their origins.

The garden is also home to a number of trees that were planted on ceremonial occasions.

Barbican Estate

At a glance: Nestled in the northwest corner of the City, the Barbican Estate is both hard to miss but easily overlooked. Thanks to the Romans, Luftwaffe and 1960s developments the estate is actually home to several gardens including Beech Gardens, Defoe Gardens, Barbican Wildlife Garden, Lakeside Gardens and Lakeside Terrace.

Site location: Barbican, Silk Street
Postcode: EC2Y 8BR
Grid ref: TQ323818
Size in hectares: 3.2
Type of site: Housing Estate Landscaped Gardens and Public Gardens
Date(s): 1963-1982; 2018.
Designers: Chamberlin, Powell and Bon with Ove Arup & Partners
Listed structures: Section of the Roman Wall and the Barbican Estate
Site ownership: City of London Corporation Barbican Estate
Site management: City of London Corporation Open Spaces Department
Open to public?: Yes
Opening times: 24/7
Public transport - Tube Station: St Paul's (Central), Barbican (Hammersmith & City, Circle, Metropolitan)

Contains OS data © Crown copyright and database rights 2019

History

What is now the Barbican Estate replete with public, communal and domestic gardens, courtyards and squares and waterways was once northwest corner of Londinium and though there isn't much sign of the old gates, the Roman wall is still evident along with later fortifications.

By the 19th century the area was one of industrial warehouses which perhaps goes some way to explaining why during WWII some 35 acres were destroyed by aerial bombardment. In 1951 it was proposed that part of the area should be developed as a new residential neighbourhood.

When they were built, the 400 feet high tower blocks were the tallest in Europe and over 6,500 people call the Barbican their home. You won't find roads and cars in the Barbican, that was never in the grand plan but instead there are raised walkways, gardens and pools of water as well as quite a few public sculptures, seating areas and flowerbeds.

There is even a canal that borders the old churchyard of St Giles Church. It's well worth visiting inside, particularly for those with an interest in John Wesley whose family played a part here, or if you have any interest whatsoever in the political philosopher Milton who is buried here.

North of the church are a series of rectangular and semi-circular raised beds in which C18th and C19th gravestones are set. The lamp posts might look Victorian but are only from the 1980s! Across the gated bridge it is possible to see secluded communal garden incorporating excavated footings of the old Roman Wall, the remains of which lead south bounding the east side of a lawn to the east of the Museum of London, and beyond which is the Barber-Surgeons' Hall Gardens.

There is also a conservatory in the Barbican within which are tropical trees and plants and even an aviary. There are several other areas to see in the Barbican and in brief there is ample to see here. One of the highlights is the Barbican Wildlife Garden, where volunteers have created a hidden gem that even some Barbican residents have never visited, which is a shame as it is only open to the public at large during the Open Garden Squares Weekend.

Looking across the canal from St Giles Cripplegate to the Roman / Medieval City Wall and Bastion

The first time you visit the Barbican you may likely get lost; in fact you might do on the tenth visit but you'll come out the better for it. Whether you appreciate the architectural style of the towers is another matter!

Barnard's Inn

At a glance: Harking back to a time when it was home to the legal establishment, two small paved courtyards just off Fetter Lane, Holborn.

Site location: High Holborn and Fetter Lane

Postcode: EC1N 2HH

Grid ref: TQ312815

Size in hectares: 0.0943

Type of site: Square

Date(s): 15th century, 1894 and 1989-1992

Listed structures: Barnard's Inn Hall and neighbouring structures

Site ownership: Great Portland Estates

Site management: Great Portland Estates

Open to public?: Yes

Opening times: Subject to management

Public transport - Tube Station: Chancery Lane (Central Line)

Contains OS data © Crown copyright and database rights 2019

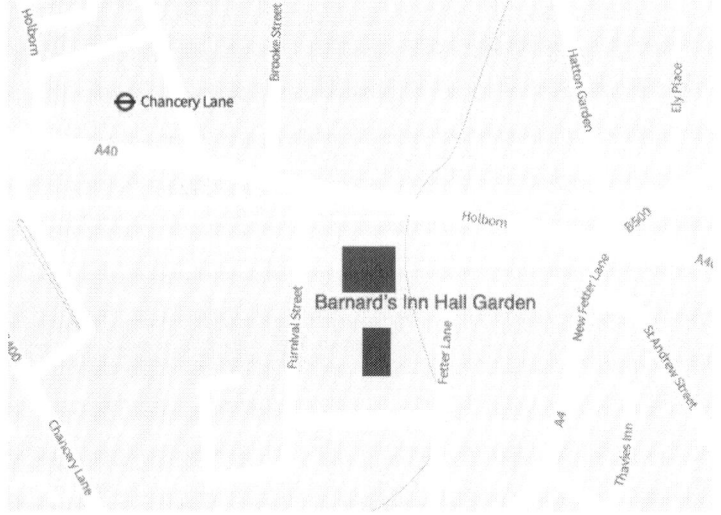

History

This one is a little harder to find with the central courtyard that was formerly the garden of Barnard's Inn, one of the Inns of Chancery, whilst fans of Charles Dickens may recall it is featured in *Great Expectations*.

The late 14th-century Barnard's Inn Hall survives and has its origins as once being the home of John Macworth, Chancellor to Henry V and Dean of Lincoln. The name 'Barnard' comes from Lionel Barnard who had the tenancy in the mid-15th century before the site began being used by law students.

Though the name remains, the legal trade moved out towards the end of the Victorian era, possibly hampered by the lack of potential to expand. After a century as a school and then offices, the site was redeveloped in 1988 and some of the old buildings were restored. Since 1991 Gresham College has been here. The college has its origins in 1597 when Sir Thomas Gresham gave free public lectures in his Bishopsgate home.

Both courtyards are largely paved, with the southern one having raised planters and shrubs. Of the two, the northern courtyard porhaps retains more of an original charm with seating and shrubbery in raised beds and large containers all overshadowed by a mature tree. Not too far away, though not as attractive, is Salisbury Square.

Blackfriars Bridge South Garden and Blackfriars Underpass

At a glance: The compact gardens of Blackfriars Underpass were opened in the 1960s at a ceremony attended by amongst others Dame Barbara Castle.

Looking towards Blackfriars Rail Bridge and the River Thames

Site location: Blackfriars Bridge/Queen Victoria Street/Victoria Embankment
Postcode: EC4Y 0DH
Grid ref: TQ315808

Type of site: Public Gardens

Date(s): Early 20th century and Post War 1960s

Listed structures: Blackfriars Bridge and drinking fountain

Site ownership: City of London Corporation

Site management: Transport for London

Open to public?: Partly

Opening times: The traffic island is theoretically open access but due to fences and busy roads, not easily accessible from some sides. A quieter narrow strip of landscaped public space near the river is a much easier proposition.

Public transport - Tube Station: Blackfriars (District, Circle). **National Rail:** Blackfriars

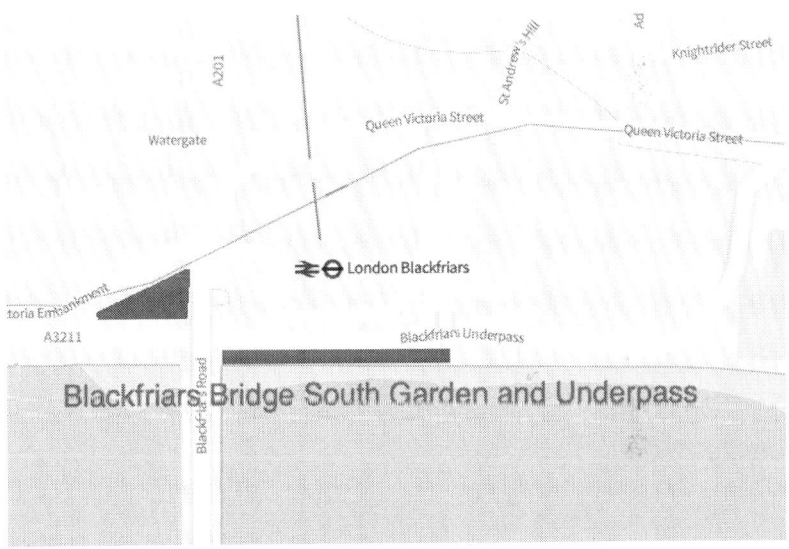

Contains OS data © Crown copyright and database rights 2019

History

Even in the 1920s there was a Blackfriars Bridge Garden. .The current landscaping dates from the 1960s Blackfriars Underpass opening. There is a narrow landscaped strip along the river which has a commemorative stone that is quite easy to access, but also areas of grass and flowerbeds that are for all intents and purposes traffic islands.

Venture inland from the river a few minutes to find St Andrew-by-the-Wardrobe.

Brewers' Hall Garden

At a glance: Brewers' Hall garden is adjacent to London Wall so it can be noisy for much of the week. It largely consists of a number of raised beds with trees and seating on a broad pavement.

Site location: London Wall
Postcode: EC2V 7HR
Grid ref: TQ324815
Type of site: Public Gardens
Date(s): 1960s
Site ownership: City of London Corporation
Site management: City of London Corporation
Open to public?: Yes
Opening times: 24/7

Public transport - Tube Station: Moorgate (Hammersmith & City, Circle, Metropolitan). **Rail:** Moorgate

Contains OS data © Crown copyright and database rights 2019

History

The Brewers' Company is one of the oldest Livery Companies in the City of London and one of the first Guilds to have its own hall, which by the early 15th century was let out for use to not just other City Livery Companies but also to groups and associations including 'footballpleyers', surely one of the first mentions of 'the people's game'.

The existing hall is the third with the previous structures destroyed by Great Fires and the Luftwaffe though it stands on exactly the same spot as the others. The present Hall was constructed in 1960 with responsibility for the garden being taken up by the City of London Corporation.

Interestingly one of the benches has a brass plaque which holds the following dedication: DEDICATED TO THE OPPRESSED LABOURERS WHOSE SUFFERING ULTIMATELY RENDERED THIS DISPLAY OF CORPORATE AFFLUENCE POSSIBLE.

In the middle of the garden next to the footpath is the statue of 'The Gardener' which was relocated here from Moorgate in the early 21st century.

St Mary Aldermanbury is just to the south, whilst cross the at times busy London Wall road to visit St Alphage Gardens.

Bridgewater Square

At a glance: Built in the early 16th century on the site of the mansion and gardens of the Earl of Bridgewater. Having survived the Great Fire, unfortunately Bridgwater House burnt down in 1687 which caused the deaths of the 3rd Earl's eldest sons and tutor with the house itself not being subsequently rebuilt.

The residential square was latterly developed around a central garden and for all intents and purposes is now part of the Barbican Estate and used as a playground for a children's nursery. Just to the north is Fann Street Wildlife Garden which is accessible to residents of the estate.

Site location: Bridgewater Square
Postcode: EC2Y 8AH
Grid ref: TQ321819
Size in hectares: 0.2173
Type of site: Housing Estate Landscaped Garden
Date(s): 17th century and 1926-1928
Site ownership: City of London Corporation Barbican Estate
Site management: Open Spaces Dept; Bright Horizons City Child Nursery (Fann Street Wildlife Garden: Barbican Wildlife Group)
Open to public?: No
Opening times: Privately run nursery; Fann Street Wildlife Garden accessible to residents of Barbican estate only
Public transport - Tube Station: Barbican (Metropolitan, Hammersmith & City; Circle). **Rail:** Moorgate

Contains OS data © Crown copyright and database rights 2019

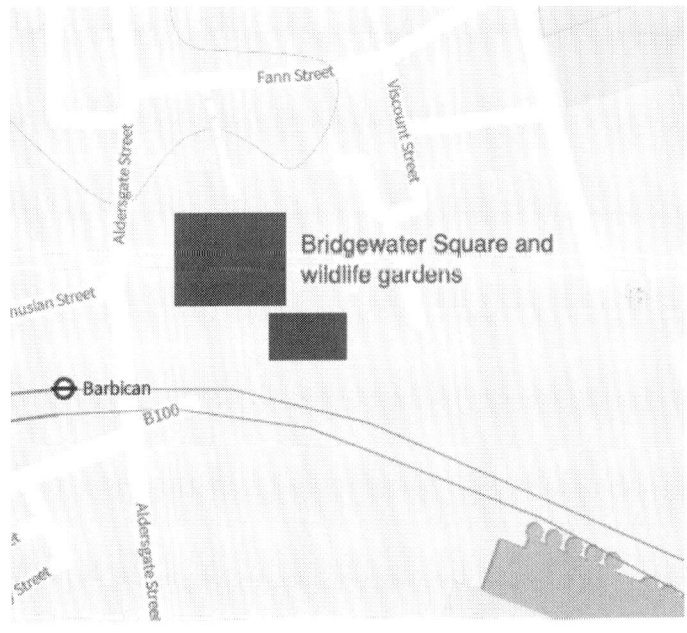

History

Following the Great Fire of 1666 a number of the wealthy people who lived in the City moved elsewhere to less populated and more fashionable districts to the west of London, and the area was rebuilt under the tutelage of Sir Christopher Wren amongst others.

It was a beautiful square in the 18th century and, following a campaign to save the garden as public space in 1926, it was acquired for £5,000 with the money raised from the public and laid out as public gardens, and opened to shortly thereafter for 'use by local workers'.

It suffered severe damage in WWII as did much of the Barbican Estate area and is now used as a children's play area along with being home to a number of trees.

Carter Lane Garden

At a glance: Carter Lane Gardens is very centrally located for tourists and locals alike under the shadow of the magnificent St Paul's. It is a small public space divided into two areas by a wide pathway that takes one from St Paul's to the Millennium Bridge and the Tate Modern.

Site location: Carter Lane
Postcode: EC4M 8BX

Grid ref: TQ320810
Size in hectares: 0.1576
Type of site: Public Gardens
Date(s): 1955 and 2007
Site ownership: City of London Corporation
Site management: City of London Corporation
Open to public?: Yes
Opening times: 24/7 Information Centre: 9.30am-5.30pm Mon-Sat, 10am-4pm Sun
Public transport - Tube Stations: St Paul's (Central); Mansion House (District, Circle) **Rail:** Thameslink

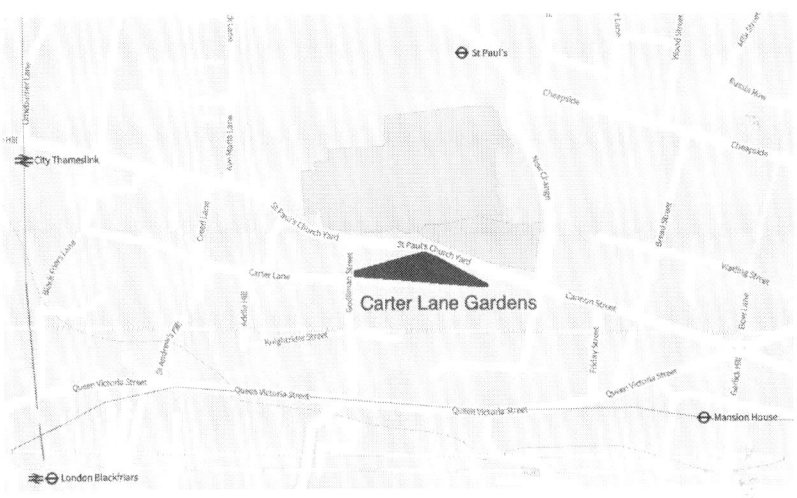

Contains OS data © Crown copyright and database rights 2019

History

After WWII the area where the gardens now are had been earmarked for a road scheme but this never came to pass, and it follows the footprint of the pre-war buildings that were obliterated during the war.

Of the two sections, the western is more informal and secluded from the traffic, with a lawn seating, a number of plane trees and shrubs, whilst the triangular area to the east is more formal with flowerbeds set into lawn with changing floral displays, and a number of ornamental trees.

Carter Lane Gardens was re-landscaped in 2009 with a new tourist information booth, and further planting took place in 2012 along with new and additional seating.

To the east of the lawns is a beautiful Victorian drinking fountain, which in a previous life was situated outside St Lawrence Jewry Church and was also reconstructed in the garden, after many years in storage.

No visit to the gardens is complete without spending a moment at the evocative Fire Brigade War Memorial of 1991 by John W Mills which remembers amongst other things the sacrifices made to protect St Paul's from fire during WWII.

Despite its central and high profile location, Carter Lane Gardens often provides a surprisingly tranquil respite from the bustle of nearby attractions, and if you come in December it is also home to a fabulous Christmas tree which always looks a treat given the treasured building in the background.

There are several gardens nearby; why not try Old Change Court or the brand new Distaff Lane Garden which are adjacent to each other.

Christchurch Greyfriars Church Garden

At a glance: A beautiful garden to enjoy, just a short walk from St Paul's tube station, Christchurch Greyfriars Church Garden is on the site of the Franciscan Church of Greyfriars.

Site location: King Edward Street
Postcode: EC1A 7BA
Grid ref: TQ320813
Size in hectares: 0.0815
Type of site: Public Gardens
Date(s): 13th century, 17th century, 1989
Listed Structures: Remaining structure of Christ Church
Site ownership: City of London Corporation
Site management: City of London Corporation
Open to public?: Yes
Opening times: 24/7
Public transport - Tube Station: St Paul's (Central Line)

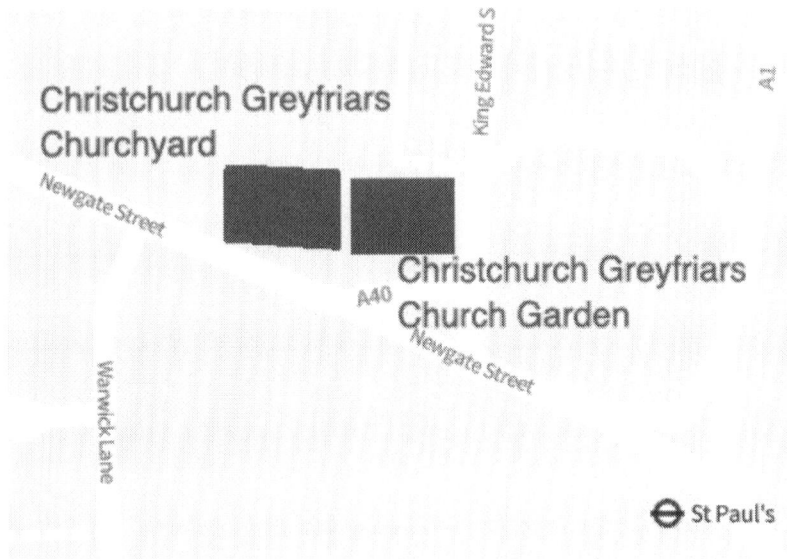

Contains OS data © Crown copyright and database rights 2019

History

This garden is located on the site of the Franciscan Church of Greyfriars, which was established in 1225, following the arrival from Italy in 1224 of 9 monks of the Franciscan order, called Greyfriars because of the colour of their clothing.

It soon became a booming centre and with royal approval at the start of the 14th century, the second largest medieval church in London was built here as well as a library built by the famed Lord Mayor, Richard Whittington. It is the resting place for royalty from across the British Isles.

Things obviously had to change for the Priory with the Dissolution and after a brief period as a Tudor treasure trove, Christ's Church within Newgate was founded with the backing of King Henry VIII, with it being tasked with amongst other things attending the prisoners at the notorious Newgate when required.

Putting a number of the Greyfriars' buildings to good use, a Christ's Hospital was founded in 1552 and it remained here until the school moved to pastures new in 1902. The grand old medieval church was destroyed though in the 1666 Great Fire, and Wren worked on a smaller replacement which being situated so close to St Paul's Cathedral, it was all but inevitable that the body of the Wren church was gutted in 1940.

The church garden stands in the ruins of the old Blitz ravaged church

As a cost saving measure, Christchurch was one church that it was decided not to rebuild although in 1960 the steeple was restored by Lord Mottistone. Incredibly to us and also to many then, road widening in the 1960s by the Corporation of London led to the destruction of the east wall of the church, something that understandably caused an outcry.

In 1989 a rose garden was planted which copies the floor plan of the church with rose beds and box hedge outlining features of the old church. Climbing plants also represent the locations of the pillars that once held up the roof.

In 2019 a small memorial to Christ's Hospital School's 350 years' presence in the City of London, 1552-1902, was erected on a wall of the garden. Whilst you're here, make sure you walk a few feet down the road to Christchurch Greyfriars Churchyard.

Christchurch Greyfriars Churchyard

At a glance: Immediately to the west of the church steeple is all that remains of Christchurch Greyfriars, an old burial ground. It was in 1872 that the railed churchyard became a garden albeit a minimal one with just grass and a few mature trees. There are though two chest tombs and a number of headstones which give an indication as to its previous primary purpose.

Site location: Newgate Street
Postcode: EC1A 7BA
Grid ref: TQ319813
Size in hectares: 0.1231
Type of site: Public Gardens
Date(s): 1680s and 1872
Listed Structures: Remaining structure of Christ Church
Site ownership: Diocese of London
Site management: City of London Corporation
Open to public?: Yes
Opening times: 24/7
Public transport - Tube Station: St Paul's (Central Line)

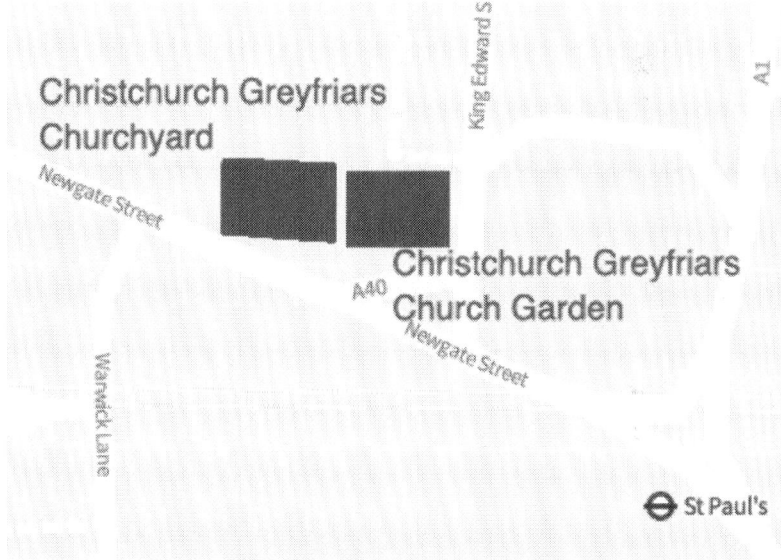

History

Enjoying the same history as the preceding Christchurch Greyfriars Church Garden, this walled and railed churchyard became a garden and public open space in 1872. From 1931 an annual grant was paid by the Corporation of London towards its maintenance as an open space, though perhaps the maintenance sum is not as great as others as the space is largely grass.

The garden is bisected by a central footpath which runs from the front of Vestry House and the remains of Christ Church to the gates on Greyfriars Passage. There are a wealth of gardens nearby from the beautiful Postman's Park to the gardens of St Bartholomew's Hospital and Church as well as West Smithfields. Otherwise try St Sepulchre without Newgate or Warwick Square.

Cleary Garden

At a glance: One of my favourite little gardens, and one that couldn't be easier to find, just a short walk from Mansion House underground station. Cleary Garden is a terraced garden originally created following bomb damage in WWII built on a series of terracing to reflect its fascinating past.

Site location: Queen Victoria Street/Huggin Hill
Postcode: EC4V 4HQ
Grid ref: TQ322809
Size in hectares: 0.1119

Type of site: Public Gardens
Date(s): 1940s; 1982 and 2007
Site ownership: City of London Corporation
Site management: City of London Corporation Open Spaces Department
Open to public?: Yes
Opening times: 24/7

Public transport - Tube Station: Mansion House (Circle and District Lines), St Paul's (Central Line) **Rail:** Cannon Street

Contains OS data © Crown copyright and database rights 2019

History

Cleary Garden is a modern terraced garden sloping down Huggin Hill to the east and down towards where the Thames, whose northern shores would have been much closer 2,000 years ago. Huggin Hill appears in the history books in 1260 when it was called 'Hoggenelane', and likely named as such due to it being a place where hogs were kept.

Each level of the garden represents an era of London's history. The lowest level represents Roman, then medieval, the Great Fire, Victorian and modern at street level. Towards the base of Huggin Hill is part of the retaining wall of the Roman baths, which was discovered in 1964. The baths were probably built around 80 AD and were later expanded but fell out of favour and were demolished towards the end of the 3rd century. A thousand years later the area was used by vintners who both traded and grew grape vines here.
Following the catastrophic Blitz in 1940, much of the area was flattened including the house that had been on this site, leaving only the cellars in situ.

The site was laid out as a public open space after WWII bomb damage in the Blitz of 1940 by a shoemaker called Joe Brandis who despite all of the rubble on site, started to collect mud from the river banks and even brought soil from his own garden in Walthamstow to the site. His success was such that on 29th July 1949 Queen Elizabeth the Queen Mother visited the new garden.

Looking through the Roman inspired pergola

Things remained little changed until a fresh round of landscaping in 1985 when the pergolas and seating were erected along with the planting of a variety of bushes and trees.

You would have thought all of this would mean this place would be called Brandis gardens but instead they are named after Frederick Cleary who made it his mission in life to increase the number of green spaces within the city and on the 28th July 1982 he planted a golden acacia in the gardens.

The gardens have received countless awards in recent decades and much effort is also made to make it wildlife friendly. On a hot sunny day, there is nowhere better than to sit amongst the vines and climbers that were added during the most recent works in 2007.

If you're enjoying a moment of quiet solitude and hear an underground train nearby, don't be alarmed as the garden also houses an old exhaust vent from Mansion House underground station which you can see from the platform level.

Walk down Huggin Hill and turn left at Upper Thames Street and soon you will be at St James Garlickhythe. Alternatively cross over Upper Thames Street into Queenhithe and visit the only remaining Anglo-Saxon dock in the world with a fabulous mosaic explaining its history.

Coleman Gardens

At a glance: A great spot to get away from the hustle and bustle of Moorgate, One Coleman Street Gardens is a small, modern public garden in the City of London creating a contemporary space as a relief from the hard surrounding streets. The garden contains a leafy grove of lush planting with areas for seating as well as lawn areas for use during the summer months.

Site location: Basinghall Avenue/Coleman Street

Postcode: EC2V 5DD
Grid ref: TQ3256481477
Size in hectares: Unknown
Type of site: Public Garden
Date(s): 2002-2007
Designer(s): David Walker Architects
Site ownership: City of London Corporation
Site management: City of London Corporation Open Spaces Department
Open to public?: Yes
Opening times: 24/7
Public transport - Tube Station: Liverpool Street (Central, Circle, Hammersmith & City, Metropolitan) **Rail:** Liverpool Street

Contains OS data © Crown copyright and database rights 2019

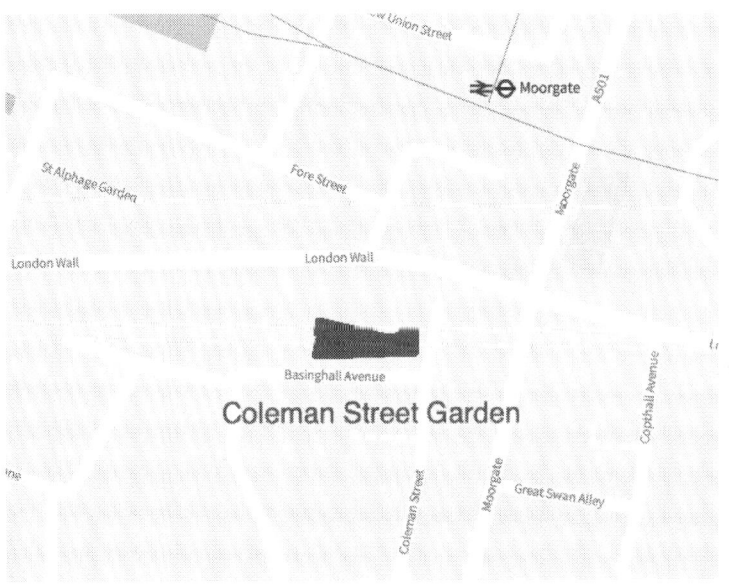

History

Despite the fact that most of it runs along Basinghall Avenue, it's actually part of the modern office block on the adjacent side road which is why this is known as One Coleman Street Gardens.

Basinghall Avenue was once an actual avenue that was destroyed in WWII post-war bomb site clearance that saw the alley converted into a road, and the burnt out remains of the buildings on the site demolished.

The garden consists of a vibrant green lawn area, with an avenue of managed planting and some pleasant benches to sit on. Amelanchier trees and Liquidambar form a delicate canopy over areas of seating whilst a variety of long grasses are planted around and about. A few feet away is Girdlers' Hall Garden.

Cutlers Gardens in Devonshire Square

At a glance: Known as Cutlers Gardens in the 20th century, this is now an office, retail and residential development but with some thoughtful landscaping befitting a historic site dating back to Roman times.

Site location: Cutlers Gardens in Devonshire Square

Postcode: E1

Grid ref: TQ334815

Size in hectares: 0.5743

Type of site: Housing Estate Landscaped Gardens

Date(s): 1978-1982
Designer: Russell Page
Listed structures:
LBII: Warehouses and gate piers to warehouses on Cutler Street
Site ownership: Devonshire Square Management
Site management: Devonshire Square Management
Open to public?: Yes
Opening times: Monday - Friday 7am - 10pm or Dusk.
Public transport - Tube Station: Liverpool Street (Central, Hammersmith & City, Metropolitan, Circle). **Rail:** Liverpool Street.

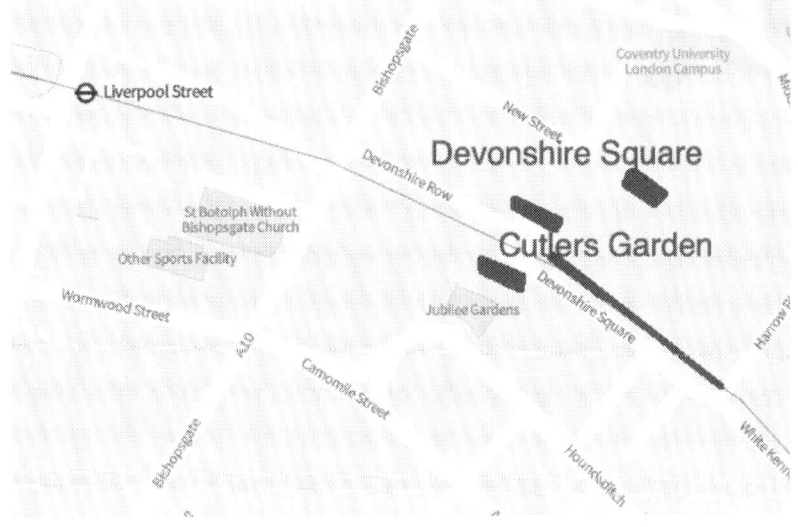

Contains OS data © Crown copyright and database rights 2019

History

In the heart of East London, it can be a little surprising to come across such an interesting garden and with an incredible history to boot.

Back in the 2nd-4th centuries the area was used for burials but in the 10th century the land was granted to the Cnihtengild, who were a group of 13 knights. Then in the early 12th century the Holy Trinity Priory in Aldgate created a convent garden here. However 600 years later the area was covered with tenements, workshops and small industries until the arrival of the East India Company who started building large developments here.

The present incarnation of the site began in 1978 when some of the old buildings were restored, financed no doubt by the construction of new developments.

Landscaped courtyards are the order of the day here and from the main entrance an avenue paved with cobbles sits between rows of miniature hornbeams in raised beds.

In Central Court, amongst the plane trees and sitting atop a lawn is a sculpture commemorating the 13 knights of the Cnihtengild which was unveiled by the Lord Mayor of London in 1990.

Whilst you're here, try and find Devonshire Square which is just a short walk away.

Dean's Court

At a glance: A garden belonging to the Bishop of London's Ministry which has been behind hoardings for the last year or so undergoing repair and improvement works which are due to be completed later in 2020.

Site location: Dean's Court

Postcode: EC4   **Grid ref:** TQ319810

Type of site: Private Garden   **Date(s):** 1670

Site ownership: St Paul's Cathedral

Site management: St Paul's Cathedral

Open to public?: No   **Opening times:** No

Public transport - Tube Station: St Paul's (Central Line) **Rail:** Thameslink   Contains OS data © Crown copyright and database rights 2019

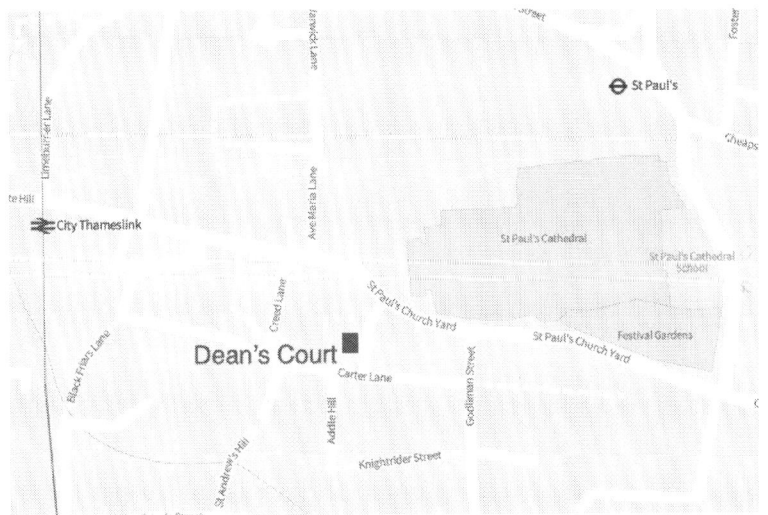

History

In 1670 St Paul's Deanery was built in Dean's Court and is still home to the Bishop of London today. A rare mansion house in the City, designed by Sir Christopher Wren himself.

It is quite well hidden located behind an imposing wall but at least we get to see the mature plane trees rising high up into the sky.

There are a flurry of small gardens nearby in around Distaff Lane Garden.

Devonshire Square

At a glance: The Earl of Devonshire owned this area until 1675 and this was the location of the garden for his mansion house. Almost everything has changed in the intervening centuries and the present incarnation came about following a 2004 landscaping with new paving and some tasteful seating along with a delightful circle of 12 pleached lime trees.

Site location: Devonshire Square
Postcode: EC2M 4TH
Grid ref: TQ333814
Size in hectares: Unknown
Type of site: Unknown
Date(s): 1787-1780 and 2002
Site ownership: City of London Corporation

Site management: City of London Corporation Open Spaces Department

Open to public?: Yes

Opening times: 24/7

Public transport - Tube Station: Liverpool Street (Central, Circle, Hammersmith & City, Metropolitan) **Rail:** Liverpool Street

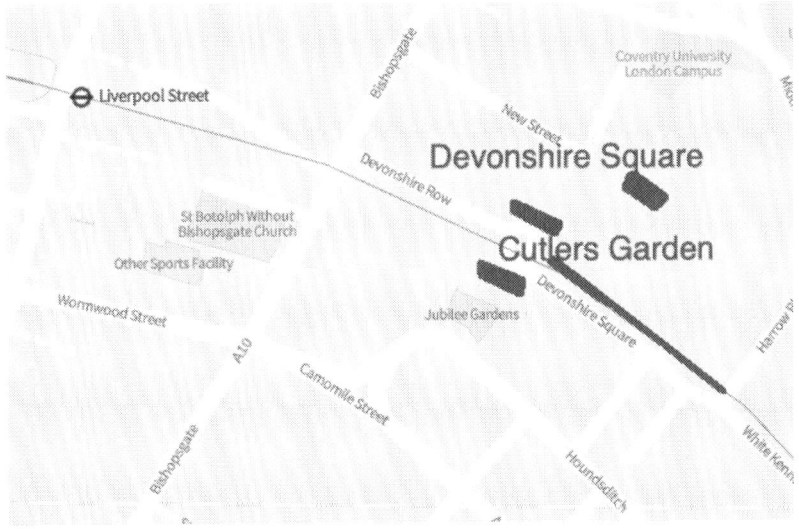

Contains OS data © Crown copyright and database rights 2019

History

Following the Great Fire, the Earl of Devonshire sold his lands here to Dr Nicholas Barbon, an entrepreneur from Holland, who created Devonshire Square between 1678-1708 as well as several other notable properties further west.

There remains two wonderful mid-18th century houses (numbers 12 and 13). Number 13 has since 1958 been the Coopers' Company Hall as their earlier and more auspicious building was destroyed in WWII.

A small oval street garden with flowers, shrubs and small trees crossed by paths can be found at the centre of the square and surrounded by the road where a circle of 12 pleached lime trees were planted.

Whilst you're here, try and find Cutlers Garden which is just a short walk away.

Statue of King Edgar

Distaff Lane Garden

At A Glance: A brand new pocket park in the heart of the City of London which only opened to the public in 2019 and consists mainly of birch trees but with a garden feature that harks back centuries.

Site location: Distaff Lane /2-6 Cannon Street
Postcode: EC4M 6YH
Grid ref: TQ320811
Type of site: Public Gardens
Date(s): 2019
Designer(s): Tom Stuart-Smith
Site ownership: Pembroke Real Estate
Site management: Pembroke Real Estate
Open to public?: Yes
Opening times: 24/7
Public transport - Tube Station: St Paul's (Central Line), Mansion House (Circle and District Lines) **Rail:** Blackfriars

Contains OS data © Crown copyright and database rights 2020

History: A pocket garden mainly of birch trees in the heart of London, in between St Nicholas Cole Abbey and St Paul's Cathedral. The former is dedicated to St Nicholas of Myra, the patron saint of fishermen, and in Elizabethan times there was an important fish market here.

An organic web of interweaving paths divides the space, allowing for the creation of a variety of intimate and open spaces. The birch trees allow for delicate filtering of views across the garden which in winter act as bright white sculptures. There is a solitary pin oak which acts as a connection between the garden and the predominant street trees on Distaff Lane. The garden is meant to read as a small cluster of trees, rather like a copse.

A peek into Distaff Lane Gardens, created just months ago but densely planted.

An existing sculpture of Icarus by Michael Ayrton was relocated to the middle of the garden. And a water wall inspired by fish scales acts as a bookend to the garden and gives us a connection back to the Elizabethan fish market.

The water wall at the far end harks back to the Elizabethan fish market here

Drapers' Hall Garden

At A Glance: A beautiful if largely unvisited long private garden that had its origins with Thomas Cromwell in the early 16th century. It can be found along the lower part of Throgmorton Street between Austin Friars and Drapers' Hall, just a few minutes' walk from the Bank of England.

Site location: Throgmorton Avenue/Throgmorton Street/Austin Friars
Postcode: EC2N 2DQ
Grid ref: TQ328814
Size in hectares: 0.0571
Type of site: Private Garden
Date(s): 16th century and 1928
Designer(s) 1928: Heaton Comyn, Drapers' Company surveyor
Listed structures: Drapers' Hall
Site ownership: Worshipful Company of Drapers
Site management: Worshipful Company of Drapers
Open to public?: Occasionally
Opening times: Sometimes open for has opened for Open Garden Square Weekend and Open House London. Visits by appointment through the Chief Executive
Public transport - Tube Station: Bank (Central, DLR, Northern); Moorgate (Hammersmith & City, Northern) **Rail:** Moorgate and Liverpool Street

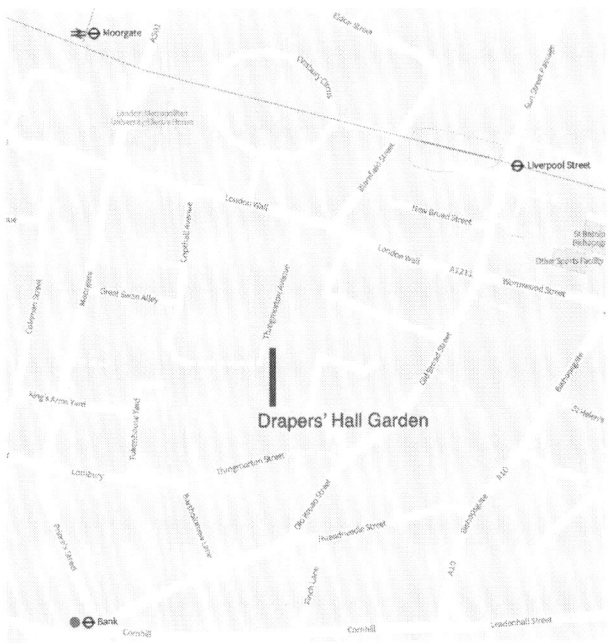

Contains OS data © Crown copyright and database rights 2019

History

Thomas Cromwell acquired land here from the 1530s when it is likely the garden was replete with walks, arbours, knot and herb gardens. His fall from grace provided the perfect opportunity for the Drapers' Company to purchase his mansion house in 1543 which was swiftly covered into Drapers' Hall along with a garden for its members.

A century or so later mulberry trees were planted to encourage the silk industry but with the Great Fire of 1666 both the Hall and the garden were destroyed, though the garden itself acted as something of a firebreak itself and was key to saving a number of nearby properties. Both Hall and garden were then restored in the early 1670s and the garden even open to members of the public.

A new design was put in place in 1928 which included York paving, roses and a new fountain, and this same design is largely what we have today with the addition of some mulberry trees in remembrance of times past, one of which was planted by a very young Queen Elizabeth II in 1955.

Walk north along Throgmorton Avenue and you will come out almost opposite Finsbury Circus Gardens.

Fenchurch Place

At A Glance: A relatively large paved square outside London's smallest mainline railway station. Disconnected from the tube network and down a small side street, it can be busy during the working week but largely deserted at weekends.

Site location: Fenchurch Place, off Fenchurch Street
Postcode: EC3M 4AJ
Grid ref: TQ333809
Size in hectares: 0.1473
Type of site: Public Square
Date(s): Ongoing
Designers: Townshend Landscape Architects (2014)

Listed Structures: Fenchurch Station frontage

Open to public?: Yes

Opening times: 24/7

Public transport - Tube Station: Tower Hill (Circle and District Lines); Aldgate (Circle and Metropolitan Line) **Rail:** Fenchurch Station!

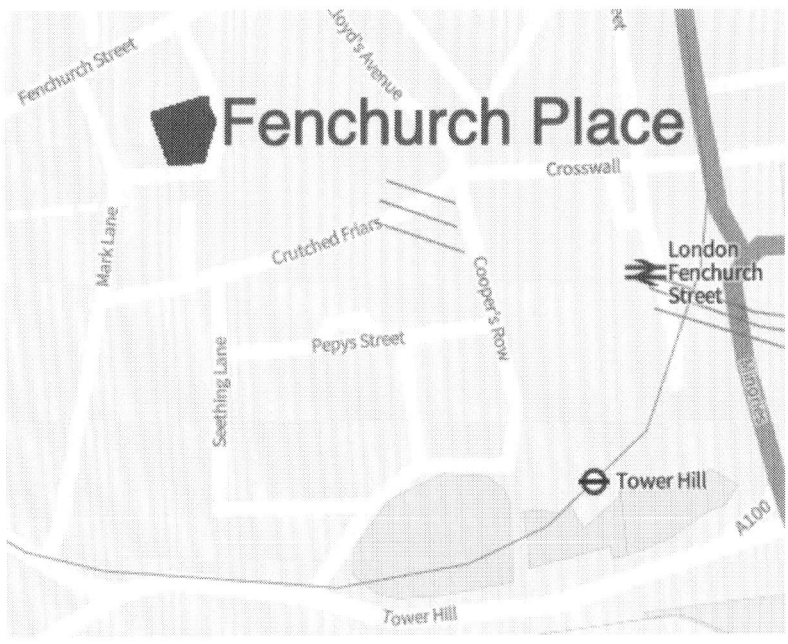

Contains OS data © Crown copyright and database rights 2020

History

The original building designed by William Tite opened on 20th July 1841, serving the London and Blackwall Railway (L&BR), replacing a nearby terminus at Minories that had opened in July 1840. It had two platforms connected via a stairway to the booking hall. Steam locomotives did not use the station until 1849 because before this time trains were dragged uphill from Blackwall to Minories, and ran to Fenchurch Street via their own momentum. The reverse journey eastwards required a manual push from railway staff. William Marshall's railway bookstall established at the station in 1841 was the first to be opened in the City of London.

The area around Fenchurch Street is one of the oldest inhabited parts of London; the name "Fenchurch" derives from the Latin *faenum* (hay) in reference to the hay markets in the area. The station was the first to be granted permission by the Corporation of London to be constructed inside the City of London, following several refusals against other railway companies.

Fenchurch Station and its services long suffered from a poor reputation and it was seen as something of an embarrassment by the local Conservative MPs who used the line from Essex. In July 1994, shortly before privatisation, the station closed for seven weeks for an £83 million project to replace signals, track and electrification works. It was the first significant closure of a London terminal station.

Work was also carried out on Fenchurch Place in the 1990s and the square was further upgraded around 2014 with additional and mostly stone seating along with minor planting to supplement the existing trees.

The Fenchurch area is still somewhat tired, and work has been scheduled both inside and outside Fenchurch Station during the 2020s to both ease transit and encourage a greater use of the area.

Not too far away you will find the moving Fen Court which is overlooked by The Garden at 120. Alternatively turn east along Fenchurch Street and hidden away on the right is St Katherine Coleman Churchyard.

Fen Court

At A Glance: Perhaps my favourite square garden in the City of London, Fen Court is the site of the former churchyard of St Gabriel Fenchurch, which was destroyed in the Great Fire of London but afterwards not rebuilt.

1960 saw it gain a new lease of life as a paved open space with a few trees and a few raised beds with seating amongst three impressive looking 18th century chest tombs. Decades later it was re-landscaped and though the new paving, seating and planting is very welcome, what really makes Fen Court special is the 2008 thought-provoking public sculpture entitled 'Gilt of Cain' which was unveiled by Archbishop Desmond Tutu.

Site location: Fen Court just off Fenchurch Street
Postcode: EC3M 5BA

Grid ref: TQ332809

Size in hectares: 0.0522

Type of site: Square

Date(s): 14th century, 1960 and 2008.

Site ownership: Private

Site management: Private but planters maintained by City of London Corporation

Open to public?: Yes

Opening times: 24/7

Public transport - Tube Stations: Monument (District, Circle)/Bank (Central, DLR, Northern, Waterloo & City) **Rail:** Fenchurch Street.

Contains OS data © Crown copyright and database rights 2019

History

This is the site of the former churchyard of St Gabriel Fenchurch which was around by at least 1108 but which was destroyed by the Great Fire of London of 1666 and not rebuilt.

When the Romans arrived, London was largely marshland and as with the marshy fens in East Anglia it is likely that this might have influenced the naming of the area along with the established hay trade.

A plaque on Fenchurch Street by Parchment House records the site of the church, which might have belonged to the Cnihtengild and been given to Holy Trinity Priory at Aldgate in 1108.

The churchyard was present by the early 14th century and soon walled off; it remained surrounded by railings and closed to the public beyond WWII. 1960 saw it gain a new lease of life as a paved open space with a few trees and raised beds with seating amongst three impressive looking 18th century chest tombs. One of which dates from 1762 for Anne Cotesworth with the inscription stating that she was 'born in the parish and her nearest relatives being buried in the next vault'.

What really makes Fen Court special is the 'Gilt of Cain' sculpture that was unveiled by Archbishop Desmond Tutu in 2008. It commemorates the movement to abolish the transatlantic slave trade and depending on how one looks at it, is evocative of both a pulpit and a slave auctioneer's podium whilst the columns can be either stems of sugar cane, a crowd at a slavers' auction or a church congregation.

The moving Gilt of Cain sculpture

The artwork also features a powerful poem by Lemn Sissay which cleverly combines Old Testament text with the language of the Stock Exchange. This garden is close to the old St Mary Woolnorth where prominent anti-slavery campaigner Reverend John Newton preached, though he is best remembered by many these days for his incredible hymn, 'Amazing Grace'.

For a totally different garden experience, go round the corner and up into the lift to experience The Garden at 120.

Festival Gardens

At A Glance: These grandly named gardens date from 1951 as the Corporation of London's contribution to the Festival of Britain. Located close to St Paul's and offering a relatively large green open space.

Site location: New Change/Cannon Street
Postcode: EC4M 6QQ
Grid ref: TQ321810
Size in hectares: 0.1896
Type of site: Public Gardens
Date(s): 1951
Designer(s) Sir Albert Richardson
Site ownership: City of London Corporation
Site management: City of London Corporation Open Spaces Department
Open to public?: Yes
Opening times: 24/7
Public transport - Tube Station: St Paul's (Central); Mansion House (District, Circle)

Contains OS data © Crown copyright and database rights 2019

History

The Festival Gardens like nearby Carter Lane Garden follow the footprints of buildings that were wiped out during the Blitz and were on a street known for centuries as Old Change.

As part of the City of London Corporation's effort towards the Festival of Britain, these gardens were laid out in 1951 by Sir Albert Richardson.

Though surrounded by raised paved terracing and plenty of seating, trees and hedging, the Festival Garden are in essence a sunken lawn with a water fountain. An eye-catching work of art known as 'The Young Lovers' was added in the early 1970s and was created by Georg Ehrlich (1897-1960).

In the 21st century, further improvements were made in conjunction with those just across the road at Carter Lane Gardens to enhance the surroundings of St Paul's Cathedral and make the district more suitable for such a stunning and significant location.

Just across New Change you will find the gardens at 25 Cannon Street or alternatively head south down Distaff Lane to find Distaff Lane Garden round the corner on the right.

Finsbury Circus Gardens

At A Glance: Usually a beautiful and expansive garden as it has been since at least 1900, for the last decade, much of it has been off limits and marred due to the Crossrail construction project which seems to have an end date forever in perpetuity.

Site location: Finsbury Circus
Postcode: EC2M 7EA
Grid ref: TQ328816
Size in hectares: 2.2
Type of site: Public Gardens

Date(s): 1815-1817 and 1900
Designer(s): George Dance the Younger
Listed structures: 1902 Drinking fountain. Surrounding houses: LBII*: 1-6 Finsbury Square (Lutyens House) & 94-100 Moorgate.

LBII: 16-18 & 26-31 Eldon Street, 25 London Wall Buildings, 31 Salisbury House.

Site ownership: City of London Corporation

Site management: City of London Corporation Open Spaces Department

Open to public?: Yes

Opening times: 8am-dusk weekdays and weekends April-Sept (closed weekends Oct-March) The site has taken part in Open Garden Squares Weekend

Public transport - Tube Station: Moorgate (Hammersmith & City, Circle, Northern, Metropolitan) **Rail: Moorgate**

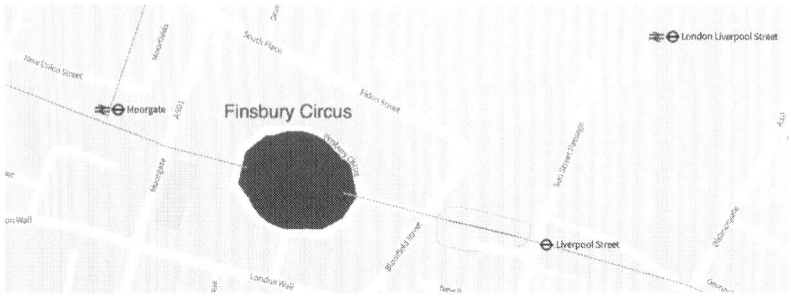

Contains OS data © Crown copyright and database rights 2019

History

For centuries there was a moor here. The old Roman wall caused drainage issues with rivers and streams flowing south towards the Thames resulting in the ground outside of the city walls to be boggy like a moor. Later the area was part of the Finsbury Manor Estate which in the early 16th century was drained with gravelled paths laid out over what were then open fields.

More formal gardens and lawns bounded by trees took shape a century later, with the 13th-century Bethlehem Royal Hospital moving nearby and when the old Roman wall in this part of the city was demolished the time was ripe for a grand redevelopment in 1815 based on a slightly earlier plan by George Dance for an oval amphitheatre here.

A precursor to our modern Crossrail woes arrived in 1864 when the Metropolitan Railway Company cut a tunnel right through the site, though at least they paid an annual £100 which was to go towards the maintenance of the gardens.

It wasn't until 1900 that the garden was taken up by the City Corporation. New seating and planting was put in place and there remains some traces of this today, and as the century progressed greater leisure facilities were added including a bowling green and a post-war bandstand.

North of the bowling green is a pink granite drinking fountain dating from 1902, designed by John Whitehead & Son of Westminster, with a shelter based on a design of a well by Philip Webb for William Morris's Red House in Bexleyheath.

The beautiful gardens have bedding plants, camellias, bamboos, and plenty of shrub bedding in fact as well as more unusual specimens such as Japanese aralia, a pagoda tree as well as the tried and trusted London plane trees.

Sadly for the last decade most of the gardens have been inaccessible due to construction work on Crossrail which perhaps allows us to sympathise with residents during WWII when the gardens were home to a barrage balloon. It has been promised that the gardens will be fully restored upon completion, though when this will actually be is anyone's guess.

Head down Throgmorton Avenue and you will find Drapers' Hall Garden, alternatively walk east down London Wall to All Hallows-On-The-Wall and past that St Botolph Without Bishopsgate.

Fishmongers' Hall Garden

At A Glance: A small and largely paved garden near London Bridge. You can just about see over the wall of this private garden from the Thames Path whilst also having a great view of the river, Southwark Cathedral and The Shard.

Site location: Just off Swan Lane and Lower Thames Street
Postcode: EC4R 9EL
Grid ref: TQ328806
Size in hectares: 0.0701
Type of site: Private Garden
Date(s): 1831-1835 and 1977-78
Listed structures: Fishmongers Hall
Site ownership: The Worshipful Company of Fishmongers

Site management: The Worshipful Company of Fishmongers

Open to public?: Occasionally

Opening times: Only through open days, tours and appointments through the Fishmongers' Company

Public transport - Tube Station: Monument (District, Circle)/Bank (Central, DLR, Northern, Waterloo & City); Cannon Street (District, Circle). **Rail:** Cannon Street

Contains OS data © Crown copyright and database rights 2019

History

Two thousand years ago this area was a Roman quayside. The Fishmongers' Company isn't quite that old with its origins in at least the 1200s with the Stockfishmongers (fresh wet fish) and Saltfishmongers (fish preserved by salt) and was granted its first Charter in 1272.

The medieval Fishmongers Hall was destroyed in the Great Fire in 1666 although due to its close proximity to the river, many important items from within the building were saved.

The current Hall was built in 1831-35 to replace an earlier hall when part of its site was needed for the new London Bridge Approach. In 1977 when new building work took place facing Upper Thames Street there was the opportunity to improve upon the original old courtyard and as such it was opened up as a small garden that faces straight out to the river, albeit behind some imposing walls.

From what I saw, the garden is on two levels and largely paved with a simple flowerbed and a few trees. It does though feature perhaps the most impressive climbers I've seen in the city, covering the side of a building several storeys high.

Carry on eastwards under London Bridge and soon on your left you will come to St Magnus The Martyr Churchyard.

Gardens of Inner Temple (Includes Hare Court and King's Bench Walk)

At A Glance: Just off the western end of Fleet Street is The Honourable Society of the Inner Temple, one of the four Inns of Court, along with Middle Temple, Lincoln's Inn and Gray's Inn. It is an astonishingly beautiful collection of lawns, squares, gardens and picturesque lanes that dates back to the times of the Knights Templar in 1160 AD.

Site location: The Inner Temple, Middle Temple Lane, Victoria Embankment
Postcode: EC4Y 7HL
Grid ref: TQ312808
Size in hectares: 1.7
Type of site: Gardens of an Institution
Date(s): Medieval; 17th, 19th & 20th centuries
Designer(s): 19th century Robert Marnock, William Robinson
Listed structures: Inner Temple Hall Buttery, gates, gate piers & steps, Crown Office Row. LBII; Gateway to Tudor Street., 5 lamp standards in King's Bench Walk; 1 lamp standard in Hare Court; 2 lamp standards outside Inner Temple Hall
Site ownership: The Honourable Society of the Inner Temple
Site management: The Honourable Society of the Inner Temple
Open to public?: Yes - Private but with public access.
Opening times: Inner Temple Garden: weekdays 12.30-3pm (unless closed for private function or maintenance)

Public transport - Tube Station: Blackfriars and Temple Stations both Circle and District Lines

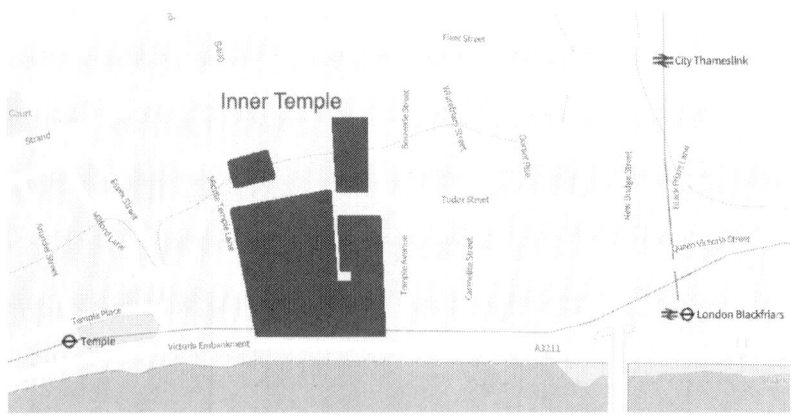

Contains OS data © Crown copyright and database rights 2019

History

Even above the gardens themselves, the highlight here is obviously the Temple Church built back in the era of the Knights Templar. In the 14th century the property was leased to law students by the Knights of the Order of St John of Jerusalem, who inherited the property by order of Parliament in 1324 after the Knights Templar movement was forcibly disbanded and shut down by the Pope.

The Great Garden of the Inner Temple was created by the building of an embankment to control the Thames in 1533; another embankment in 1770 doubled its size and it was again enlarged in the 1870s when the Embankment was constructed. There are lawns, a fine collection of trees, rose beds, a peony garden, seasonal displays in the High Border and a woodland garden.

Amongst the earlier surviving gardens in both Inner and Middle Temple are the 240 metres that stretch along the Embankment to the south along with the gorgeous Fountain Court, which stands to the north-west of Middle Temple Garden. Though sadly mainly used as a car park, Kings Bench is also an old space.

The gardens were already renowned for their roses in Shakespeare's time and he set the dispute between Richard Plantagenet and John Beaufort that led to the War of the Roses here (Henry VI Part 1, Act 2). More roses were added to make the most of the Shakespearean heritage on the west of the Paper buildings.

The High Border is on either side of the main gates and is known for having quite wonderful displays. From the sundial are steps which date from 1730 down to the gardens to the south, on either side of which are displays mainly devoted to Mediterranean species. The Peony Garden is also a highlight.

The gardens have been enlarged on a number of occasions including following the construction of Blackfriars Bridge which led to the erection of a new embankment, completed in 1770 that effectively allowed the Great Garden to double in size. When the present day Embankment was constructed in 1864-70, direct access to the river was unfortunately but unavoidably lost, though in some measure of recompense, the gardens grew in size again.

The present layout of the northern and central sections is largely that of the early 19th-century redesign, and it was then that the annual chrysanthemum show which was held here grew so large that due to complaints by the members of the legal profession it was moved out of the gardens a few miles to the west, where we know it now as the Chelsea Flower Show.

Sadly, Temple buildings were badly bombed in WWII when Lamb Building was lost, its site commemorated by a plaque in Church Court. The present Middle Temple and Inner Temple Gardens have wonderfully large lawns with antiquated walls, railings and mature plane trees.

The rest of the Inner Temple Garden has extensive lawns with scattered trees including the perennial favourite flowering cherry, white-beam, cedar, magnolia and gingko. Harking back to the medieval orchards there are also fruit trees, a black mulberry and a Japanese Blood Walnut.

Within the Inner Temple precincts there are also various courtyards, some of which are landscaped, including Hare Court.

Gardens of Middle Temple (including Fountain Court, Elm Court, Pump Court, Church Court, Brick Court, New Court)

At A Glance: The Honourable Society of the Middle Temple is one of the four Inns of Court, along with Inner Temple, Lincoln's Inn and

Gray's Inn. A simply gorgeous collection of squares, gardens and picturesque lanes that dates back to the times of the Knights Templar in 1160 AD.

Site location: The Temple, Middle Temple Lane, Victoria Embankment
Postcode: EC4Y 9AT
Grid ref: TQ311809
Size in hectares: Middle Temple 0.484; Fountains Court: 0.198
Type of site: Gardens of an Institution
Date(s): Medieval; 17th, 19th & 20th centuries
Listed structures: Middle Temple Hall; Middle Temple Gatehouse; Gateway to New Court from Devereux Court. LBII: Lodge at Victoria Embankment Gateway; Fountain basin in Fountain Court; pair of lamp standards in New Court
Site ownership: The Honourable Society of the Middle Temple
Site management: The Honourable Society of the Middle Temple
Open to public?: Private but with public access.
Opening times: Middle Temple Garden May-Sept: Mon-Fri 12.30-3pm. Also takes part in the Open garden Squares event.
Public transport - Tube Station: Blackfriars and Temple Stations both Circle and District Lines

History
Without repeating too much of the history of adjacent Inner Temple it is recorded that the first ever performance of Shakespeare's *Twelfth Night* was performed in these gardens in 1602 and just a few years later in 1608 the Temple land was granted by a Charter of King

Fountain Court

James I to the Benchers of the Inner and Middle Temple, 'their heirs and assigns for ever, for the habitation and education of the students of law'.

Middle Temple Gardens and buildings were reworked in the mid to late 17th century and it was then that they were enclosed by a tall wall to keep out the Thames. Following this work new spaces were created including Benchers' Garden.

In 1681-82 Fountain Court was formed and the fountain is reputedly the oldest permanent fountain in London. Charles Dickens would often feature the disparity between the rich and poor in London and characters used legal proceedings to seek their rightful justice, and as such areas such as Lincoln's Inn Field and Middle Temple feature heavily in his work with this fountain being the location in *Martin Chuzzlewit* where Ruth Pinch meets John Westlock. Keep an eye out for the two mulberry trees which were planted here in 1887 to commemorate Queen Victoria's Jubilee.

Elm Court

There is so much to see here and a rich variety of planting with a lovely herb garden to the south of Middle Temple Hall, whilst if you edge round to the west of the hall you can see amongst other specimens both the roses of York and Lancaster. Steps lead up to Fountain Court, which has an altogether different ambience.

Within the Middle Temple precincts are numerous landscaped courtyards. Elm Court has a formal garden with fountain. Brick Court and Pump Court also have plenty of mature trees.

Many of these courtyards and passageways as well as being the location for Dickens have been seen in several television programmes including *Downton Abbey*.

George Yard

At A Glance: Despite it being just a few minutes' walk from Bank, George Yard gardens are well hidden away, perhaps because for centuries George Yard existed as a narrow alleyway, but was opened out in 1929-32 to provide a large paved courtyard as offices were constructed around and about and in doing so begat George Square.

Site location: George Yard
Postcode: EC3V 9EA
Grid ref: TQ328810
Size in hectares:

Type of site: Square
Date(s): 1929 -1932 and 1986-1994
Site ownership: City of London Corporation
Site management: City of London Corporation
Open to public?: Yes
Opening times: 24/7
Public transport - Tube Station: Bank (Central, DLR, Northern, Waterloo & City) and Monument (Circle, District).

Contains OS data © Crown copyright and database rights 2019

History

Since its creation from yard to square in 1929-1932, the square has changed over the 20th century as new building works took place, particularly when Barclays Bank, which has had premises on Lombard Street since 1728, decided on building new premises in 1986.

Five decorative reliefs were commissioned in 1946 from Sir Charles Wheeler for Barclays when its HQ was at 54 Lombard Street was relocated here. The courtyard is almost entirely hard landscaped with just a small amount of flowerbeds, two small trees and seating.

Just across George Square is the small garden of the former churchyard of St Edmund the King and Martyr.

Girdlers' Hall Garden

At A Glance: An award winning garden with its origins going back centuries. Having stood since 1431 AD, the first hall of The Worshipful Company of Girdlers was destroyed in 1666 and rebuilt in 1680-81, but this building was unfortunately destroyed by bombing raids in 1940 and then rebuilt, opening in 1961 with a rear garden that charmingly features a mulberry tree grown from a cutting of a tree most likely planted in 1750.

Site location: Basinghall Street/Basinghall Avenue

Postcode: EC2V 5DD
Grid ref: TQ325814
Size in hectares: 0.0479
Type of site: Private Garden
Date(s): C15th, C18th, 1961, 2009
Designer: Jago Keen in 2009
Site ownership: The Worshipful Company of Girdlers
Site management: The Worshipful Company of Girdlers
Open to public?: No
Opening times: Visible only through railing but has taken part in the Open Garden Squares event.
Public transport - Tube Station: Moorgate (Hammersmith & City, Circle, Northern, Metropolitan); Liverpool Street ((Hammersmith & City, Circle, Central, Metropolitan). **Rail:** Liverpool Street

Contains OS data © Crown copyright and database rights 2019

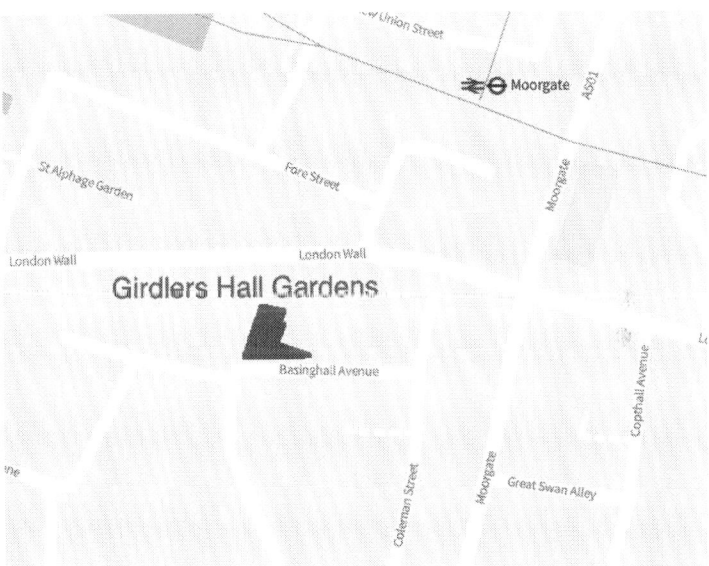

History

Basinghall Street was a long favoured location for the Livery Companies due to its close proximity to the Guildhall which of course is central to the City of London Corporation. Along this road the Coopers, Masons, Weavers all had halls from the around 15th century until the latter half of the 19th century. The Girdlers' Hall is the last to remain here and the patron saint of the Girdlers' is St Lawrence, whose church of St Lawrence Jewry stands nearby adjacent to Guildhall Plaza.

The first Hall and its garden was destroyed in the Great Fire of 1666. It was rebuilt 15 years later on an enlarged plot of land with the garden then containing fig trees, vines and a mulberry as well as roses and all manner of bedding plants.

Like with so many other places, Girdlers' Hall and garden were destroyed in the Blitz in 1941 with the exception of the mulberry tree and fig tree which survived unscathed.

The orientation of the area was however entirely changed post-war as the City of London Corporation compulsory purchased 177 acres around Guildhall allowing them to create a masterplan of post-war reconstruction that we see today.

A new Girdlers' Hall was designed by Waterhouse and Ripley which opened in 1961 with both the hall and garden roughly on their original site.

During 2007-2008 the hall was refurbished and also enlarged upon with an additional floor added. 2009 saw further landscaping although the rear garden still contains a mulberry tree grown from a cutting of a previous tree. Of course there is a well-kept lawn surrounded by paving stone paths shrubs, trees and a small fountain with a cherubic figure.

Cleverly the annual colour schemes in the garden reflect the colours of the Livery and of the ancient carpet that hangs in the Hall interior.

Even to this day The Worshipful Company of Girdlers still presents the sword belt for the Sword of State and Stole for the coronation of a new monarch.

Golden Lane Estate

At A Glance: As with the nearby **Barbican** district, this part of London suffered terribly from the Blitz and in the post-war years was reborn as the Golden Lane Estate in a car-free design mixing blocks of flats with hard landscaping and areas of green space.

Site location: Golden Lane/Fann Street/Goswell Road
Postcode: EC1Y 0SH
Grid ref: TQ321820
Size in hectares:
Type of site: Housing Estate Landcaped Gardens

Date(s): 1953-62

Designer(s): Chamberlin, Powell and Bon

Listed structures: Bowater House, Cuthbert Harrowing House, Community Centre, Basterfield House, Bayer House, Great Arthur House, Stanley Cohen House, garden feature near Golden Lane, Cullum Welch House, Recreation Centre

Site ownership: City of London Corporation

Site management: City of London Corporation Open Spaces Department

Open to public?: Partially

Public transport - Tube Station: Barbican (Metropolitan, Circle, Hammersmith & City); Liverpool Street (Central, Metropolitan, Circle, Hammersmith & City). **Rail:** Liverpool Street

Contains OS data © Crown copyright and database rights 2019

Golden Lane Estate

History

Golden Lane Estate was built for the Corporation of London a decade or so after WWII. The estate was designed to be traffic-free and the aim was to provide accommodation for people working in the City, with 10 blocks around 4 courts, which were largely hard landscaped, the architects regarding the whole scheme as urban. One of the architects is quoted to have said "We have no desire to make the project look like a garden suburb" and if so then it was mission accomplished.

Back on the ground one can find several courtyards and also grassy communal gardens, though there are some trees and a rather splendid fountain.

2019 saw the first openings of the Great Arthur House Roof Garden which had been closed for almost 40 years following a spate of suicides and vandalism from the top of what had been one of the tallest residential buildings at the time.

Gough Square

At A Glance: Whilst there is not much to see in the way of planting, half the joy of this square is to discover it, hidden away in the maze of alleys that lead north off Fleet Street. Once you're there it is quite lovely and that's before you set foot in the home of its most famous son.

Site location: Gough Square with access from Pemberton Row
Postcode: EC4A 3EA
Grid ref: TQ313812
Size in hectares: 0.05
Type of site: Square

Date(s): 17th century and 1990s.

Listed structures: Dr Johnson's House No 17 Gough Square and No 16 Gough Square

Site ownership: City of London Corporation

Site management: City of London Corporation

Open to public?: Yes

Opening times: 24/7

Public transport - Tube Station: Blackfriars (District, Circle); Chancery Lane (Central)

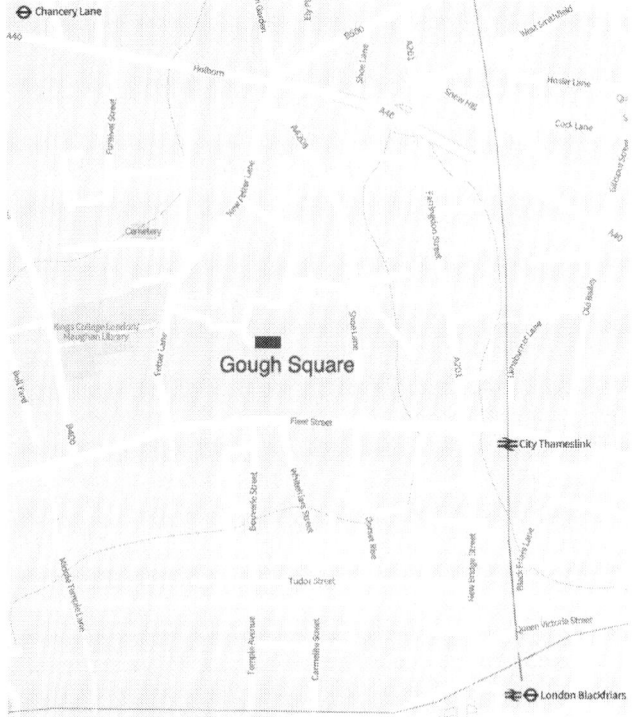

Contains OS data © Crown copyright and database rights 2019

History

Gough Square was originally laid out in the late 17th century as part of a housing development, unsurprisingly by the Gough family.

17 Gough Square is famous for being the house where Dr Samuel Johnson lived in the years between 1748 and 1759 and it was here where he compiled his pioneering Dictionary whilst working in the attic. The house was restored as a museum to Dr Johnson by Alfred Burr in 1911 and at this time the Curator's House to the south with a small garden was also built.

The home of Dr Johnson was actually hit during WWII and though mercifully the damage was comparatively slight, one can still see the charred timbers on the top floor when inside.

The north and east sides of Gough Square were rebuilt in the 1950s and further refurbishment took place in the 1990s after LBC Radio moved out. The square has a solitary tree and is paved with granite stone and laid out with reproduction gas-lights and old cast iron bollards. Vehicular traffic can arrive here through an atmospheric covered carriageway in the north-west corner.

At the far end of the square from the home of Dr Johnson is a statue of his cat, 'Hodge' which has been here since 1997.

Not too far away to the northwest you can find St Dunstan-in-the-West Burial Ground, to the south of Fleet Street is Salisbury Square and further to the west the gardens of the Inner and Middle Temple.

Grocers' Hall Courtyard

At A Glance: A very small private courtyard, rather hidden away from the busy streets of Bank though not the most scenic of gardens if truth be told.

Site location: Grocers' Hall Court, off Prince's Street
Postcode: EC2R 8AD
Grid ref: TQ326812
Type of site: Private Garden
Date(s): 1889-1893 and 1970s
Site ownership: The Grocers' Company
Site management: The Grocers' Company
Open to public?: Yes
Opening times: Monday-Friday 8.30am-5.30pm
Public transport - Tube Station: Bank (Central, DLR, Northern, Waterloo & City)/Monument (Circle, District)

History

The Grocers' Company emerged from the Guild of Pepperers recorded in 1180 AD, and in 1427 purchased the house of Lord Fitzwalter in 1427 which was then part of a much larger piece of real estate, and allowed them to set to work building their hall here.

The Hall was damaged in the Great Fire of 1666 and has been rebuilt several times since then. The Hall had a substantial garden at one point but much was lost when the surrounding streets were realigned at the turn of the 19th century and again a century later when neighbouring buildings (banks) were extended. All of this means just a small amount of planting remains on this triangular courtyard and this is often obscured by cars as well as a statue St Anthony of Vienne at the entrance.

Contains OS data © Crown copyright and database rights 2019

Interestingly this guild sprung off from an association of spice traders known as The Guild of Pepperers. They specialised in bringing in exotic produce from the Byzantine Empire and if nothing else today give us the expression 'peppercorn rent' which derives from the antiquated habit of using pepper as a form of currency.

For something more expansive, 3 minutes' walk away is Guildhall Yard and Piazza

Guildhall Yard and Piazza

At A Glance: One never forgets the first time when on an aimless wandering one happens across the Guildhall and its largely hard landscaped square hidden almost out of sight of Gresham Street. A fantastically expansive open space practically in the middle of nowhere for tourists but right in the heart of old London.

The Guildhall with the rounded outline of the Roman amphitheatre on the paving

Site location: Gresham Street, Aldermanbury Basinghall Street
Postcode: EC2V 5AA

Grid ref: TQ324813

Size in hectares: 0.3251 (South) and 0.1868 (North)

Type of site: Square

Date(s): 12th century to modern day

Listed structures: St Lawrence Jewry Church; Guildhall, former Guildhall Library. The Mayor's & City of London Court; Irish Chamber; Police Callbox. Roman Amphitheatre in Guildhall Yard

Site ownership: City of London Corporation

Site management: City of London Corporation

Open to public?: Yes

Opening times: 24/7

Public transport - Tube Station: St Paul's (Central Line)

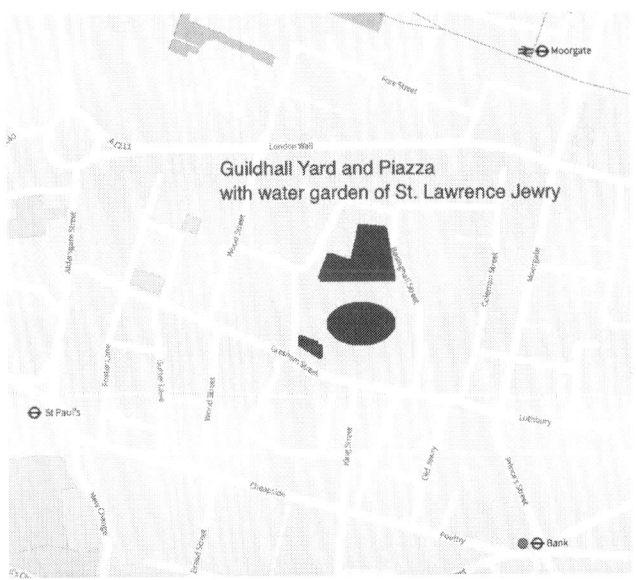

Contains OS data © Crown copyright and database rights 2019

History

Although the building today is 15th-century, the Guildhall was established 300 years earlier. Long gone buildings from that era included a chapel, a library and a gatehouse and all other things that would come with such a prestigious body as a library. Much of the broad piazza was once the churchyard for the 12th century St Lawrence Jewry.

The water feature in the garden of St Lawrence Jewry

The Great Fire of 1666 destroyed the church, which was rebuilt by Christopher Wren, and necessitated some rebuilding of the Guildhall.

A planned rebuild was delayed by 50 years when the Blitz gave a pretty blank canvas to make some far-reaching changes to the area.

Guildhall Piazza and Guildhall Yard are largely hard landscaped, the area to the south adjoining the church having that rare thing in the City, a good sized pond as well as some appropriate planting. The piazza to the north has a number of sculptures.

Beneath the site is a Roman amphitheatre which was only discovered in the 1980s when foundations were being laid for modern building works. It was known there must have been a Roman amphitheatre somewhere in London due to the size and wealth of the city, but later civilisations had made off with and repurposed the stonework.

Whilst not exactly like the Coliseum in Rome, it's well worth going for a look. You'll find the entrance 30 feet under the entrance to the gallery. For those who prefer to stay on the surface, the outline of the placement of the amphitheatre can be seen in the black stone paving blocks that run across the main square.

Just 2 minutes' walk up is St Mary Aldermanbury Garden and nearby Aldermanbury Square.

Jubilee Gardens

At A Glance: Near the top of Houndsditch in the east of the city is this small public garden created for the Queen's Silver Jubilee in 1977.

Contains OS data © Crown copyright and database rights 2019

Site location:
Postcode: EC3A 7AD
Grid ref: TQ333814
Size in hectares: 0.0481
Type of site: Public Gardens
Date(s): 1977 and 2004
Site ownership: City of London Corporation
Site management: City of London Corporation Open Spaces Department
Open to public?: Yes
Opening times: Daylight hours
Public transport - Tube Station: Liverpool Street (Central, Metropolitan, Circle, Hammersmith & City) **Rail:** Liverpool Street

History

As its name might suggest Jubilee Gardens was created for the Queen's Silver Jubilee in 1977. It is a small garden with a scheme of raised brick planters with box hedging within a paved area and some seating that was last refurbished in the early years of the Millennium. Head up Barbon Alley and you will be in Devonshire Square.

King George's Field

At A Glance: Like countless others created under the same scheme, Portsoken Street Garden was created after WWII with financial assistance from the King George's Fields Foundation and is the smallest King George's Field in the country.

Site location: Portsoken Street

Postcode: E1 8BN

Grid ref: TQ337809

Size in hectares: 0.0821

Type of site: Public Gardens

Date(s): Post war and 1980s

Site ownership: City of London Corporation

Site management: City of London Corporation Open Spaces Department

Open to public?: Yes

Opening times: 8am - 7pm (or dusk if earlier)

Public transport - Tube Station: Tower Hill (Circle); Tower Gateway (DLR) **Rail:** Fenchurch Street

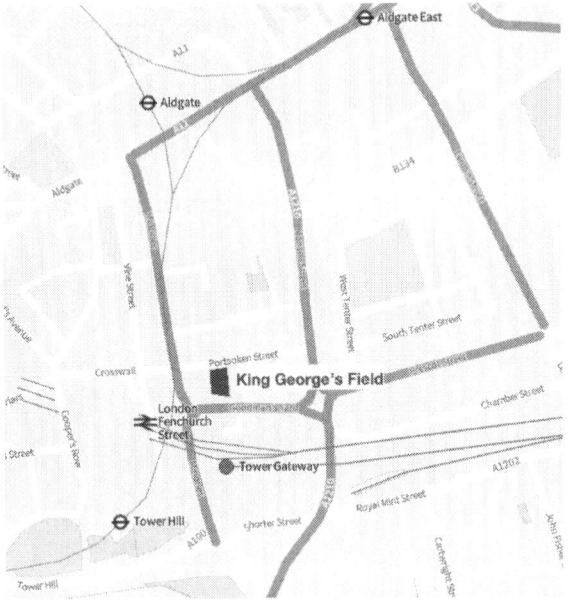

Contains OS data © Crown copyright and database rights 2019

History

Following the King's death in 1936, a foundation was set up to create or improve upon 471 parks and gardens in memory of King George V.

It was thought that the late King would have approved as it would benefit the 'individual well-being and the general welfare of the nation', particularly for young people.

Each new playing field was to be known as King George's Field and it was a condition of the grant that the tenure of the site was sufficiently secure that it would provide a meaningful legacy to the king's memory; the land must have been acquired only for the purpose of public recreation and the original layout and design had to be approved by the foundation.

A water feature with fountain and pools within circular brick walls was integral to a 1980s revamp which also included a perimeter path, some seating and much additional planting, and a decade ago the park was remodelled to include a children's play area, the only other being Tower Hill Gardens. So much has changed that there isn't really much of a resemblance to the original park.

King's College London Strand Campus, Maughan Library and Information Services Centre

At A Glance: King's College London was founded in 1829 and was one of two founding colleges in the University of London in 1836 and is now spread over 5 campuses. This is the oldest one and the site of the former Rolls Chapel which came into being in 1232.

In the last 20 years or so the garden was re-landscaped as a Contemplative Garden of 'green rooms' which includes a water feature.

Site location: Fetter Lane/Chancery Lane

Postcode: WC2A 1LR
Grid ref: TQ311812
Size in hectares: 0.2923
Type of site: Institutional Gardens
Date(s): 1851-96; 1912; 2001/2
Designer(s): 2001: George Carter
Listed Structures: Public Record Office. LBII: Walls, railings and lamps. Gatehouse, gateway and screen wall in Clifford's Inn Passage
Site ownership: King's College London
Site management: King's College London. Garden contractor
Open to public?: Private
Opening times: By appointment only but has taken part in the Open Garden Squares Weekend event.
Public transport - Tube Station: Chancery Lane (Central), Temple (District and Circle Lines)   Contains OS data © Crown copyright and database rights 2019

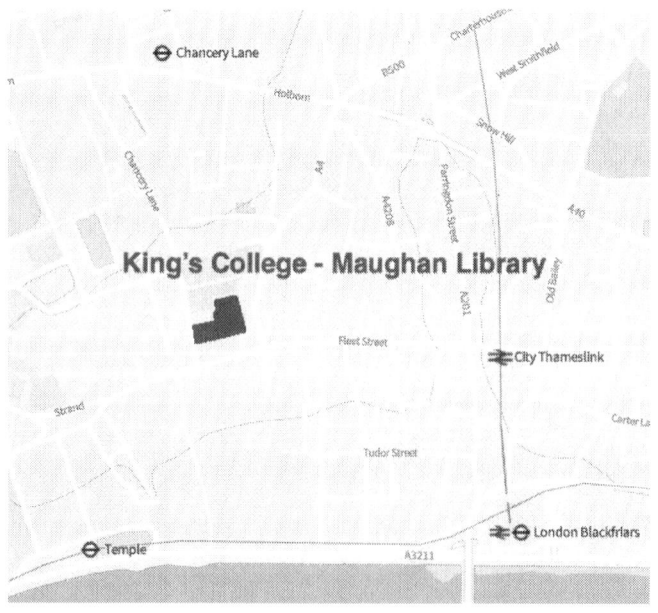

History

Kings College London was founded by King George IV and the Duke of Wellington in 1829, and along with University College London became the founding colleges of the University of London in 1836.

This garden was originally the site of the former Rolls Chapel, which was founded in 1232 by Henry III for Jews who had converted to Christianity. Later the Rolls Estate had responsibility for keeping governmental records and eventually turned into what we know as the Public Record Office which eventually moved to Kew in 1997.

In 2001 the gardens here were reopened to the public as part of King's College London Strand Campus. It has been designed to complement the main features of the adjacent building, and the planting of hornbeam, lime and yew offer links to the past. There is quite an abundance of seating here to take in the garden, water feature and sculpture.

Incidentally 2 minutes' walk away at Cliffords Passage which leads onto Fleet Street you can see some incredibly intact urine deflectors, designed to persuade men to go elsewhere.

London Wall - Moorgate

At A Glance: A small area of landscaping at the road junction of London Wall and Moorgate.

Site location: London Wall/Moorgate

Postcode: EC2

Grid ref: TQ326815

Type of site: Public garden

Date(s): 1959 and 2005

Site ownership: City of London Corporation

Site management: City of London Corporation Open Spaces Department

Open to public?: Yes

Opening times: 24/7

Public transport - Tube Station: Moorgate (Hammersmith & City, Circle, Northern, Metropolitan) **Rail:** Moorgate

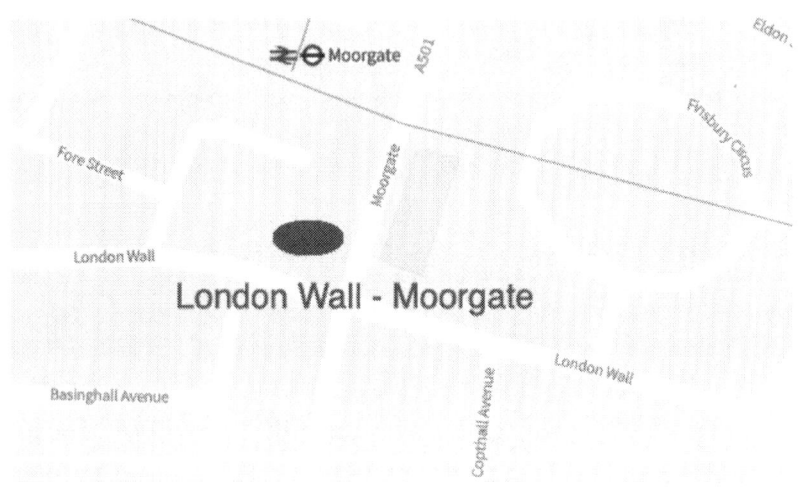

Contains OS data © Crown copyright and database rights 2019

History

As part of the epic repair work following WWII, the road junction of London Wall and Moorgate was one of the first sections to be opened to traffic in 1959. Surrounded by low brick walls, the landscaping consisted of shrub planting, an oak tree and a small area of lawn.

The rather hard to access old gardens down Cliffords Inn Passage, off Fleet Street

The area was more recently re-landscaped as part of realignment of the roads, and the site now consists of an oval area of grass with a series of gentle undulations and an oak tree with the brick wall replaced by hedging.

Until 2005 there had also been a sculpture, 'The Gardener' but this was subsequently moved to Brewers' Hall Garden.

Merchant Taylors' Garden

At A Glance: The Merchant Taylors' Garden is the oldest surviving Livery Company garden. It suffered badly in the Great Fire and the WWII bombings leading to extensive redesigns in 1984-86 when the garden was redesigned by raising the fountain and its surround. The flowerbeds were moved to the outer edge and new stone was laid.

Site location: 30 Threadneedle Street
Postcode: EC2R 8JB
Grid ref: TQ329812
Size in Hectares: 0.0331
Type of site: Private Garden
Date(s): 1406; 1573; 1912; 1986
Listed Structures: Merchant Taylors' Hall
Site ownership: Worshipful Company of Merchant Taylors
Site management: Worshipful Company of Merchant Taylors
Open to public?: By appointment only
Opening times: Contact the Beadle for the possibility of a private visit.
Public transport - Tube Station: Bank (Central, DLR, Northern, Waterloo & City)/Monument (Circle, District)

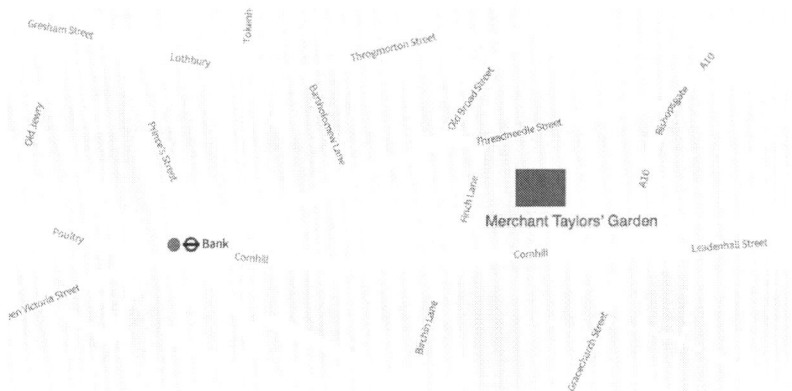

Contains OS data © Crown copyright and database rights 2019

History

This is the oldest surviving Livery Company garden in the City of London and has remained on the same site since at least 1406. The hall though is a post WWII reconstruction but on its original foundations.

A century before the Great Fire the garden had a bowling alley, a terrace, herb garden and 'Knottes' along with stone paving, thought to be Purbeck. In 1598 the garden was converted into grass plots and alleys. It must have been a popular place as visitors to the Hall were blamed for 'spoiling and defacing' the knots by draping washing over them, one of the few problems we don't seem to have in parks and gardens today.

It took several years after the Great Fire before the garden was restored to splendour given the more pressing task of rebuilding the destroyed properties, but sadly all was destroyed in the 1940s.

Following the end of WWII, the garden was laid out much as it might have been in the Edwardian period with its fountain, flowerbeds and a number of ornamental urns and planters. Latterly in 1984-86 the garden was redesigned, the flowerbeds moved and the fountain raised with new paving and box hedging.

Mitre Square

At A Glance: One of the most improved squares of recent years. Still small but recently refurbished into public gardens with a unique and famously grisly history.

Site location: Mitre Square (off Mitre Street/Dukes Place)
Postcode: EC3A 5DE
Grid ref: TQ334811
Size in Hectares: 0.0552
Type of site: Public Garden
Date(s): 1108, 1534, 19thC and 2018/19
Site ownership: City of London Corporation
Site management: City of London Corporation
Open to public?: Yes
Opening times: 24/7
Public transport - Tube Station: Aldgate (Circle and Metropolitan Lines)

History

This history of Mitre Square goes back almost a millennium when the Holy Trinity Priory was founded around 1108 by Queen Matilda, first wife of King Henry I, and later two of the children of King Stephen were buried here as was London's first Mayor, Henry FitzAilwin.

Contains OS data © Crown copyright and database rights 2019

The adjoining Mitre Street was the nave whilst Mitre Square itself occupies the site of what was the cloister of Holy Trinity Priory, Aldgate.

Sadly of course the Priory suffered under the Dissolution of the Monasteries of King Henry VIII with it lying derelict for a number of years before being handed to the nearby church of St. Botolph Without.

If you take a peek through the windows of the building at the junction of Mitre Street and Leadenhall Street you can still see some of the ruins and indeed the old water-well if you can blag your way inside. For those who can't, it likely connects to the famous Aldgate Pump of Death across the road, restored in September 2019.

For much of the 20th century and early 21st century Mitre Square was a grim old place with just a small raised flowerbed on top of a ventilation outlet and another flanked by wooden benches, approximately at the spot for which the square is most notorious.
For here in the south corner of the square was the site of the murder of Catherine Eddowes by Jack the Ripper. Her mutilated body was found there at 1:45 in the morning on 30 September 1888 just an hour after she had been released from prison for being drunk in public. This was the westernmost of the Whitechapel Murders and the only one located within the City of London.

One has to use a little imagination now but St James's Passage, Creechurch Place and across the road through the blue gate the passage to St Katherine Cree Churchyard give a little bit of an idea of the old maze of streets that Jack the Ripper operated in.

In 2017-18 Mitre Square was finally redeveloped and now has peaceful lawn areas and raised flowerbeds surrounded by curved stone seating.

As well as visiting works of public art, Mitre Square is home to a very welcoming Illy café which makes it hard to believe what terrible events unfolded here over 130 years ago and shows that sometimes change can be a good thing. Just a few minutes away to the east is the expansive Aldgate Square but for something a whole lot more secluded then just across Mitre Road is St Katherine Cree churchyard which you can find behind a blue gate.

The newly developed Mitre Square. Catherine Eddowes was murdered where the photo was taken.

Monkwell Square

At A Glance: Just to the north of the busy London Wall road is Monkwell Square. It was formed after WWII on the site of Monkwell Street, the name probably originating from the medieval Muchewella family.

Site location: Monkwell Square   **Postcode:** EC2Y 5BL
Grid ref: TQ323816   **Size in Hectares:** 0.58
Type of site: Public Gardens   **Date(s):** Post WWII and 1980s
Designer(s): Terry Farrell Partnership
Site ownership: Private
Site management: City of London Corporation Open Spaces Dept
Open to public?: Yes   **Opening times:** 24/7
Public transport - Tube Station: Barbican and Moorgate (Circle, Metropolitan, Hammersmith & City) **Rail:** Moorgate

Contains OS data © Crown copyright and database rights 2019

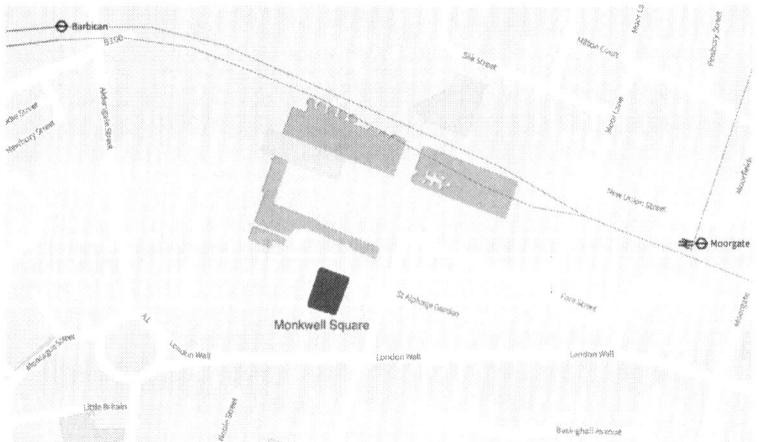

History

Monkwell Square was originally formed after WWII on the site of Monkwell Street. Originally there was a formal layout with grass and circular planters. There was also an area of hexagonal paving with plenty of seating.

The Alban Gate development of the 1980s which was named after the nearby Wren church of St Alban in Wood Street resulted in the square not just being redesigned but becoming considerably smaller in size.

Though there is residential property bordering much of the square, it is also adjacent to the Barber Surgeons' Hall whose garden lies to the west.

I often feel that the current garden could be worked on a little, even though perhaps little can be done about the neighbouring buildings, but there are plenty of trees and an area surrounded by balustrades which add some interest here.

Museum of London

At A Glance: A Rotunda Garden in the middle of the Museum of London which was set up in the 1960s and refurbished in 2011. Access is through the high-level walkways.

Site location: Aldersgate Street/London Wall
Postcode: EC2Y 5HN
Grid ref: TQ321816
Size in Hectares: 0.0634
Type of site: Museum gardens
Date(s): 1968
Listed Structures: None
Site ownership: Museum of London
Site management: Museum of London
Open to public?: Yes
Opening times: Museum opening times: Mon - Sat 10am - 5.50pm; Sun 12 to 5.50pm last admission 5.30pm. Nursery Garden April-Oct only. Rotunda visible from walkway.
Public transport - Tube Station: St Paul's (Central Line); Barbican (Hammersmith & City, Circle and Metropolitan Lines)

History

As part of the massive rebuilding effort following WWII, it was decided that a new museum be built alongside the parallel new road and the numerous developments in the Barbican area. Work actually began in 1968 and the museum opened in 1976.

In the centre of the circular Museum building is a sunken Rotunda Garden overlooked by City Walkway that leads to the museum entrance, and very close by is a striking memorial to John Wesley.

Contains OS data © Crown copyright and database rights 2020

There is also a Nursery Garden which was created in 1990 with over 20 historic nurseries evoking the history of the nurserymen who have worked in London over the last 1,000 years.

The Museum of London is scheduled to relocate to nearby Smithfields in a few years' time so plans are uncertain as to what will become of the garden here.

Noble Street Gardens

At A Glance: Noble Street Gardens is a sunken garden adjacent to Plaisterers' Hall Suffering heavily from WWII aerial bombings, the aftermath saw the excavation of Roman ruins which give this unusual garden its unique feeling.

Contains OS data © Crown copyright and database rights 2019

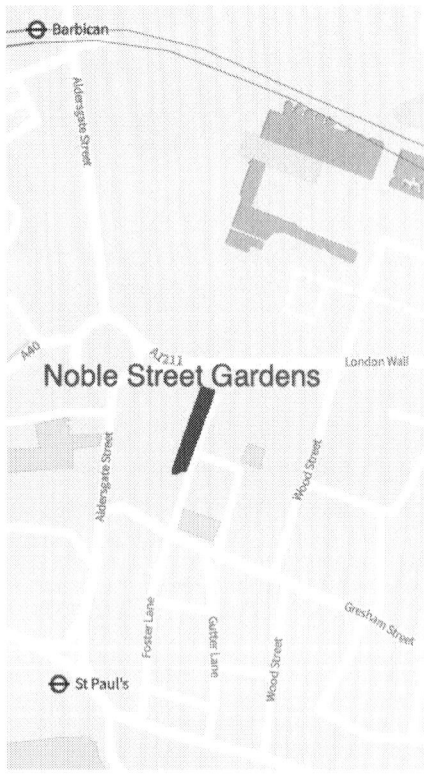

Site location: Noble Street/ London Wall

Postcode: EC2V 7JU

Grid ref: TQ322814

Size in Hectares: 0.0653

Type of site: Private Garden

Date(s): 1970-83 and 2002.

Listed Structures: Remains of Roman Wall

Site ownership: Plaisterers' Company

Site management: City of London Corporation Open Spaces Dept

Open to public?: No but designed to be viewed by the public from Noble Street

Opening times: Has taken place in the Open Garden Squares Weekend.

Public transport - Tube Station: St Paul's (Central Line); Barbican (Hammersmith & City, Circle and Metropolitan Lines)

History

Originally Noble Street was named after Thomas Noble who was a landowner in these parts during the 14th century.

The Worshipful Company of Plaisterers was incorporated in 1501 and its original hall was built in 1556 in Addle Hill off Carter Lane, rebuilt first after the Great Fire of 1666 and then in 1882 after another fire.

Noble Street Gardens with the Roman foundations visible alongside the later modified wall. Note the bee hives, an indication of the importance these gardens are to nature.

This part of London suffered heavy bomb damage in WWII, and the sunken garden is set with and against the old Roman and later medieval walls.

The garden is laid out with grass, seating, and some planting, with creepers growing over the remains of the wall. There are some beehives present which serve as a reminder of the importance of these small gardens to the biodiversity of the City of London.
Almost across the road to the north is St Olave Silver Street whereas at the opposite end of the street is the Churchyard of Saint John Zachary.

Old Change Court

At A Glance: Old Change Court was laid out in the 1960s. It is part of the of the City Walkway and just off Carter Lane and a short walk from the very well-known St Paul's, moderately well-known Festival Gardens and the largely unknown St Nicholas Cole Abbey.

Site location: Carter Lane
Postcode: EC4M 8EN
Grid ref: TQ321810
Size in Hectares: 0.2386
Type of site: Public Gardens
Date(s): 1960s and 2010s
Site ownership: City of London Corporation

Site management: City of London Corporation Open Spaces Department
Open to public?: Yes
Opening times: 24/7
Public transport - Tube Station: St Paul's (Central Line), Mansion House (Circle and District Lines) **Rail:** Blackfriars

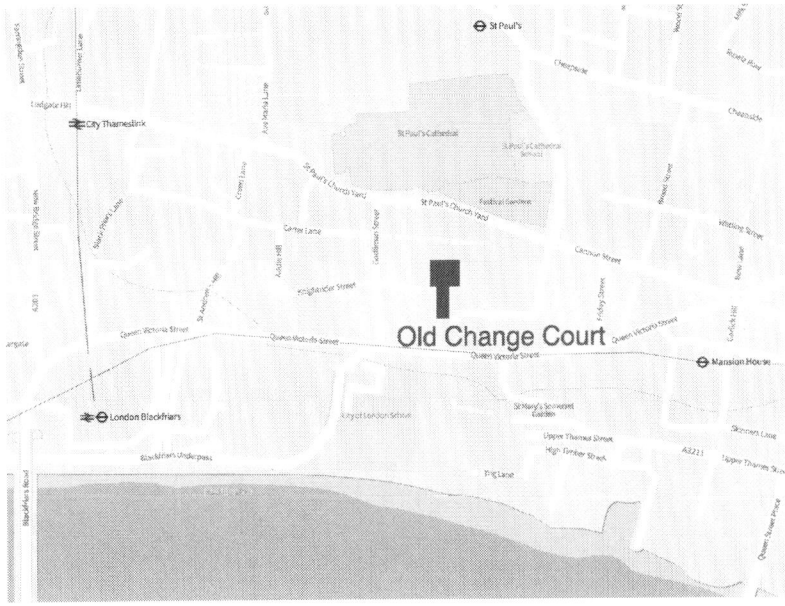

Contains OS data © Crown copyright and database rights 2019

History: Old Change Court has recently been remodelled and is now a largely hard furnished garden. There are four mature trees in raised planters on the upper level, each surrounded by seating, whilst down a few steps are six large planters with seasonal flowers, accompanied by wooden benches.

In 2019 the neighbouring Distaff Lane Garden opened to the public.

One New Change

At A Glance: Originally constructed in 1953-60 for the Bank of England, the building faced all-round derision despite it being home to a formal sunken garden facing Bread Street complete with 18th-century style fountains and lawns. This building was demolished in 2007 and replaced in 2010, with new pedestrian routes and public access to a rooftop garden.

Site location: New Change/Bread Street
Postcode: EC4M 9AD
Grid ref: TQ321811
Size in Hectares: 0.099 (garden area)
Type of site: Private open land.
Date(s): 1953-1960 and 2005-2010
Designer(s): 1953-60: Ernest Gillick (landscape architect); Victor Heal (architect); 2005-10 Jean Nouvel
Site ownership: Land Securities
Site management: Land Securities
Open to public?: Yes
Opening times: 10am until evenings

Public transport - Tube Station: St Paul's (Central Line) Mansion House (Circle and District Lines), Bank (Central, DLR, Northern, Waterloo & City) **Rail:** Cannon Street

Contains OS data © Crown copyright and database rights 2019

History

Situated in what had once been part of the market area of the City of London (Bread Street), rather unusually for the post-war reconstruction in the City, New Change Buildings were built by the Corporation of London in 1953-60 in a traditional rather than modernist style. This reflected prevailing opinion in the Corporation that sought to preserve the setting of St Paul's Cathedral in the post-war reconstruction through classically inspired buildings. However almost upon completion the build faced a wealth of detractors.

The central courtyard was famously described as 'disastrously bleak' by Nikolaus Pevsner with a plain fountain, some planting and for some reason, replica 18th-century-style lead cisterns. So underwhelming was it that it became something of a car park. As such it was a relief to many when the demolition of New Change Buildings began in 2007. The new scheme became known as One New Change and was completed in December 2010.

The unparalleled view of St Pauls from the rooftop gardens of One New Change

One New Change has a roof garden but reaching it can be something of a trial for the first time, and requires passing through the retail-lined ground floor from New Change to Bread Street, which is crossed by a second pedestrian route from Cheapside to Watling

Street. In the centre where the two routes meet, a lift provides public access to new rooftop gardens where a variety of restaurants and bars can be found.

There isn't too much for horticulturalists here but it is hard to find a better view of St Paul's and it makes for a fine place to sit and rest for a while. One of the wall also has some artwork too but really the dome of St Paul's is the star attraction here.

If all of this doesn't sound like your cup of tea then the garden at 25 Cannon Street is much easier to access.

One Tree Park

At A Glance: This small, predominantly paved area was once the Upper Burying Ground of the parish of St Botolph by Billingsgate which was never rebuilt after its destruction in the Great Fire. There is a small plaque stating this in the courtyard paving with the garden largely consisting of the one tree.

Site location: Monument Street/Botolph Lane
Postcode: EC3R 8BT
Grid ref: TQ330806
Size in Hectares: 0.0141
Type of site: Private Garden
Date(s): Medieval and 20th century
Site ownership: Private

Site management: Private
Open to public?: No
Opening times: None but visible from the street
Public transport - Tube Station: Monument (District and Circle) Lines, Bank (Central, DLR, Northern, Waterloo & City Line

Contains OS data © Crown copyright and database rights 2019

History

The burial ground was established in 1392 AD though the stone piers and old gate at the corner of Monument Street possibly are only from the 18th century. Standing to the east of the churchyard, south of Lower Thames Street, the church of St Botolph Billingsgate dated from the 12th century and was rebuilt around 80 years before it was destroyed in 1666 in the Great Fire of London, and then was not rebuilt as part of the site was used for the widening of Thames Street.

These days we think of St Christopher as the patron saint of travellers but St Botolph was the Anglo-Saxon patron saint of travellers, and as a result churches with this dedication were usually located at city gates.

Interestingly in the late 19th century the area was a playground for Billingsgate Ward School but it is now a private courtyard for a residential building, with minimal planting and a solitary circular planter.

For something a little greener try St Mary at Hill Churchyard.

Paternoster Square

At A Glance: Paternoster Square has long been a sacred space by its association with Paternoster Row where the clergy of St Paul's used to walk in procession, reciting the Paternoster prayer. It was once the site of the Newgate Meat Market and now is one of the largest open squares in the City and home to numerous works of art and temporary cultural and artistic events.

Site location: Paternoster Square, near St Paul's Cathedral.

Postcode: EC4M 7DX

Grid ref: TQ319812

Size in Hectares:

Type of site: Square

Date(s): 1960s and 1996-2004.

Designer(s): William Holford in the 1960s and latterly William Whitfields

Listed Structures: Temple Bar

Site ownership: Mitsubishi Estate Co

Site management: Mitsubishi Estate Co

Open to public?: Yes

Opening times: 24/7

Public transport - Tube Station: St Paul's (Central Line) **Rail:** City Thameslink

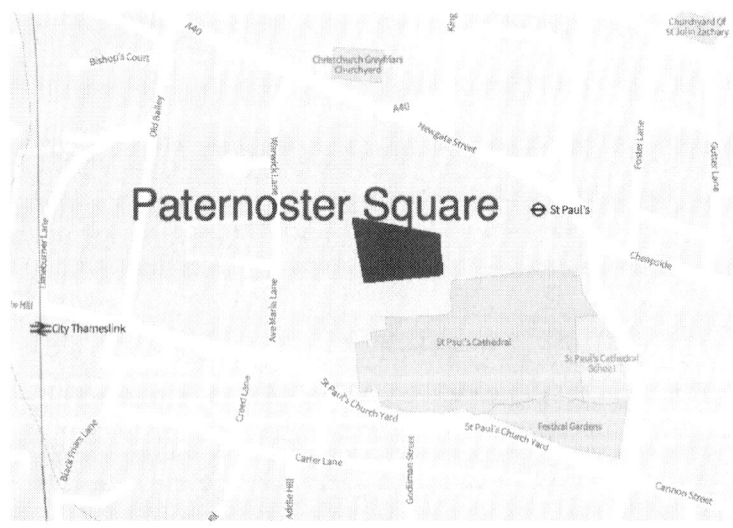

Contains OS data © Crown copyright and database rights 2019

History

Being adjacent to St Paul's Cathedral, the area was heavily bombed during WWII and its first reincarnation was never all that engaging so a 1989 plan was adopted to create the high-end retail, business and leisure space we see today.

There are a number of works of art that give an insight to the history of the district including a bronze sculpture by Elisabeth Frink, 'Paternoster - Shepherd and Sheep' which was commissioned for the Square in 1975 and harks back to the old meat market.

Paternoster Square from the dome of St Pauls

Looking rather like its taller and more famous cousin (Monument) is the Paternoster Square Column; it is a 23m high Portland stone Corinthian column at the top of which is a flaming copper urn covered with gold leaf, which is illuminated by fibre-optic lighting at night. As with the famous Monument there is a gold flame sat atop the column and this is to remember both the Great Fires of London; 1666 and 1940.

In 2004 the historic Temple Bar was re-erected as the entrance to the Paternoster Square having previously marked the boundary between City of London and City of Westminster. Originally commissioned by Charles II, the Portland stone arch was designed by Christopher Wren. During the 18th Century the heads of traitors were mounted on pikes and splayed from the roof! By the Victorian era it had long become an impediment to traffic and so was dismantled in 1878 when the Corporation of London needed to widen the road, and for a century or so the 2,700 stones were erected in a private garden in Enfield before being brought to what is hopefully their final and suitably impressive location.

Paternoster Square is often home to temporary exhibitions, cultural and sporting events but if you want something quieter then at the far end of Rose Alley you will see
Christchurch Greyfriars Garden.

Postman's Park

At A Glance: This greatly loved park was laid out as a public garden in 1880, from the churchyard of St Botolph Aldersgate, and later enlarged to incorporate the adjacent disused graveyards of St Leonard's Foster Lane and Christchurch, Newgate Street, resulting in it going from one of the smallest to one of the largest parks in the City.

So named due to its popularity with workers at the adjacent Post Office sorting office, it is particularly revered due to the erection of the memorial shelter with its wall of tablets commemorating the heroic deeds of ordinary men and women who lost their lives to save

Looking up from the Aldersgate Street entrance

others, which was proposed to mark the Golden Jubilee of Queen Victoria in 1887 though it wasn't constructed until 1899.

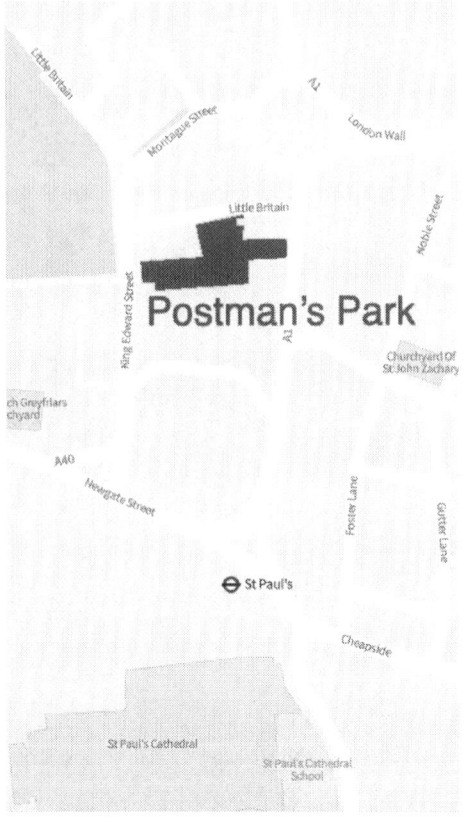

Contains OS data © Crown copyright and database rights 2019

Site location: St Botolph Aldersgate/Aldersgate Street
Postcode: EC1A 4AS
Grid ref: TQ321814
Size in Hectares: 0.2648
Type of site: Public Gardens
Date(s): 1348 AD, 1880s and 1900.
Listed Structures: St Botolph's Church. Gates & railings to church on Aldersgate St; Memorial Shelter; Drinking fountain on Aldersgate St. SAM: remains of Roman Wall/ Bastion
Site ownership: City of London Corporation
Site management: City of London Corporation Open Spaces Department and Friends of St Botolph's Aldersgate and Postman's Park

Open to public?: Yes
Opening times: Daylight hours
Public transport - Tube Stations: St Paul's (Central Line), Barbican (Circle, Hammersmith and Metropolitan Lines)

History

There has been a church here since at least the 12th century if not earlier, although only St Botolph's remains following the destruction during the Great Fire of London and the Blitz of St Leonards Foster Lane and Christchurch respectively.

Enclosed by 19th-century railings, the park is a long and narrow site and its layout was based on a series of focal points: a pool with luxurious planting around it and surrounded by round-headed railings; the memorial shelter; a central flowerbed, and a tree which in times past once had a circular seat around it.

A number of mature plane trees create shady areas along with sometimes exotic trees and shrubs including, chestnut, lime and fig.

The entrance from Aldersgate Street retains the original ornamental metal railings and gates. There is a still functioning memorial which dates back to 1870 as well as a plaque commemorating John Wesley who is also featured in one of the stained glass windows within the church near the door, though it is best seen from within. In fact there is a plaque above the door of a residence towards the end of Little Britain where Charles Wesley had his evangelical conversion and it is from this house that John Wesley went for a walk and himself encountered the Holy Spirit at the Museum of London.

St Botolph Aldersgate and Postmans Park

There are plenty of headstones along the perimeter of Postman's Park and a few tombs scattered around too. A circular pond with a fountain complete with some rather large golden fish is in the pathway from Aldersgate Street and the flowerbeds from there to the Watts Memorial Shelter are always host to seasonal planting and supplemented by tree ferns.

The undoubted highlight of Postman's Park is the Memorial to Heroic Self-sacrifice. It is a wall of ceramic tiles each commemorating the heroic deeds of ordinary people who as a result of their actions lost their own lives, and all under a shelter. There are 53 glazed plaques in total; 13 designed by Watts, 30 by his widow, with five added in 1930 and subsequently one more in recent years. Apparently it has been decided that no more memorials will be added which I think is rather a shame as the deeds of good people are so quickly forgotten and are surely needed now more than ever.

The view from the Kind Edward Street entrance

Two minutes away is the garden at St Anne and St Agnes.

Queen Street

At A Glance: A small private garden tucked away off Cannon Street on a newly pedestrianised stretch of Queen Street.

Site location: 27 and 28 Queen Street
Postcode: EC4R 1BB
Grid ref: TQ324809
Size in hectares: Unknown
Type of site: Private Garden
Date(s): 1850s
Listed structures: 27 and 28 Queen Street
Site ownership: Formcut
Site management: Formcut
Open to public?: No
Opening times: None but visible from the street
Public transport - Tube Station: Mansion House (Circle and District) **Rail:** Cannon Street

History

It might be hard to tell today but the raised forecourt of the splendid looking 18th-century houses at numbers 27 and 28 Queen Street are part of the site of the former burial ground of the church of St-Thomas-the-Apostle.

St Thomas-the-Apostle was first recorded in 1170 AD and later rebuilt in 1371, having been destroyed and not rebuilt in the Great Fire of London with the parish joined with St Mary Aldermary. The

churchyard survived longer however, and remained until 1851 when
Queen Street was widened.

Contains OS data © Crown copyright and database rights 2019

The human remains from these works were interred in a vault on the
east side where there is still a detached burial ground. The forecourt
garden itself is accessed by a flight of steps each side, and is paved
with one large plane tree and shrubs. Look out for the old plaque
which is laid into the wall.

Nearby you have St James Garlickhythe Church and Whittingdon
Garden.

Royal Exchange Gardens

At A Glance: Right in the very heart of the City of London, outside
the Bank of England and the Royal Exchange buildings are these

two small gardens, most notable perhaps for the numerous works of art which they contain but with a history going back to at least the 10th century.

Site location: Threadneedle Street/Cornhill/Royal Exchange Buildings
Postcode: EC3V 3LF
Grid ref: TQ328811
Size in Hectares: 0.1106 (east side + 0.0773 (west side)
Type of site: Square
Date(s): 1840s and 20th century
Listed Structures: Royal Exchange. Statue of Wellington, 1914-18 War Memorial, 2 drinking fountains in Royal Exchange Square, statue of George Peabody, No 2 Royal Exchange Buildings
Site ownership: City of London Corporation
Site management: City of London Corporation Open Spaces Department
Open to public?: Yes
Opening times: 24/7
Public transport - Tube Station: Bank (Central, DLR, Northern, Waterloo & City Lines) and Monument (Circle and District Lines)
Rail: Cannon Street

History

London's first Exchange was founded by Sir Thomas Gresham in 1566-70, and the original was lost in the Great Fire and promptly replaced during 1667-71 by what was described as 'the grandest monument of artisan classicism in the City'. Sadly it too was destroyed by a fire in 1838 leaving us the still splendid Exchange building we have today.

Contains OS data © Crown copyright and database rights 2019

General trading took place here until the outbreak of WWII after which it became home to a number of specialist exchanges. The building has a sumptuous central courtyard which was covered all the way back in 1883 and now houses upmarket establishments such as Fortnum & Mason.

To the western end of the Royal Exchange is a paved area with a number of wonderful military statues including one of the Duke of Wellington from 1844 and a 1919 Great War memorial. The garden area at the junction of Threadneedle Street and Cornhill was re-landscaped in 1985 and is home to low walls, some shrubs and seats as well as splendid looking cast-iron lamps.

The Royal Exchange Square lies to the east of the Royal Exchange. It's a paved pedestrian area that was created in 1906 and is home to a number of sculptures and a fountain.

There is also a drinking fountain commemorating the Jubilee of the Metropolitan Drinking Fountain and Cattle Trough Association at the south end. Intriguingly this is a copy of the original one that was stolen in 1911.

Before any of this development, the site was home to the long destroyed church of St Benet Fink.

A few minutes' walk through some atmospheric alleys, fine pubs and past the oldest coffee house in London you will find the churchyard garden of St Michael Cornhill.

Saddlers' Hall Garden

At A Glance: A small private garden belonging to The Worshipful Company of Saddlers who, being formed in 1395 by Royal Charter, are one of the oldest Livery Companies in the City of London.

Site location: 44 Gutter Lane
Postcode: EC2V 6BR
Grid ref: TQ322812
Size in Hectares: 0.0257
Type of site: Private Garden

Date(s): 15th century and 1989
Designer: James Welch (1989)
Site ownership: The Worshipful Company of Saddlers
Site management: The Worshipful Company of Saddlers
Open to public?: By appointment only
Opening times: Possibly by appointment but visible through the railings.
Public transport - Tube Station: St Paul's (Central Line)

Contains OS data © Crown copyright and database rights 2019

History

The first Saddlers' Hall was built on this site as soon as a Royal Charter was granted to the Saddlers' Company in 1395 AD. Both it and two successive buildings were destroyed through events such as the Great Fire of London and the Blitz with the current Neo-Georgian styled building dating from 1958.

Saddlers' Hall courtyard garden itself was last re-landscaped in 1989 and consists of a cobbled path with raised bedding adjacent to it. There are also a number of planters and, rather fittingly, a sculpted horse's head. On the south wall is a carved pediment originally from the third Hall and formerly on the Foster Lane entrance.

For something easier to access then St Vedast alias Foster Churchyard is only a few seconds away.

Salisbury Square

At A Glance: Salisbury Square was once a grand front yard for a house which belonged to the Bishops of Salisbury, hence the name. They settled here around 1200 AD though any obvious signs of their time have been lost.

Whilst there is some tasteful 18th-century housing here, it is somewhat overwhelmed by less tasteful late 20th-century office blocks. However there is a seated area amongst trees next to a rather splendid looking obelisk.

Site location: Salisbury Square

Postcode: EC4Y 8AE

Grid ref: TQ314811

Size in Hectares:

Type of site: Square

Date(s): 18th century and 1990s

Designer(s): epr Architects Ltd (1990s)

Listed Structures: Obelisk

Site ownership: City of London Corporation

Site management: City of London Corporation Open Spaces Department

Open to public?: Yes

Opening times: 24/7

Public transport - Tube Station: Blackfriars (District, Circle). Rail: Blackfriar   Contains OS data © Crown copyright and database rights 2020

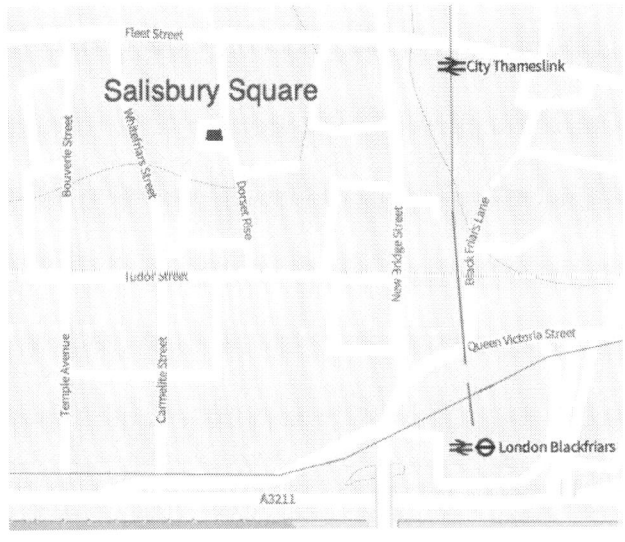

History

Following its time being the home of the Bishops of Salisbury, the property was purchased by the Sackville family in 1565. They were obviously well to do as they were soon granted the title the Earls of Dorset which explains the naming of nearby Dorset Rise street.

Salisbury Square with an uninspiring backdrop

The square still has some 18th-century housing but is sadly dominated by more recent developments, particularly a rather awful 1960s office block.

In the centre of the square on a low circular plinth is a granite obelisk brought here in 1975 from Bartholomew Close. The obelisk commemorates Lord Mayor of 1823-24 Robert Waithman.

Surrounding the obelisk, the area is paved with seating and a raised brick planter with shrubs and small trees, and the road around this central landscaping is cobbled which helps to add a little character.

Whilst Salisbury Square may never be the most picturesque or richly planted garden it makes for a welcome detour off busy Fleet Street and is just a short walk from St Bride's Church.

Salters' Garden

At A Glance: The Salters' Garden is one of London's hidden gems, with a portion of the London Wall and the surrounding open spaces making it something special. Originally opened in 1981, this contemporary garden was redesigned as a knot garden by David Hicks FRSA and reopened in 1995 to commemorate the 600th anniversary of the Worshipful Company of Salters.

This lovely secluded garden, which is sunk below road level and has the old Roman city wall as its southern boundary, is formally laid out with areas of lawn, hedging, pergolas and fountains. In summer, it is full of beautiful and fragrant roses.

Site location: Salters' Hall, London Wall Place/Fore Street

Postcode: EC2Y 5DE

Grid ref: TQ324816

Size in Hectares: 0.0796

Type of site: Private Garden

Date(s): 1981; 1995 and 2019

Listed Structures: Section of the Roman Wall

Site ownership: Salters' Company

Site Management: Salters' Company

Open to public?: Yes

Opening times: Generally open to the public 9am-5pm Mondays - Fridays.

Public transport - Tube Station: Moorgate (Circle, Hammersmith & City, Metropolitan and Northern Lines), St Paul's (Central Line). **Rail:** Moorgate

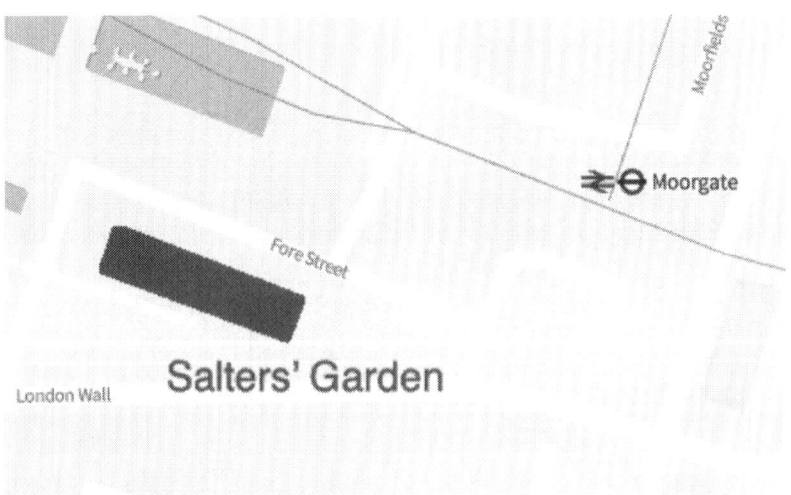

Contains OS data © Crown copyright and database rights 2020

History

The Worshipful Company of Salters was founded in 1394 and based in Bread Street before moving to Oxford House on St Swithin's Lane, the site of the house of the first Lord Mayor of the City of London. Sadly this Hall was damaged beyond repair during WWII and so the Salters moved here in the 1970s. The wrought iron gates with birds at the Fore Street entrance date from 1887 and have moved from the previous site at St Swithin's Lane.

Looking into Salters Garden with the old city wall on the left

The new garden is sunk below road level and has the old city wall as its southern boundary. It's rather formally set out with areas of lawn, hedging and pergolas complete with both paving and gravel paths. The garden is also home to three fountains, one adjacent to the building and one at each end of the garden.

The eastern side of the garden was remodelled around the time the new high-level walkways were installed (circa 2018) and consist of modern paved terrace with low-level planting on each tier, sometimes festooned with modern art.

There are all manner of gardens to the north but just to the south is St Alphage Garden and St Alphage Extension Garden.

Seething Lane Gardens

At A Glance: A recently redeveloped garden not too far from the Tower of London with close connections with the famed diarist Samuel Pepys, who worked here at the Navy Office.

Site location: Seething Lane
Postcode: EC3N 4AT
Grid ref: TQ333807
Size in Hectares: 0.0861
Type of site: Public Gardens
Date(s): 1950 and 2018
Listed Structures: No. 2 Seething Lane

Site ownership: City of London Corporation

Site management: City of London Corporation Open Spaces Department

Open to public?: Yes

Opening times: 24/7

Public transport - Tube Station: Tower Hill (Circle and District Lines) **Rail:** Fenchurch Street **DLR:** Tower Gateway

Contains OS data © Crown copyright and database rights 2020

History

A recently redeveloped garden with close links to the famed diarist Samuel Pepys who lived and worked here at the Navy Office. The original office survived the Great Fire but was destroyed by fire in 1673 with Sir Christopher Wren building a new one in 1682-3 which lasted only until 1788, when warehouses were built for the East and West India Docks Company.

Previously the last significant remodelling of the garden was in 1950 when it used to be locked at night. It was then closed for several years in the previous decade to facilitate the work being done on neighbouring Trinity House before reopening in a much improved style in 2018.

New features of the garden include a formal lawn area almost double the size of the previous garden, as well 14 new trees. A former service road running between the garden and 10 Trinity Square was closed, resulting in a net increase in the area of the garden by 20%. With an eye to the environment, rainwater harvested from the roof of 10 Trinity Square is used to irrigate the garden.

As well as the customary blue plaque there is a fantastic bust of Pepys by late British sculptor Karin Jonzen, which in many ways is the centrepiece of the new garden.

New stone paths feature work by sculptor Alan Lamb depicting scenes from Pepys' life and diaries such as the Great Fire, pesky plague fleas and of course his eponymous cheese account.

The addition of new trees and shrubs aims to improve the biodiversity of the area and will become an important habitat for wildlife within the urban landscape.

There are also some red roses to commemorate the date in 1381 when the wife of Sir Robert Knollys seethed about chaff blowing across from the land opposite her house. She promptly bought out the offenders and built a bridge across a stream that once flowed

The plague doctor and rat, one of engravings in the stone paving
stones of Seething Lane Gardens

down the street. However she did so without permission, which was retrospectively granted for which the City charged Sir Robert one red rose each summer. This is still marked by an annual ceremony arranged by the Company of Watermen and Lightermen of the River Thames who present the Lord Mayor with the first rose of the summer.

It should be said that the word 'Seething' is more likely to come from the medieval word 'sifethen' meaning 'full of chaff' than anyone being angry!   Whilst you're here be sure to visit St Olave just across the road.

Senator House Gardens

At A Glance: A small contemporary public space created in combination with the upgrading of a 1980's office block.

Site location: Senator House Gardens
Postcode: EC4V 4AB
Grid ref: TQ32235 80894
Type of site: Public Gardens
Date(s): 1980's and 2019
Designers: Parmabrook
Site ownership: City of London Corporation
Site management: City of London Corporation Open Spaces Department

Open to public?: Yes

Opening times: 24/7

Public transport - Tube Station: Mansion House   (Circle and District Lines) **Rail:** Cannon Street & Blackfriars

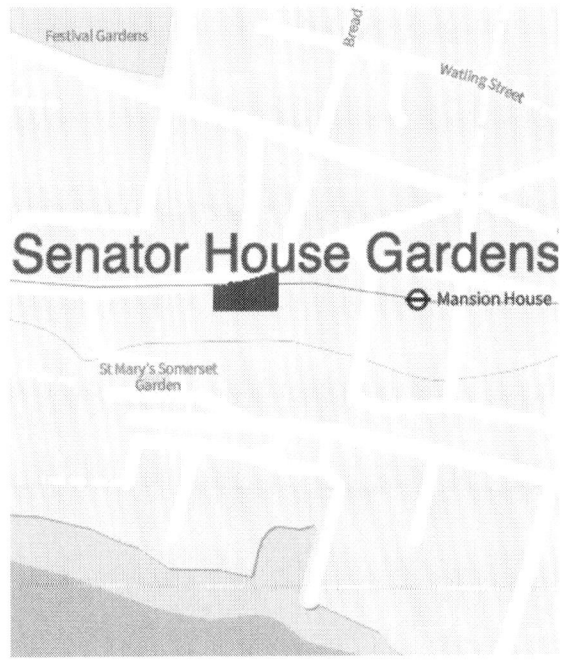

Contains OS data © Crown copyright and database rights 2020

History

The gardens are situated towards what was the northern end of Fye Foot Lane which at one time extended to Old Fish Street but was truncated with the construction of Queen Victoria Street over a century ago.

The previous garden had a pair of fairy mature trees and a large expanse of lawn but as it was all bounded by a raised bed on the street-side, it wasn't particularly open or inviting to visitors.

November 2019 saw the conclusion of a site renovation project and the garden has been substantially reworked. The lawns are now reduced in size but there are improved pavements through the garden and a number of wooden seats are in place.

Looking east towards Cleary Gardens and Mansion House
Underground Station

The original trees remain and have been supplemented by additional trees, low growing shrubs and ornamental grasses with a pergola in place over one of the pathways which will in time provide an additional focal point.

The garden was clearly designed to fit in with neighbouring **Cleary Gardens** and has also improved access to Fye Foot Lane which provides an alternative and in many ways more interesting route to the River Thames and if nothing else provides a fine view of **St Mary Somerset** from the bridge over Upper Thames Street.

Serjeants' Inn Courtyard

At A Glance: Hidden away south of Fleet Street, a large but largely soulless square, predominantly cobbled with a few planters to break the monotony.

Site location: Off Fleet Street/Old Mitre Court/Lombard Lane
Postcode: EC4Y 1BQ
Grid ref: TQ313811
Size in Hectares: 0.0097
Type of site: Square
Date(s): 12th, 15th and 18th Centuries, 1950s and 2012
Designer(s): Devereux and Davies (1950s)
Listed Structures: 49 and 50 Fleet Street

Site ownership: The Honourable Society of the Inner Temple, leased to Apex Hotels Ltd
Site management: Apex Hotels Ltd
Open to public?: Yes
Opening times: 24/7
Public transport - Tube Station: Temple Station (Circle and District Lines) **Rail:** City Thameslink

Contains OS data © Crown copyright and database rights 2020

History

This is the former site of one of the Serjeants' Inns, which accommodated the Serjeants-at-Law. They were an order of barristers which possibly originated back as far as the 11th century.

This site out of the three they held became the senior one by the 16th century and remained so, and following its inevitable fiery destruction and rebirth in the 1660s eventually became the home to the Amicable Society life insurance company in 1706 that in the late 19th century amalgamated with Norwich Union.

The last Serjeant-at-Law, Lord Lindley, died in 1921 and with him so did the Order and so after WWII the buildings were repurposed for commercial office use and the courtyard came to resemble its current form.

There are attractive archways from the courtyard which lead to Fleet Street and another to Mitre Court in Inner Temple. In 2001 the Honourable Society of the Inner Temple obtained the freehold with the intention of using the buildings for barristers' chamber but the costs of rebuilding and refurbishment proved too much and in March 2008 the Society granted a long lease to Apex Hotels Ltd for hotel development of Nos. 1-2 Serjeants' Inn who have incorporated part of the square into the entrance of their hotel reception.

Much of the square remains purely for car parking and vehicular access. There are some modern planters and seating near the hotel. There are some raised brick beds in the western section of the square along with some bushes planted in the Southwestern corner.

A little to the left is Temple Churchyard and the wider gardens in the area.

Sky Garden

At A Glance: The 'sky garden' at the top of the building was claimed by the developer to be London's highest public park, but since opening there have been debates about whether it can be described as a 'park', and whether it is truly 'public' given the access restrictions.

The garden spans the top three floors, which are accessible by two express lifts and include a large viewing area, terrace, bar and two restaurants. Fourteen double-deck lifts (seven low-rise up to the 20th floor, seven high-rise above the 20th floor) serve the main office floors of the building.

Site location: 20 Fenchurch Street
Postcode: EC3M 8AF
Grid ref: TQ 33071 80875
Type of site: Private/Public Garden
Date(s): 2015
Designer: Rafael Viñoly
Site ownership: CBRE's Asset Services

Site management: CBRE's Asset Services

Open to public?: Yes if pre-booked three days in advance
Opening times: 10am-6pm week days and 11am-9pm at weekends for non-paying restaurant customers.
Public transport - Tube Station: Monument (Circle and District Lines)

Contains OS data © Crown copyright and database rights 2019

History

The Sky Garden, which was described as a large and free public viewing space at the top of the building, was part of the justification for the planners allowing such a vast office block to be built on the edge of a conservation area. Advance computer visualisations shown to the planners included a glade of full-height trees, but the garden as constructed has a slope with ferns and succulents instead.

Free access to the general public is limited to one-and-a-half-hour slots which must be booked three days in advance, and visiting ends at 6pm, after which the garden is available only to paying customers of the catering facilities.

The Garden has been criticised for these restrictions, and for its extent and quality failing to meet pre-construction expectations. Oliver Wainwright, architecture critic of *The Guardian*, described it as "a meagre pair of rockeries, in a space designed with all the finesse of a departure lounge".

The City of London Corporation's former chief planner, Peter Rees, who approved the structure, said: "I think calling it a sky garden is perhaps misleading. If people [are] expecting to visit it as an alternative to Kew, then they will be disappointed."

In July 2015 it was reported that planners are to consider a landscape architect's alterations to the layout, following claims it is not consistent with illustrations submitted with the original planning application. The 'sky garden' was a key feature in sealing approval for the building, which is situated outside the main cluster of skyscrapers in the City.

There is another roof garden nearby at The Garden at 120 or for something very different try Fen Court.

St Alban's Tower

At A Glance: A tiny garden but on a site with one of the longest histories. It won't take you long to see everything but its quirkiness will stay in your mind.

Site location: Wood Street/Love Lane
Postcode: EC2V 7AF
Grid ref: TQ323814
Size in Hectares: 0.0156
Type of site: Public Open Land
Date(s): 8th century/17th century and 20th century
Listed Structure: Tower of former St Alban's Church
Site ownership: City of London Corporation
Site management: City of London Corporation Open Spaces Department
Open to public?: Yes
Opening times: 24/7
Public transport - Tube Station: St Paul's (Central Line), Moorgate (Circle, Hammersmith & City, Metropolitan and Northern Lines) **Rail:** Moorgate

History

St Alban's Tower is situated right in the middle of what would have been the barracks for the occupying Roman forces in Londinium.

St Alban's Church itself may have origins as far back as being an 8th-century chapel built by King Offa, founder of St Alban's Abbey.

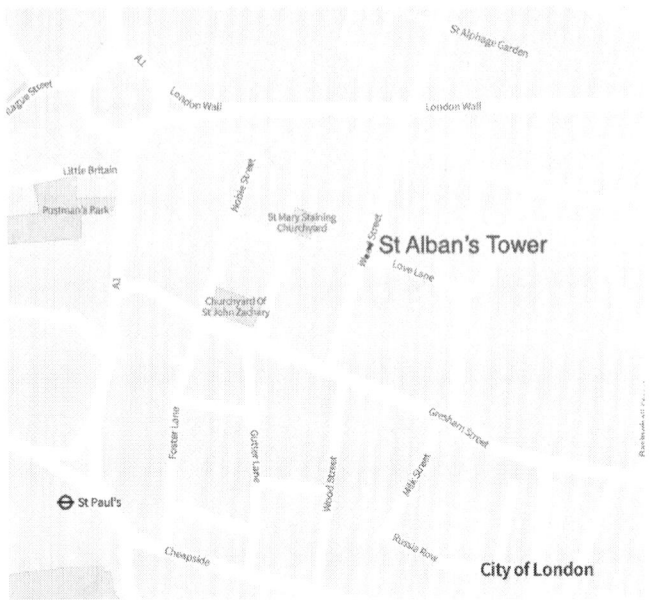

Contains OS data © Crown copyright and database rights 2019

The church was rebuilt in 1633-4 though suffered considerable fire damage in 1666 which required its rebuild by Sir Christopher Wren.

Suffering from extensive bomb damage in WWII it was demolished in 1955 apart from the steeple, which was restored in 1964 and later converted to a house which stands on an island site in the middle of Wood Street. There is a tree on the north within a small planted area. Just outside the front door is a nettle tree which has featured on the City of London's tree trail.

The churchyard had been to the north of the building, but is now entirely built over by roadways and buildings.

At the other end of Love Lane is St Mary Aldermanbury Gardens, or alternatively walk through the cover of St Albans Court to St Mary Staining.

A tree stands outside the front door
with a tiny garden to the rear.

St Alphage Garden and St Alphage Extension Garden

At A Glance: A fascinating garden in an interesting part of London Wall. Having been recently remodelled and improved upon, there is much to be seen here going back to Roman times.

Site location: St Alphage Garden, off London Wall
Postcode: EC2Y 5EL
Grid ref: TQ324816
Size in Hectares: 0.567
Type of site: Public Gardens
Date(s): 14th century; 1872 and 2018
Listed Structure: 14th century tower of former church St Alphage and a section of the London Wall
Site ownership: Diocese of London and City of London Corporation
Site management: City of London Corporation Open Spaces Department
Open to public?: Yes
Opening times: 24/7
Public transport - Tube Station: Moorgate (Circle, Hammersmith & City, Metropolitan and Northern Lines) **Rail:** Moorgate

History

Located next to the old Roman Cripplegate fort of the 2nd century; on the northern section of the current garden, the former churchyard of St Alphage became a public garden around 1870. The northern boundary of the garden actually contains a high section of the old Roman Wall and to the west of the main garden is an extension with a lower paved area.

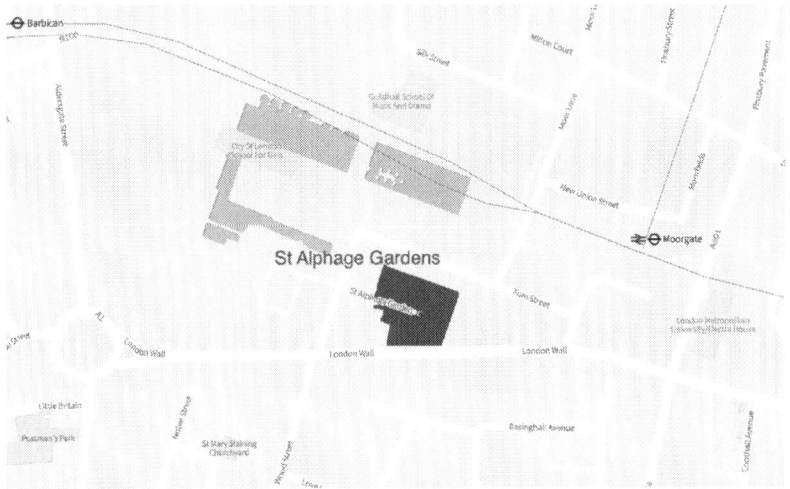

Contains OS data © Crown copyright and database rights 2019

Amongst the most severely bombed areas of London during the Blitz, the garden was enlarged upon as part of a scheme drawn up in 1954-5 by the Corporation of London to create a new business district around the London Wall area.

Provision was made for gardens and open spaces, and fragments of the old Roman city walls and older buildings also remained amidst the new architecture. Fascinatingly the garden also includes the ruined tower of St Alphage Church which is on the site of a priory church from the 14th century, which was known as Elsing Spital due to its location on the site of an even earlier hospital for the blind which was set up by William Elsing.

The newly added raised walkways and re-landscaped gardens add to the unexpectedly extensive ruins next to the busy London Wall road.

The gardens hold flowerbeds and benches with the main garden comprised mostly of grass, with a **magnolia tree and an oak tree. The southern edge of the garden has a beech hedgerow. On the other side of the Wall lies the private** Salters' Garden.

Taking advantage of the large amount of office redevelopment in the 21st century, the gardens have been extensively improved upon with the installation of a new high-level walkway that opened just a few years ago so you can now enjoy wonderful views of both the garden and the tower from above.

Almost adjacent to the north is Salters' Hall Garden and just across London Wall is Brewers Hall whilst to the west is the Museum of London Rotunda Garden and to the north-west is St Giles Cripplegate and the Barbican Estate beyond.

St Andrew's Holborn Churchyard

At A Glance: Recently refurbished gardens of what is the largest surviving Wren church in the City of London, providing a sheltered green space for nearby office workers and the general public alike with a beautiful weeping willow tree being one of the highlights.

Site location: Holborn Viaduct
Postcode: EC4A 3AB
Grid ref: TQ314815
Size in Hectares: 0.1125
Type of site: Public Gardens
Date(s): 13th century onwards

Listed Structures: St Andrew's Church. Holborn Viaduct; 5, 7 and Vicarage on St Andrew Street; wall & gate piers to garden of No. 7 St Andrew Street

Site ownership: Diocese of London

Site management: City of London Corporation Open Spaces Department

Open to public?: 5 days a week

Opening times: 8am - 7pm or dusk (whichever is earlier)

Public transport - Tube Station: Chancery Lane (Central Line) and Farringdon (Circle, Hammersmith & City, Metropolitan and Northern Lines) **Rail:** Farringdon

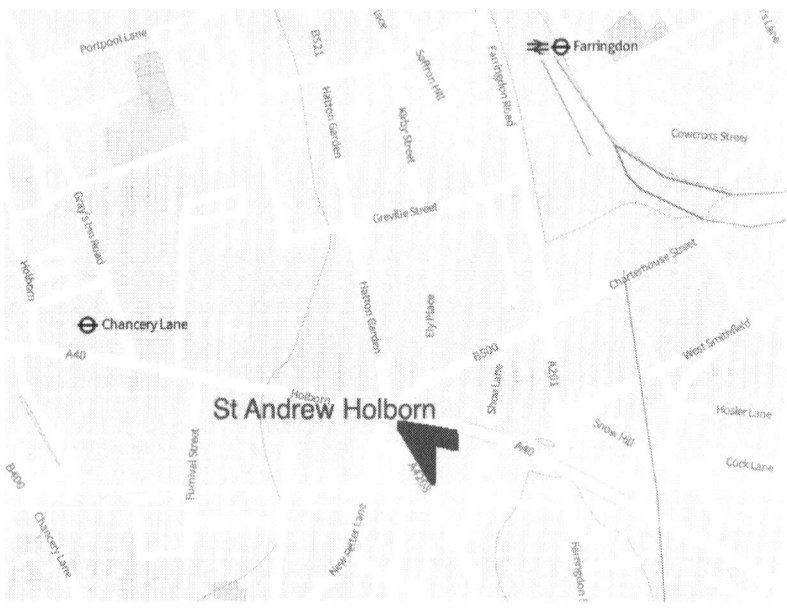

Contains OS data © Crown copyright and database rights 2019

History

Roman pottery has been found on this site and there has been a timber church since at least 951 AD, and the churchyard is known to have existed since 1348 though it is now a sunken garden.

The church survived the Great Fire of London due to a last minute reprieve in the form of a change of wind direction but it had nevertheless fallen into disrepair allowing Sir Christopher Wren to initiate widespread rebuilding around 1690. Our only Jewish Prime Minster, Sir Benjamin Disraeli, was amongst those baptised here on the 31st July 1817.

In the 1860s, the northern section of the churchyard was purchased for the Holborn Valley Improvement Scheme to make way for the new Holborn Viaduct built to link Holborn and Newgate and given the honour of an opening by Queen Victoria herself in 1869.

Many of the human remains disturbed by this work were reinterred in the crypt with others in the City of London Cemetery in Ilford. The crypt was finally cleared in 2002-03 and the bodies within were moved to the memorial at the City of London Cemetery.

The church was badly damaged by incendiary bombing during WWII and it was long thought that St Andrews would not be rebuilt, but finally the decision was made to rebuild it stone by stone and brick by brick in 1960.

One of many idyllic views in this garden

The gate piers to the churchyard from Holborn Viaduct date from approximately 1870 with the actual gates being from the post-war reconstruction efforts.

In 2015 improvements to the garden were completed which include a fully accessible entrance to the Church and gardens, a new boundary wall and metal railings, improved and increased paving and seating, new garden planting that includes a variety of mixed shrubs and herbaceous planting which concentrates on colour, form and biodiversity.

The garden is also screened off, in part, with a Taxus (yew) hedge that provides some privacy in the form of an evergreen element from one of the surrounding roads.

Do visit the church and look out for the statue of Captain Thomas Coram who worked so tirelessly to create the Foundling Hospital in Coram Fields. Whilst you're here pop along to see St Andrew Street Garden and Holborn Circus Garden.

St Andrew Street Garden and Holborn Circus Garden

At A Glance: Just to the west of St Andrew's Churchyard, a simple garden on the site of an old bank that was destroyed in WWII.

Site location: Holborn Circus-viaduct/St Andrew Street
Postcode: EC4A 3AB
Grid ref: TQ314815
Size in Hectares: 0.0712 + 0.0655
Type of site: Public Gardens
Date(s): Post WWII, 1960s and 21st century
Listed Structure: Statue of Prince Albert (Holborn Circus)
Site ownership: City of London Corporation
Site management: City of London Corporation Open Spaces Department
Open to public?: Yes

Opening times: 24/7

Public transport - Tube Station: Chancery Lane (Central Line) **Rail:** Farringdon

Contains OS data © Crown copyright and database rights 2019

History

Sometimes known as the Engineers' garden, this site in honour of the Holborn Viaduct was the first flyover in London. This garden is on the site of an old bank destroyed in WWII, and the garden was developed post-war and originally was on land earmarked for post-war highway improvements.

In the 1960s it was simply laid out with fencing, grass and some a little planting. The fences were later removed to be replaced by hedges which allowed it to become rather more secluded and the later additions of public seating, trees and a public chequerboard table! Further works were carried out in 2004 which sensibly created access between the churchyard and public garden.

Holborn Circus Garden is directly opposite the road and like much of the land here became public gardens as a result of improvements to the roadways after WWII. It is triangular in shape with grass, flowerbeds and a few trees.

Taken together, both gardens do a great deal to create an oasis of calm around what can be a rather busy thoroughfare.

Whilst you're there, you might want to cross into Ely Place, an old enclave of Cambridgeshire and home to a lovely old church and perhaps the hardest to find pub in London...or Cambridge come to that! Alternatively if you want to stick to London proper then a few minutes east along the A40 will bring you to St Sepulchre Without Newgate and the rather fine Viaduct Tavern.

St Andrew Undershaft Churchyard

At A Glance: A small paved churchyard which stands at the junction of Leadenhall Street and St Mary Axe. The garden is rated with two memorial seats, a tree, small flowerbeds and a number of slate tombs, all bounded by railings.

Site location: Leadenhall Street/St Mary Axe
Postcode: EC3A 6AT
Grid ref: TQ332812
Size in Hectares: 0.0254
Type of site: Public Gardens
Date(s): 12th, 14th and 16th Centuries and 1883.
Listed Structures: St Andrew Undershaft Church; LBII: Gates and railings to church on St Mary Axe
Site ownership: Diocese of London
Site management: City of London Corporation Open Spaces Department
Open to public?: Yes
Opening times: 24/7 for the garden but the church is open by arrangement with St Helen's Bishopsgate
Public transport - Tube Station: Aldgate (Circle and Metropolitan Lines)

History
St Andrew Undershaft has been standing here since at least the 12th century though its steeple is a relative latecomer from the 15th century.

Contains OS data © Crown copyright and database rights 2019

It was around this time that the church became known as St Andrew Undershaft, the shaft here being the maypole or shaft that was put up every year by the door until the 1st May 1517. It was destroyed 1549 having been declared idolatrous by the curate of St Katharine Cree!

We're lucky to still have this church as it was badly damaged by terrorist bombings in 1992 and 1993 but happily full repairs were made almost immediately.

Just across the road there is the famous 'Cheese grater' building with its new St Helen's Square garden. Two minutes' walk further up St Mary Axe you get to the Gherkin with some simple stone benches for the public to admire the modern architecture and find the resting place of a young Roman.

St Andrew-by-the-Wardrobe Churchyard

At A Glance: Initially this church was known as St Andrew's juxta Baynard's Castle due to its proximity to a fortification on the banks of the Thames that had been constructed by one of the important backers of William the Conqueror, the Baynard family.

These days the castle has gone and the churchyard is now much reduced in size due to road constructions but it makes for an interesting diversion in this quiet corner of the city.

Site location: Queen Victoria Street/St Andrews Hill
Postcode: EC4V 5DE
Grid ref: TQ318810
Size in Hectares: 0.0228
Type of site: Public Gardens
Date(s): 13th, 17th and 19th centuries
Listed Structures: St Andrews Church
Site ownership: Diocese of London
Site management: City of London Corporation Open Spaces Department)
Open to public?: Yes
Opening times: 24/7 (Church open Mon-Fri 10am-4pm)
Public transport - Tube Station: Blackfriars (Circle and District Lines) **Rail:** Blackfriars

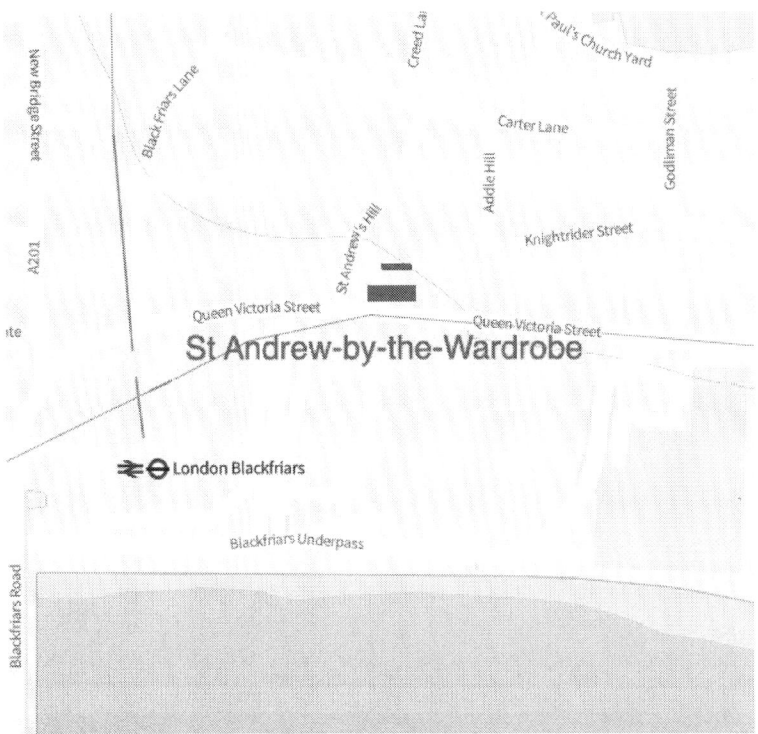

Contains OS data © Crown copyright and database rights 2019

History

St Andrew-by-the-Wardrobe was likely built in the early years of the 13th century. The aforementioned Baynard's Castle was at one point the property of the Crown and even at times used as a Royal residence.

The Royal Wardrobe moved to present day Wardrobe Place from the Tower just over a century later which explains the church becoming

St Andrew-by-the-Wardrobe, but all of these structures were lost in 1666 with the Great Fire of London.

Sir Christopher Wren rebuilt the church which was damaged by though survived WWII with it being fully restored in 1960.

The construction of Queen Victoria Street destroyed much of the churchyard to the south in 1871. The heavily inclined terraced garden that lies between the church front and Queen Victoria Street was planted in 1901 when the front wall with urns and ornamental wrought iron gates was erected. Amongst the mature trees and shrubs is an old crucifix.

The north side of the church is a rather forlorn paved area with seats and tubs, all that remains of the old churchyard.

St Ann Blackfriars Burial Grounds: Church Entry and Ireland Yard

At A Glance: Two small and almost adjacent gardens that are largely hard landscaped and surrounded by brick buildings deep in the muddle of medieval passageways between St Paul's Cathedral and Blackfriars.

Site location: Church Entry and Ireland Yard
Postcode: EC4V 5EX

Grid ref: TQ317810

Size in Hectares: 0.0467 (2 sites)

Type of site: Public Gardens

Date(s): 1666 Ireland Yard and 1597 Church Entry

Listed Structures: Fragment of rubble wall in Ireland Yard; St Anne's Vestry Hall at Church Entry

Site ownership: Diocese of London

Site management: City of London Corporation Open Spaces Department

Open to public?: Yes

Opening times: Weekdays 8am - 7pm or dusk if earlier

Public transport - Tube Station: Blackfriars (Circle and District Lines) **Rail:** Blackfriars   Contains OS data © Crown copyright and database rights 201

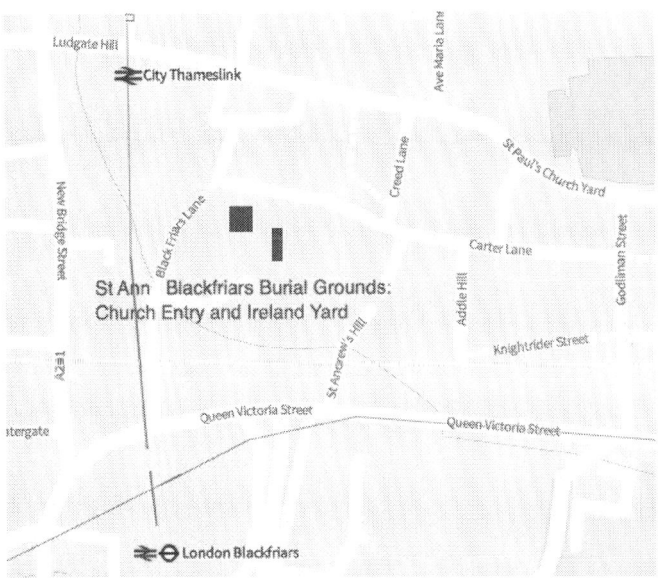

History

Established after the dissolution of the 13th century Friary of the Dominicans, the parish of St Ann Blackfriars is of course so named due to the colour of the clothing this particular order of Friars wore.

The Priory church had been demolished but the local residents were very vocal in their displeasure that they had lost their local place of worship and so St Anne Blackfriars came to be in 1597 and was built on part of the old Priory hall.

St Ann's burnt down in the Great Fire of 1666 and was not rebuilt, forcing the parish to amalgamate with that of St Andrew-by-the-Wardrobe, and the church site became a burial ground.

The two churchyards closed in 1849 and were later laid out as public gardens, largely paved, both raised and containing a number of tombstones.

St Anne and St Agnes

At A Glance: A beautiful, peaceful green garden in the grounds of St Agnes and St Anne Church which was originally established early in the 12th century.

Site location: Noble Street/Gresham Street
Postcode: EC1A 4ER

Grid ref: TQ321814

Size in Hectares: 0.1323

Type of site: Public Gardens

Date(s): 13th century, 1677-87; 1966 and 1970s.

Listed Structures: St Anne and St Agnes Church

Site ownership: The churchyard is Diocese of London with the Noble Street extension falling under the City of London Corporation.

Site management: City of London Corporation Open Spaces Department

Open to public?: Yes

Opening times: 24/7

Public transport - Tube Station: St Paul's (Central Line)

Contains OS data © Crown copyright and database rights 2019

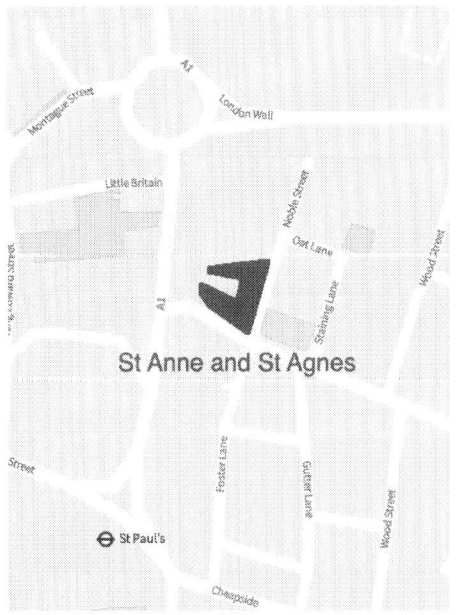

History

In the early 12th and 13th centuries the church here is recorded variously as St Agnes and St Anne, both saints being referred to here by the mid-15th century. The original churchyard is equally ancient and is recorded as being here by the mid-13th century.

Sadly the church was largely destroyed in the Great Fire of 1666 and a replacement was built in 1677-1687 by Sir Christopher Wren, which was itself later damaged by bombings in WWII before being restored in 1963-68 in keeping with Wren's designs.

The churchyard was extended on the south and east side as a result of bomb damage, with a garden created in the early 1970s composed of an area of lawn with some tombstones near the church. The garden is set off by low planting walls surrounding it and a number of different types of maturing trees.

When Noble Street was widened the churchyard garden was united with public gardens to the north to create one public open space with seating and shrubberies.

Across the road is the wonderful gardens at St John Zachary.

St Bartholomew's Hospital including St Bartholomew-the-Less Church

At A Glance: A little bit of an unusual place to go hunting for a garden but there is a lot more than might be expected here and all topped off with some incredible architecture too.

Site location: West Smithfield
Postcode: EC1A 7BA
Grid ref: TQ319815
Size in Hectares:
Type of site: Hospital Grounds
Date(s): 12th century, 1730-59; 1850s
Designers: Courtyard: James Gibbs 18th century and Philip Hardwick 19th century. Mary Keen in 2019 for the Princess Alice gardens.
Listed Structures: The Gatehouse on West Smithfield, North Wing, West Wing, East Wing. Screen wall and colonnade, St Bartholomew-the-Less Church. North-east block, Memorial to Sir William Wallace, Medical School, Pool & fountain and 3 lamp standards in the courtyard
Site ownership: St Bartholomew's Hospital; Barts and The London NHS Trust
Site management: City of London Corporation Open Spaces Dept. (Friends of St Bartholomew-the-Less)
Open to public?: Private but accessible to public
Opening times: Church itself daily 7am-8pm

Public transport - Tube Station: Barbican and Farringdon stations (Circle, Hammersmith & City and Metropolitan lines); St Paul's (Central Line) **Rail:** Farringdon

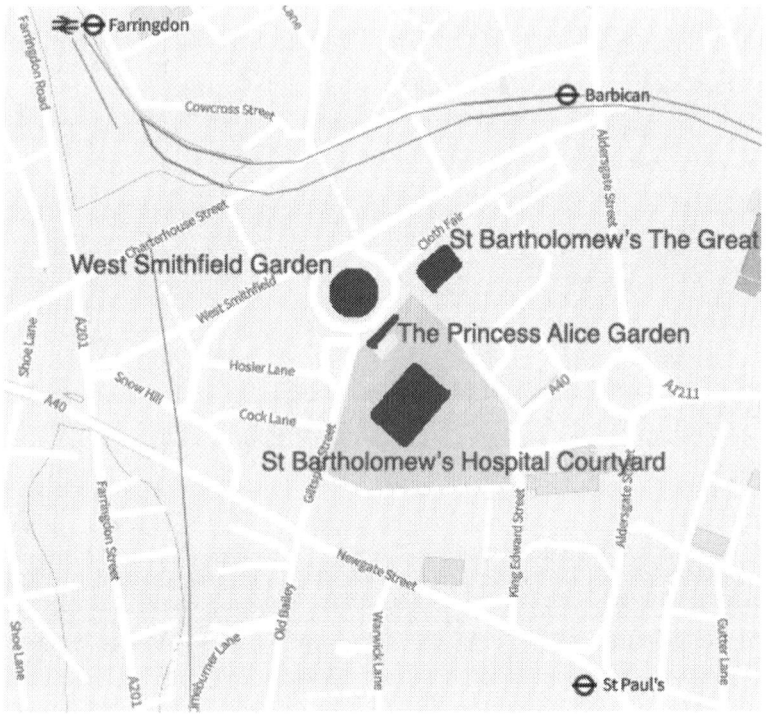

Contains OS data © Crown copyright and database rights 2019

History

St Bartholomew's Hospital is the oldest hospital in London, being established in 1123 AD by Rahere who was a courtier for King Henry I. Rahere also established a Priory centred on the adjacent St

Bartholomew-the-Great after falling ill overseas and encountering a vision of St Bartholomew, promising to create facilities for physical and spiritual wellbeing back in London should he be so fortunate as to make an unlikely recovery from his illness.

The water feature in the central courtyard

The Hospital and Priory became separate institutions by 1420. St Bartholomew-the-Less within the Hospital walls was originally one of 4 priory chapels, becoming the parish church in 1547. At the same time the only public statue of King Henry VIII in London was erected over the new gate to West Smithfields.

Remains of its churchyard are to the north and east of the church, one of 4 burial grounds within the hospital site, the remainder since built over.

One of several quiet spots in the hospital, this being the refurbished Princess Alice Garden

The 18th century saw the hospital develop as it became wealthier. A new north gate was erected in 1702, and in 1723 a new hospital was commissioned from James Gibbs, consisting of 4 blocks around a central square.

In 1859 a fountain was erected in the centre of the square, and the lamp posts and shelters date from the 1890s. It provides patients, visitors and curious outsiders a welcome serene area that is surprisingly magnificent for a hospital.

The churchyard north of the church was laid out as the Princess Alice Garden in 2001 and refurbishment works on the Garden started in March 2019, with a plan devised by the renowned landscape gardener Mary Keen to rearrange, refresh and restore the planting of the garden. Shrubs are being used more than perennials for simplicity, and some plants from Princess Alice's original list are being introduced.

St Bartholomew-the-Great Churchyard

At A Glance: St Bartholomew-the-Great was originally the church of the Priory founded here in 1123 AD by Rahere, who also founded the adjacent St Bartholomew's Hospital. Rahere was buried here in 1143 and there is a 15th-century monument to him within the church. In 1133 the Priory established Bartholomew Fair, which became the largest cloth fair in the country and ran until 1855.

As part of the Dissolution, the Priory was closed in 1539 with the nave of the church being criminally demolished and the churchyard created here, although the wonderful Priory gateway is still in place.

Site location: West Smithfield/Little Britain

Postcode: EC1A 7JQ

Grid ref: TQ319817

Size in Hectares: 0.0744 + 0.0171 (small private rear garden)

Type of site: Public Gardens

Date(s): 12th century, 1698, 1893

Listed Structures: St Bartholomew-the-Great Church and the Gateway on West Smithfield.

Designer: Fanny Wilkinson 19th century

Site ownership: Diocese of London

Site management: City of London Corporation Open Spaces Department

Open to public?: Yes

Opening times: 24/7 (not including private garden to rear of the church) Church open Sun 8.30am-1pm/2.30-8pm; Tue-Fri 8.30am-5pm; Sat 10.30am-1.30pm.

Public transport - Tube Station: Farringdon and Barbican (Circle, Hammersmith & City) and Metropolitan Lines), St Paul's (Central Line) Rail: Farringdon

History

St Bartholomew-the-Great is full of history within and without. It starts even before you reach the fantastic gateway to the churchyard with plaques and memorials to Wat Tyler, John Ball and the Peasants Revolt that came to its conclusion here. Here too is where William Wallace (Braveheart) met his unfortunate end as well as bishops who were burned alive for refusing to recant their faith. If all of that isn't enough the craters on the wall of St Barts Hospital are from a WWI Zeppelin attack in 1917.

The gateway itself leads onto the forecourt and churchyard which are the remains of the Augustinian Priory that stood where the church is now, with a straight path which leads to the church entrance. This gatehouse was restored in 1932 and has served as a school and currently a domestic residence.

Contains OS data © Crown copyright and database rights 2019

The main part of the churchyard that remains is now a garden on the left of the path raised by an ever increasing height as one approaches the church door, all behind an impressive knapped flint retaining wall.

The historic St Bartholomew The Great

Steps lead up to the grass which has a pathway, a number of seats and some always rather shady shrub beds. There are a number of headstones some of which are set into the grass and trees including London plane, and an English yew planted to commemorate the 850th anniversary of the Priory Church.

On the right of the path is a private garden with substantial railings in the ownership of St Bartholomew's Hospital. An informal garden is to the south-east of the church with trees including a mulberry tree.

The church itself is well worth a visit and incredibly ornate, it being the oldest church in the area that survived the Great Fire of London. Due to its use in many popular television programmes and films, it is sadly one of the few churches that charge for tourist entry though of course access for worship is free at all times.

If you leave the churchyard to Cloth Fair, take a look at the old house opposite and see if you can see the inscriptions on the first-floor window in what is said to be the oldest residential house in the City of London. They can be hard to make out if they aren't glinting in the sun but you might try as I did and take photos of them and then enlarge them on a computer screen to see such names as Winston Churchill and the Queen Mother.

If you turn left then you will soon be at West Smithfield Garden or if you head right you will find your way to the Barbican Estate.

St Benet Welsh Church

At A Glance: A church was first recorded here around the year 1111 AD. The unusual name of the church originates from Bene't which was a corruption of St Benedict, founder of the order of Benedictine monks in the 6th century. St Benet's burnt down in the Great Fire of 1666 and was rebuilt in 1678-84 by Sir Christopher Wren.

Site location: Bennet's Hill

Postcode: EC4V 4ER   **Grid ref:** TQ320809

Size in Hectares: 0.0346   **Type of site:** Public Gardens

Date(s): 12th century and 1677

Listed Structures: St Benet Welsh Church

Site ownership: St Benet's Welsh Church

Site management: City of London Corporation Open Spaces Department

Open to public?: Yes

Opening times: 24/7 though the church is by appointment only.

Public transport - Tube Station: Blackfriars and Mansion House (Circle and District Lines). Contains OS data © Crown copyright and database rights 2019

History

It can be a little tricky to find St Benet Welsh, sunk down from Victoria Street and largely surrounded by major roads, flyovers and even a tunnel.

Part of the former churchyard of St Benet Paul's Wharf is still in situ though the construction of Queen Victoria Street in the 1870s drastically curtailed its size. After this work the parish joined that of St Nicholas Cole Abbey in 1879 and the church was only saved by becoming the London Church of the Welsh Episcopalians and remains the Metropolitan Welsh Church with the services there held in Welsh.

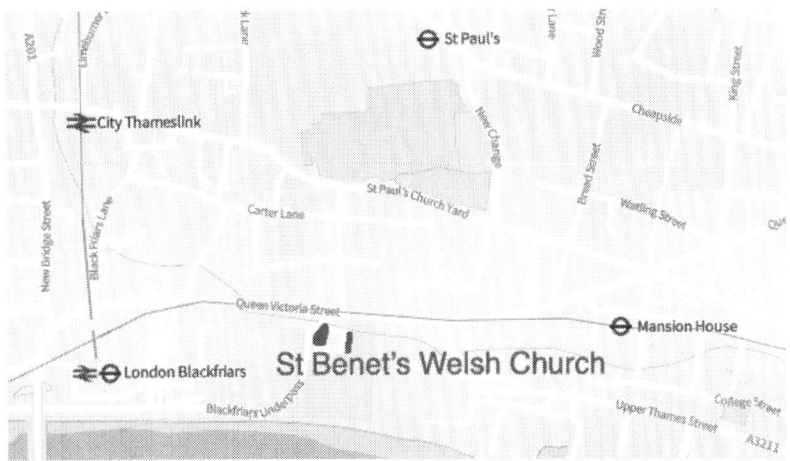

Contains OS data © Crown copyright and database rights 2019

There is quite a sizeable lawn to the west of the church and 3 small trees, handily located for the adjacent City Gardens Depot as well as a more mature tree and other foliage near the steps to Queen Victoria Street. A smaller grassy area with some low level shrubs can be found to the east.

A minute or so west on Queen Victoria Street on the other side of the road is St Andrew-by-the-Wardrobe.

St Botolph Without Aldgate Churchyard

At A Glance: A recently refurbished garden located on Aldgate High Street, just outside the old Roman Wall gateway at Aldgate. Due to its dedication to St Botolph the church is deemed to be of Saxon origin, St Botolph being the Anglo-Saxon patron saint of travellers before St Christopher usurped the role, and there is evidence of burials here since at least the 10th century.

Site location: Aldgate High Street
Postcode: EC3N 1AB
Grid ref: TQ335812
Size in Hectares: 0.1148
Type of site: Public Gardens
Date(s): Early Medieval Period, 1892 and 2019
Listed Structures: St Botolph's Church. Gateway to churchyard on Aldgate High Street
Designer: Fanny Wilkinson 1892
Site ownership: Diocese of London
Site management: City of London Corporation Open Spaces Department
Open to public?: Yes
Opening times: 24/7 (Church open Mon-Fri 10am-3pm and Sundays)
Public transport - Tube Station: Aldgate (Circle and Metropolitan Lines)

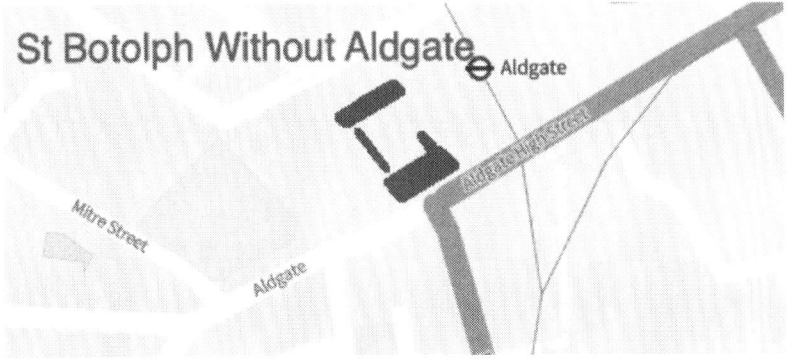

Contains OS data © Crown copyright and database rights 2019

History

The church has a raised churchyard on three sides which has been used as public gardens since the 1870s. Like many overcrowded churchyards in London, its closure came as a result of the first Burial Act of 1852.

A few years earlier a possible family member of mine, local fishmonger Edward Liddell, heard the screams of a local lady who noticed the gravedigger apparently dead at the bottom of a newly dug 20 foot deep grave for paupers. As a crowd gathered round, Edward volunteered to climb down the ladder and retrieve the body but after a single cough, collapsed and died apparently due to a cloud of unseen poisonous gas released from a millennia of decomposing bodies nearby.

You'd never know events like this had happened now with the garden being improved upon in 2019 as part of the wider Aldgate gyratory improvements work and the creation of the new Aldgate Square next door.

The church garden is enclosed by railings and has grass and flowerbeds on the north side. Gravestones have been set against the east wall with flowerbeds in front of them. The south facing area of the former churchyard is paved with flowerbeds, a few small trees, a number of graves and seats. There is also a sculpture from 1985 entitled 'Sanctuary' by Naomi Blake.

Part of the West Side gardens looking south towards the High Street

There remain a wonderful gate and railings at the south entrance of the church where you'll also find a drinking fountain against the railings which was erected in 1906 in memory of Frederic David Mocatta. The churchyard to the north of the church is less ornate being largely grass with 2 plane trees with a small number of tombs and headstones. This particular area has a chain link fence with a small area of rose beds alongside the western wall of the church with a recent water feature added too.

Do check out the old blue police box on the main street outside the church entrance, and a minute's walk away is the famous Aldgate Pump of Death which was restored in September 2019. Between the pump and the church you can see the remains of the old Aldgate priory inside a modern office block too.

Next door is the new Aldgate Square and just beyond that Mitre Square and St Katherine Cree.

St Botolph Without Bishopsgate Churchyard

At A Glance: Mention is made of St Botolph in a document which dates back to 1213 AD. There have been a number of buildings here; a Norman church was followed by a medieval church and this was eventually replaced in 1729 by the current church.

The churchyard here was one of the first to be turned into public gardens and being close to Liverpool Street Station makes a great entry point into East London. It is larger than many churchyards and a wonderfully green refuge from the busy streets outside.

Site location: Bishops Gate
Postcode: EC2M 3TL
Grid ref: TQ331814
Size in Hectares: 0.2012
Type of site: Public Gardens
Date(s): 12th century, 1727-9 and 1863
Listed Structures: St Botolph Without Bishopsgate Church. St Botolph's Church Hall; Bishopsgate Churchyard; Gatepiers, overthrows and lanterns in churchyard.
Site ownership: Diocese of London
Site management: City of London Corporation Open Spaces Department
Open to public?: Yes
Opening times: 24/7 Church: Monday - Friday 8am-5.30pm
Public transport - Tube Station: Liverpool Street (Central, Circle, Hammersmith & City and Metropolitan Lines) **Rail:** Liverpool Street

History

The old Norman church was replaced in the Middle Ages by a church that was then demolished in 1724; the current church was built in 1725-9 by James Gold and George Dance the Elder. With the exception of its west window, the church was fortunate to mostly come through WWII unscathed; sadly it suffered IRA bomb damage

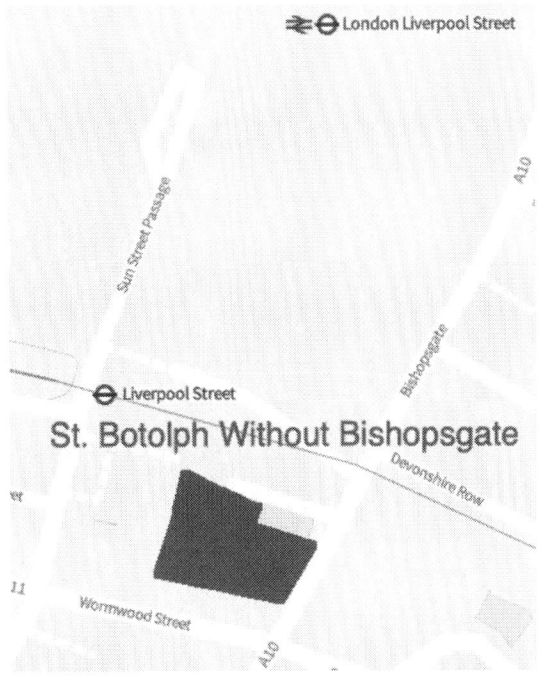

in 1993 though it was hurriedly restored.

In 1617 an area of land which was previously part of the city ditch outside the walls was added to the churchyard which expanded again in 1760. The Parish Hall which is to the west of the churchyard was a church primary school in the second half of the 19th century. A Church School for infants was built west of the graveyard in 1861 with figures of a boy and a girl placed either side of the door. Since 1905 the school has been used as the Parish Hall.

Dating from 1866, two stone pillars with drinking fountains stand at the entrance on Bishopsgate and there is a central path which runs through the churchyard garden. At one time there were seats and railings from old London Bridge here.

An autumnal day at St Botolph

There are garden areas with raised lawns in which are a number of tombs along with flowerbeds, bushes and seating.

There are in particular two interesting memorial trees here; firstly a Pride of India tree which was planted in 2001 by Lord Mayor J. M. Y. Oliver and the International Tree Foundation. That same year saw the planting of a Quercus Robur Fastigiate which was presented to the church on the occasion of the 500th anniversary of the Worshipful Company of Coopers.

Adjacent to the church is a stone memorial cross, believed to be the first memorial of the Great War to be set up in England, erected in 1916 following the Battle of Jutland and the death of Lord Kitchener, whilst there is a 1970s fountain in the south of the garden. There is also a tennis court that joins to the churchyard and this is itself on burial grounds from 1617.

Cross the busy Bishopsgate Road and you will come across Jubilee Gardens and Devonshire Square or head up Wormwood Street and you will find All Hallows-on-The-Wall and beyond that, Finsbury Circus.

St Bride's Fleet Street Churchyard

At A Glance: In an area that in the 1st and 2nd century was once Roman suburbs, this church is dedicated to the 5th-century Irish St Bride or Bridget and has reasonable claims to be the earliest site in London where Christianity has been practised. 1,500 years later a tranquil refuge can be found here especially on the north side of the church. This railed churchyard has a number of mature trees, and areas of paving and seats, with gravestones set into the ground.

Site location: Fleet Street/Bride Lane/St Bride's Passage
Postcode: EC4Y 8AU
Grid ref: TQ315811
Size in Hectares: 0.0924

Type of site: Public Gardens

Date(s): 12th century onwards

Listed Structures: St Bride's Church and St Bride Foundation Institute and Library

Site ownership: Diocese of London

Site management: City of London Open Spaces Department

Open to public?: Yes

Opening times: Mon-Sat 8am-5pm, Sun 10am-12.30pm and 5.30-7.30pm

Public transport - Tube Station: Blackfriars (District and Circle Lines) **Rail:** Blackfriars

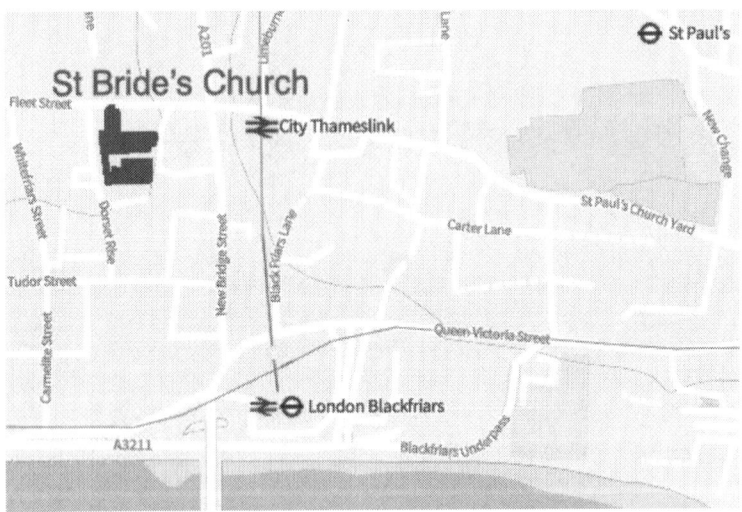

Contains OS data © Crown copyright and database rights 2020

History

With a churchyard being here since at least 1188 AD and with the old church being destroyed in the Great Fire, the stage was set for Sir

Christopher Wren to build the eighth and still the present church on this site.

The spire was not completed until 1703, the highest of Wren's steeples and is said to be the inspiration for the first tiered wedding cake. The spire was originally 234 feet above ground level but in June 1764 it was badly damaged by lightning during a storm and though restored was reduced in height by 8 feet. It is still a fabulous sight however.

The view of the church from Fleet Street was originally blocked by houses but the opportunity to enhance its surroundings came in 1825 when the nearby houses were destroyed by fire. Public fundraising allowed the purchase of the land, and the current St Bride's Avenue was created.

Situated as it is just south of Fleet Street, St Bride's is known as the Printers Cathedral and the Journalists Church due to the fact that the first printing press with moveable type was installed nearby in 1500.

Some of the notable figures with connections to the church include King John who on occasion used the church to hold council. The parents of Virginia Dare, the first European child to be born in Colonial America in 1587, were married at St Bride's. John Milton apparently lived for a time in the churchyard and Samuel Pepys was baptised here, whilst Samuel Johnson and Charles Dickens lived nearby.

St Bride's Well, a Holy Well, was once nearby in a niche below the raised burial ground at the eastern end of the church.

As one enjoys the garden it is worth remembering that during the Plague many parishioners died, with some 1,491 people buried in the churchyard between August and October 1665.

After enjoying the church and garden, it's well worth taking some time to see the incredible museum under the church with history going right back to the Roman times, and there are plenty of tried and tested pubs in the vicinity too.

At the western end of St Bride's Passage is Salisbury Square.

St Clement Eastcheap

At A Glance: A church has been here since at least 1067 AD, dedicated to St Clement who was a 1st century Roman convert to Christianity. Having long since stopped accepting burials, the former churchyard of St Clement survives as a raised garden with entrance gate and 18th-century railings on the alleyway of St Clement's Court on the north side of the church. It's hard not to feel the garden is more than a little dilapidated and run down especially when construction is occurring in neighbouring buildings.

Site location: St Clement's Court/St Clement's Lane

Postcode: EC4N 7AE

Grid ref: TQ328809

Size in Hectares: 0.0142

Type of site: Public Gardens

Date(s): Mostly 1683-87 with some medieval.

Listed Structures: St Clement's Church

Site ownership: Diocese of London

Site management: Diocese of London

Open to public?: Yes

Opening times: Week days and weekends generally during office hours but check with the church

Public transport - Tube Station: Bank (Central, DLR, Northern, Waterloo & City Lines and Monument (Circle & District Lines)

Contains OS data © Crown copyright and database rights 2020

History

With terrible timing, the church was rebuilt in 1658, soon after which it was destroyed in the Great Fire only to be rebuilt again by Sir Christopher Wren in 1683-87. As one of the smallest of his parish churches, the parish was joined by that of St Martin Orgar with the latter church becoming the burial ground for the two parishes.

The rather dilapidated St Clement Eastcheap

Most likely the church mentioned in the nursery rhyme 'Oranges and Lemons', St Clement's was worked upon several times at the end of the 19th century and again in the 1930s.

Today the old churchyard is a small raised garden which is reached by going towards the end of St Clement's Court alleyway, on the right behind some fine railings and up some steps. By and large it is covered in paving and perpetually grotty, and there are a number of tombs, trees and shrubbery. Perhaps it is one of the most sorrowful and forgotten churchyards well hidden from all except those determined to seek it out. Surely it is the City of London garden most deserving of a little bit of 21st-century TLC.

A little further west along Cannon Street you have Abchurch Yard to the north and St Laurence Pountney Graveyards to the south.

St Dunstan-in-the-East

At A Glance: In one way or the other a church has been on this site for around 950 years and by the 12th century was already in possession of a large churchyard. St Dunstan-in-the-East suffered damage in the Great Fire of 1666, after which Sir Christopher Wren made the necessary repairs whilst also adding the tower and steeple.

The church was rebuilt in 1817-21, but in 1941 was destroyed by aerial bombings though the spire was reconstructed in 1953, and the tower later restored in 1970.

Having acquired the ruins in 1967, the Corporation of London transformed the remains into a wonderful garden that opened to the public in 1971.

One of my very personal favourite spots in the whole of London, nothing warms the heart more than entering this garden and finding I have it all to myself.

Site location: St Dunstan's Hill/Idol Lane
Postcode: EC3R 5DD
Grid ref: TQ331807
Size in Hectares: 0.1526
Type of site: Public Gardens
Date(s): 17th and 19th Centuries; 1967-1971
Listed Structures: Ruin of St Dunstan's Church. LBII: walls, gate and railings to St Dunstan's Church
Site ownership: City of London Corporation with the Church falling under the nearby All-Hallows-by-the-Tower)
Site management: City of London Corporation Open Spaces Department
Open to public?: Yes
Opening times: 8am - 7pm or dusk if that comes earlier.
Public transport - Tube Station: Bank (Central, DLR, Northern, Waterloo & City Lines). Monument and Tower Hill Stations (Circle and District Lines).

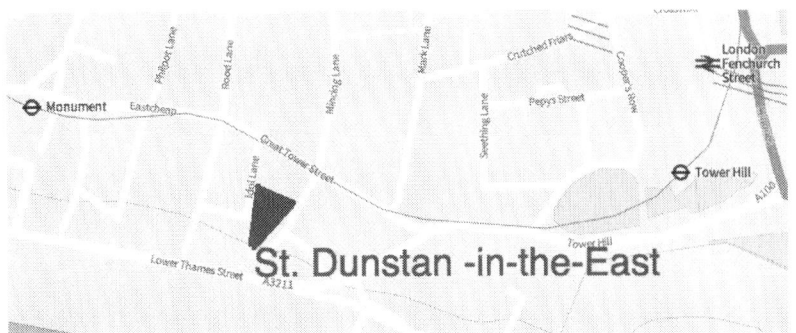

Contains OS data © Crown copyright and database rights 2020

History

Following its Wren-era repairs, the church was in a bad state of repair by the early 19th century and was rebuilt in 1817-21 but then destroyed by enemy action in 1941, and little survived although the spire was reconstructed in 1953 and the tower restored in 1970 for use.

The Corporation of London acquired the church ruins in 1967, and these and the former churchyard have been transformed into an incredibly richly planted garden centred round a circular cobbled area with a fountain.

Exotic trees, shrubs, flowers and climbers grow among the ruined arches, giving the impression in the growing season that one might have stumbled across a lost Amazonian city. Despite all the destruction, the walls, gates and railings to the churchyard are from the Wren rebuild and there is a reminder on a wall of the time when the building housed a school.

The photogenic views of St Dunstan In the East are boundless.

These gardens were the largest created by the City of London Corporation during the 20th century and have been used as a filming location in many productions of the big and small screen.

It can get busy at times but it is also easy to have it all to yourself and perhaps enjoy the most picturesque ruin in all of London.

Explore to the west and you may find St Mary-At-Hill and to the north is St Margaret Pattens or alternatively halfway to the Tower of London you'll find All Hallows-By-The Tower.

St Dunstan-in-the-West Burial Ground

At A Glance: Tucked away in the maze of routes between Fleet Street and Chancery Lane, the garden is but a fragment of the former burial ground of St Dunstan-in-the-West, the church located further south facing onto Fleet Street.   On the west side near the shrubs and along the railings are still a few old graves.

Site location: Bream's Buildings, Holborn
Postcode: EC4A 1DZ
Grid ref: TQ311813
Size in Hectares: 0.0479
Type of site: Public Gardens
Date(s): Medieval and 2009
Listed Structures: None
Site ownership: Diocese of London
Site management: City of London Corporation Open Spaces Department.
Open to public?: Yes
Opening times: 8am - 7pm or dusk if it comes earlier.
Public transport - Tube Station: Chancery Lane (Central Line)

History

St Dunstan-in-the-West first appears in historical records towards the end of the 12th century and is so named to distinguish it from St Dunstan-in-the-East.

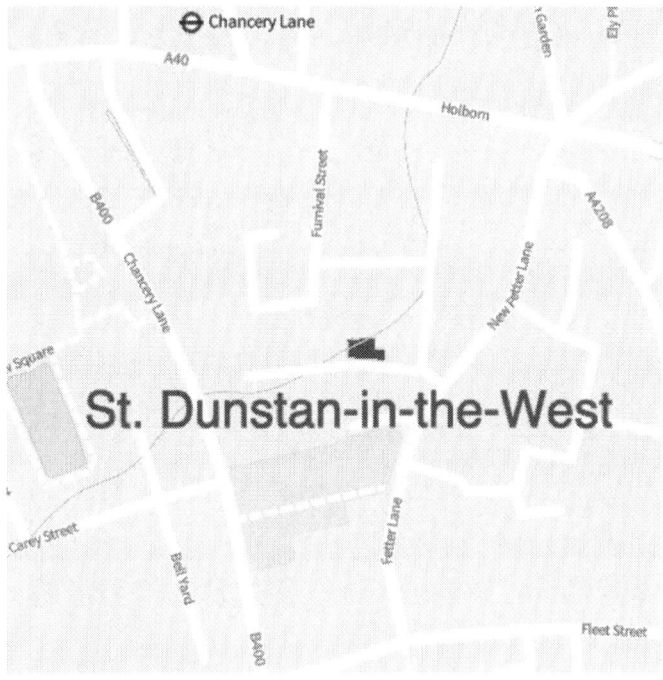

Contains OS data © Crown copyright and database rights 2020

This garden is located on what were the Bream's Buildings which was an 18th-century close which led off Chancery Lane.

Although the ancient church escaped the Great Fire in 1666, by the 19th century it was well and truly dilapidated. As a result a new church was built a little distance away.

These days 1960s-era offices overlook what is left of the churchyard which is now to all intents and purposes a small public garden. Slightly raised from the street level, it is entered up steps that bring us to the modest area of grass, trees and low-level planting amongst the remaining tombs.

To the south is King's College London Strand Campus, Maughan Library and Information Services Centre whilst the impressive Staple Inn Gardens are a bit of a walk up towards Chancery Lane underground station. At the top end of New Fetter Lane is St Andrew Holborn.

St Edmund the King and Martyr Churchyard

At A Glance: The old church has Saxon origins and is dedicated to Edmund, the King of East Anglia who died in 870 AD at the hands of the attacking Danes.

At one time the church was also known as St Edmund's Grass-church with reference to a nearby grass market that was held. It was destroyed in the Great Fire before being rebuilt soon afterwards and restored in the middle of the Victorian era and again following damaged inflicted during WWII.

Site location: Lombard Street/George Yard
Postcode: EC3V 9EA
Grid ref: TQ328810
Size in Hectares: 0.0175

Type of site: Private Garden

Date(s): 12th and 13th Centuries; 1850s

Listed Structures: St Edmund's Church

Site ownership: Diocese of London

Site management: City of London Corporation Open Spaces Department

Open to public?: By prior appointment

Opening times: By appointment, for access to garden: call 020 7621 1391 or 020 7626 5031

Public transport - Tube Stations: Bank (Central, DLR, Northern, Waterloo & City Lines) and Monument (Circle and District Lines)

Contains OS data © Crown copyright and database rights 2020

History

The origins of this small garden go back possibly to Saxon times but at least as far back as 1220 when mention is made of the churchyard here.

The churchyard closed for burials in 1853 and is now a small garden with one tree, raised beds and shrubs. It opens onto George Yard which was laid out 1929-32, and the churchyard railings date from the same period.

In 2001 St Edmund's became the London Centre for Spirituality, which moved into the Vestry Hall in that year, and it remains a consecrated church.

St Ethelburga's Centre for Reconciliation and Peace

At A Glance: The first mention of 'St Adelburga' is in 1250 though it is thought there has been a church here since at least 1180 AD. St Ethelburga was one of the oldest medieval churches in the City. Tragically, having survived the Great Fire of London and the Blitz, It was obliterated by an IRA bomb in April 1993.

Having been completely rebuilt, it reopened in November 2002 as a Centre for Reconciliation and Peace.

Site location: 78 Bishopsgate
Postcode: EC2N 4AG
Grid ref: TQ331813
Type of site: Churchyard
Date(s): Medieval and 1990s.
Designer: 2002 Peace Garden by Sylvia Crawford
Listed Structures: St Ethelburga's Church
Site ownership: Charitable Trust formed in 1997
Site management: St Ethelburga's
Open to public?: Yes
Opening times: Same as church, check website for details.
Public transport - Tube Station: Liverpool Street (Central, Metropolitan, Circle, Hammersmith & City Lines) **Rail:** Liverpool Street

Contains OS data © Crown copyright and database rights 2020

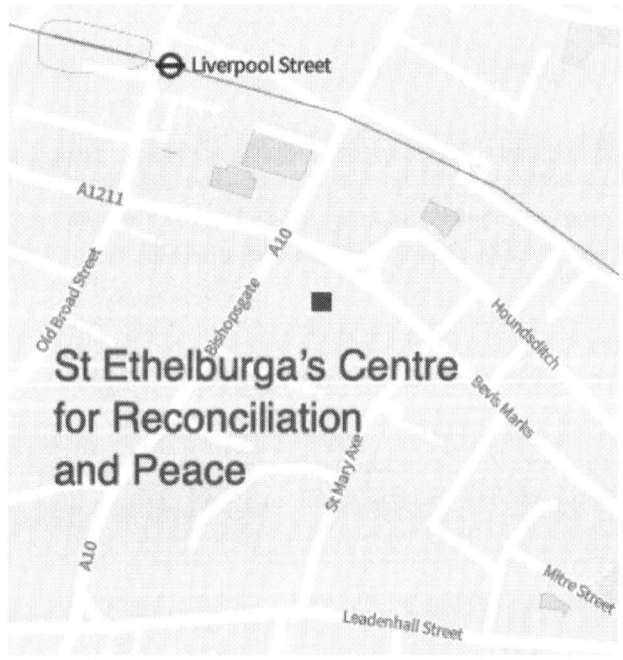

History

At the start of the 17th century this little church had a medieval porch with a little house and shops but these were eventually removed by the Corporation of London and in doing so it was said 'thereby deprived the church of almost its only distinction'!

St Ethelburga was one of the oldest medieval churches in the City having survived the Great Fire of London and the Blitz, but was gutted by an IRA bomb at Bishopsgate in April 1993.

It was completely rebuilt and reopened in November 2002 as a Centre for Reconciliation and Peace by HRH the Prince of Wales, and also re-consecrated as a church.

Before the IRA bomb, the churchyard was laid out as a garden and this has been retained though redesigned as a small peace garden and planted with a specially created St Ethelburga's Rose. There is also a statue of the saint and a fountain.

Beyond the garden wall is 'The Bedouin Tent', a space dedicated to the meeting of faiths, made of woven goat's hair in Saudi Arabia and designed by Keith Critchlow with mosaics and other decorations made in Morocco, Israel and the UK.

Nearby is St Helen's Bishopsgate and beyond that St Andrew Undershaft and also the modern St Helen's Square.

St Giles Cripplegate Churchyard

At A Glance: In 1010 AD, the body of King Edmund the Martyr reputedly rested in a church outside Cripplegate. 1090 is recorded as the date of the first church of St Giles Cripplegate but there may have been earlier churches on the site or in the vicinity. St Giles has been rebuilt and enlarged upon on several occasions since the 14th century.

Terribly damaged by WWII bombings, it was restored in 1960 within the new Barbican Estate. It is a site, though not particularly well served for nature lovers, nevertheless steeped in history and with interesting surroundings.

Site location: Barbican Estate with easy access from Fore Street and St Giles Terrace
Postcode: EC2Y 8DA
Grid ref: TQ323816
Type of site: Public Open Land
Date(s): 11th century - 1960s
Listed Structures: St Giles Church
Site ownership: City of London Corporation
Site management: City of London Open Spaces Department
Open to public?: Yes
Opening times: 24/7 for garden, church 11am-4pm Monday - Friday
Public transport - Tube Station: Barbican (Circle, Metropolitan, Hammersmith & City Lines) **Rail:** Moorgate

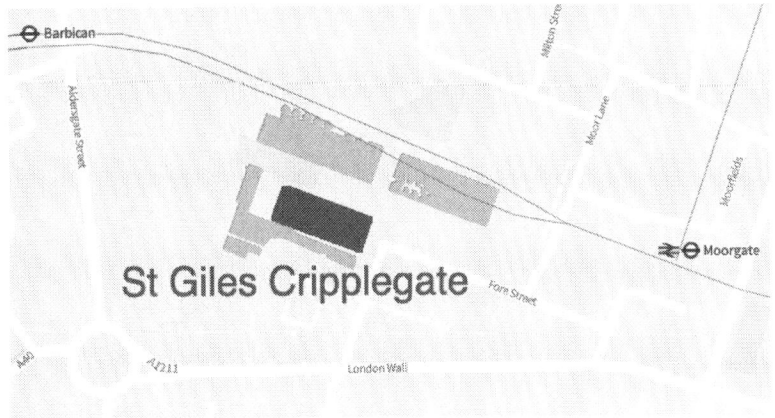

St Giles Cripplegate

Contains OS data © Crown copyright and database rights 2020

History

St Giles Cripplegate Churchyard is on the National Heritage List for England, Parks and Gardens which gives some indication of its illustrious heritage, perhaps surprisingly so given its location in the Barbican Estate.

An early church here was reputedly the resting place for the body of King Edmund the Martyr outside Cripplegate in 1010, although 1090 is given as the date of the first church here. It was founded by Alfune, who assisted Rahere in founding St Bartholomew's Priory and Hospital.

Cripplegate, an old gateway to the City, might have had an adjoining hospital for the lame or the name may simply be due to the many cripples who begged at the gate. St Giles himself was known for his works of great charity, and apparently gave away everything from his great riches down to the coat he wore.

The churchyard existed at least as far back as 1250 AD and there was a well also in the churchyard which by the mid-17th century was extended to the south in what become known as the Green Ground.

Some of the well-known figures who are buried here include preacher John Fox, the historian and map-maker John Speed and one of my personal favourite figures, John Milton (d.1608-1674) who is also commemorated by a statue within the church that once stood outside. The Wesley family have strong connections with this church also but possibly the most prominent figure linked to St Giles Cripplegate is Oliver Cromwell who married Elizabeth Bourch here on 22nd August 1622.

George Godwin in 1838 described the churchyard as 'one of the most ancient and venerable in the City, and abounds too with interesting associations, and mementos of past time'. By 1875 however it was being used as public open space, following the 1855 Burial Act saw the end of burials here and it suffered the proverbial kick in the teeth when the entire area was severely damaged by bombing in WWII with the church being later restored and reopened in 1960 within the new Barbican Estate albeit without that great history visible.

The Corporation of London acquired the site in 1965 and part of the site of the large burial ground was paved to create a new public space adjacent to an area of water. There are raised beds with old tombstones set into them and a lovely weeping willow drooping into the water. The old Victorian gas lamps that you can see here were once lighting up Tower Bridge and came here in the 1980s.

On the south side the churchyard faces onto the remains of the old London Wall with its customary ditch now a water-filled extension of the Barbican lake opposite the Barber-Surgeons' Hall Gardens.

Of interest are the remains of a Roman bastion shows where the wall turned through 90 degrees at the north-west corner of the fort of old Londinium.

St Helen's Bishopsgate Churchyard

At A Glance: Nestled amongst a forest of tall modern towers is the former churchyard of St Helen's Bishopsgate, a mostly paved semi-circular area in front of the church with mature plane trees and minimal planting.

Site location: Great St Helen's off Bishopsgate
Postcode: EC3A 6AT
Grid ref: TQ332812
Size in Hectares: 0.0402
Type of site: Public Gardens
Date(s): Medieval and 19th century
Listed Structures: St Helen's Church

Site ownership: Diocese of London
Site management: City of London Corporation Open Spaces Department
Open to public?: Yes
Opening times: 24/7 for the garden, the church 9am-5pm Monday - Friday.
Public transport - Tube Station: Liverpool Street (Central, Metropolitan, Circle, Hammersmith & City Lines) **Rail:** Liverpool Street

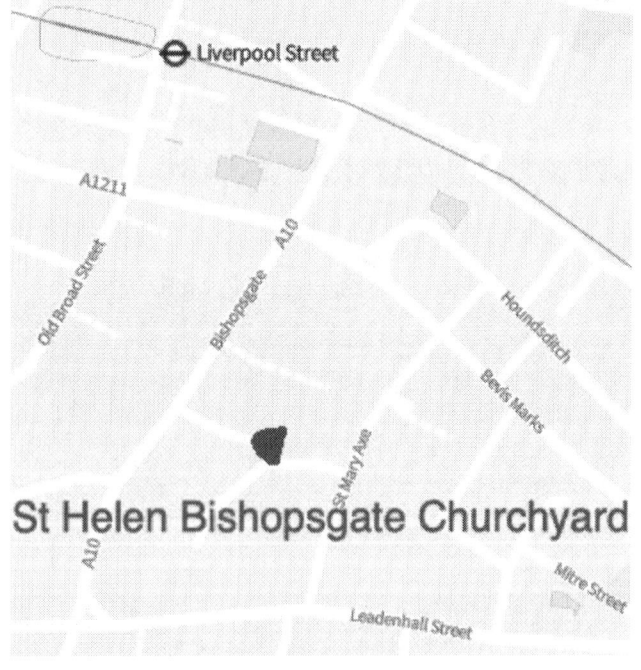

Contains OS data © Crown copyright and database rights 2020

History

The church here dates from at least the 12th century or perhaps earlier with the churchyard being established in the early years of the 13th century. Inside the church is particularly unusual as it features twin naves and this goes back to the time that the north aisle was a nuns' church for a Benedictine nunnery which was parallel to the parish church.

The church has undergone huge amounts of change over the centuries and none more so than when it suffered extensive bomb damage by the IRA in 1992 and 1993. It is now rebuilt however and still features elements of the 12th-century church.

The garden has some seating and trees behind an attractive low stone wall which once held iron railings.

Among those who are commemorated in the church are Sir Thomas Gresham who died in 1579 but not before establishing the Royal Exchange, and Martin Bond who as a young man fought against the Spanish Armada before dying in 1643 but there are several others around and about.

For a very different local experience check out St Helen's Square

St Helen's Square

At A Glance: St Helen's Square is a new public square at the foot of the Leadenhall Building.

The new square, which at 3,325 square metres is the third-largest open space in the City, provides an incredible setting for a number of modern iconic buildings, including 30 St Mary Axe, The Leadenhall Building, The Lloyd's Building and The Scalpel.

Site location: Leadenhall Street and St Mary Axe
Postcode: EC3V 4AB
Grid ref: TQ 33116 81164
Size in Hectares: 0.3325
Type of site: Square
Date(s): 2012-2018
Designer: Gillespie's
Listed Structures: None
Site ownership: Private
Open to public?: Yes
Opening times: 24/7
Public transport - Tube Station: Liverpool Street ((Central, Metropolitan, Circle, Hammersmith & City Lines) **Rail:** Liverpool Street and Fenchurch Street

Contains OS data © Crown copyright and database rights 2020

History

This pivotal space restores the site's unique authentic character albeit in a contemporary fashion. High quality paved, ramped and tiered pedestrianised walkways provide generous connections, simplifying the flow of people through this key thoroughfare.

Curved stone planters, filled with colourful planting that varies in height, colour and texture, animate the space together with integrated seating that provides opportunities for visitors to pause and relax. At night, the square is transformed through light installations that imitate 'swaying reeds' in the wind.

The redesigned space has reinvigorated the area, creating a fresh, appealing and multi-functional public plaza for people to enjoy. The space is large enough to host a range of events and performances throughout the year.

The old meets the new

Visit during the week and the square is teeming with office workers from the surrounding skyscrapers, but come the weekend and you're likely to have it entirely to yourself, but for something more spiritual try St Andrews Undershaft just across the road.

St James Garlickhythe Church

At A Glance: Situated as it is just off the busy Upper Thames Street, this will never be the most tranquil little garden. A church has stood here since around 1170 AD though has been rebuilt several times since then. Only a small part of the churchyard remains and this is largely a paved area with small planters. However adjoining the church to the west is a more expansive area with mature trees.

Site location: Upper Thames Street/Skinners Lane/Garlick Hill
Postcode: EC4V 2AF
Grid ref: TQ323808
Size in Hectares: 0.0137
Type of site: Churchyard
Date(s): Medieval and 1676
Listed Structures: St James Garlickhythe
Site ownership: Diocese of London
Site management: The church manages the small gated area whilst the landscaping to west of the church is maintained by City of London Corporation Open Spaces Department.

Open to public?: Yes
Opening times: As with the church 10am-4pm Mondays - Fridays
Public transport - Tube Station: Mansion House (Circle and District Lines) **Rail:** Cannon Street

Contains OS data © Crown copyright and database rights 2020

History

The church of St James Garlickhythe gains its name due to the hithe or wharf where garlic was landed and sold. Before the Thames was narrowed the shoreline would have been not much further away than busy Upper Thames Street is today.

Richard Lions, who was a wine merchant when Wat Tyler led his rebellion into London. Richard was beheaded in Cheapside but buried here. He is kept company by a number of pre-Elizabethan Lord Mayors of London.

Having unfortunately just enjoyed substantial repairs a few decades earlier, the church was destroyed in 1666 and rebuilt by Sir Christopher Wren 17 years later though the steeple dates from the early 18th century.

The gardens in front of St James Garlickhythe

The churchyard in front was enclosed by iron railings in 1808 and soon after a small building was erected to house the parish fire engine but this was destroyed in the Blitz.

In the 1960s the Vintners' Company donated new railings and gates complete with ornamental vine decorations which now enclose the small churchyard at the front.

There is a paved landscaped area to the west of the church complete with shrubs and trees that at least offset a little the traffic beyond them in Upper Thames Street. The area is completed with a charming bronze statue of 'The Barge Master and Swan Marker of the Vintners Company' which remembers the annual counting of the swans on the Thames which has been taking place since at least 1189.

Two minutes' walk westwards will bring you to Cleary Garden but head right past the church and it will bring you to Whittington Garden.

St John Zachary Garden (Goldsmiths' Garden)

At A Glance: One of my personal favourite gardens and a sunken one at that. The Goldsmiths' Garden is on the site of the churchyard and medieval church of St John Zachary, which was damaged in the Great Fire. Though the building remained in an increasingly ruinous condition until the Victorian times, the church was never again actively used.

The Worshipful Company of Goldsmiths acquired land here in 1339 AD and built the earliest recorded Livery Hall. Having suffered damage at the commencement of WWII, the garden that we see today was originally set out in 1941.

My two favourite plane trees in the City

Site location: Gresham Street/Noble Street
Postcode: EC2
Grid ref: TQ322814

Size in Hectares: 0.0655
Type of site: Public Gardens
Date(s): 12th century onwards; 1941; 1962 and 1995
Designers: 1962 by Peter Shepheard and 1995 by Anne Jennings
Listed Structures: Goldsmiths' Hall
Site ownership: Worshipful Company of Goldsmiths/Diocese of London (former churchyard)
Site management: Worshipful Company of Goldsmiths
Open to public?: Yes
Opening times: 24/7
Public transport - Tube Station: St Paul's (Central Line)

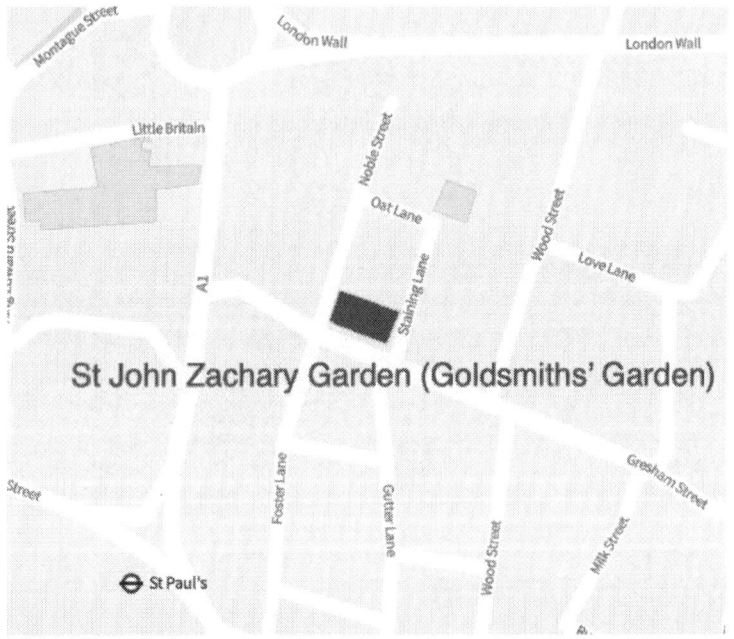

Contains OS data © Crown copyright and database rights 2020

History

After part of the Company's property was demolished in WWII, the site was laid out as a garden in 1941 by Fire-watchers and was the recipient of Best Garden on a Blitzed Site in 1950, a post-war competition run by the Gardeners' Company.

The garden was redesigned in 1962, with the west section which was the site of the former churchyard now raised above street level. The archway at the entrance/exit to the west section on Gresham Street features a gold Leopard's Head.

The garden remains simply laid out and with a number of gravestones from St John Zachary and two of the most magnificent looking plane trees in the City.

The sunken garden with its eternally well kept lawn

Steps lead down to the east section of the garden where once the church stood and having been excavated now lies some way beneath street level.

It is home to one very well-kept lawn and a catalpa tree. The fountain was added in 1995 as was some lighting, and there is seating too. In 2009, a sculpture entitled 'Three Printers' from 1957 was relocated here from another site.

There are a whole host of gardens nearby but none better than Postman's Park.

St Katherine Coleman Churchyard

At A Glance: The first St Katherine Coleman Church was already here by 1346 AD though it went through several incarnations; being rebuilt in the 15th century and then entirely replaced in 1739-40 by a new brick church which was in turn demolished in 1926.

The churchyard's stone gate piers and railings remain on St Katherine's Row and there is also a plaque that mentions the church being located here. The churchyard survives as a small public garden owned by Lloyd's Register of Shipping.

This one is easy to miss so if you're coming from Fenchurch Street look out for East India Arms pub. It is reached through an archway at 71 Fenchurch Street.

Site location: St Katherine's Row/Fenchurch Street
Postcode: EC3M 4BS
Grid ref: TQ334810
Size in Hectares: 0.0627
Type of site: Public Gardens
Date(s): 14th and 18th Centuries; 1996-2000
Designer: 1996-2000: Richard Rogers Partnership (Edward Hutchison, landscape architect)
Listed Structures: Lloyds Registry, 71 Fenchurch Street
Site ownership: Lloyd's Register of Shipping
Site management: Lloyd's Register of Shipping
Open to public?: Yes
Opening times: 8am - 6pm Monday - Fridays
Public transport - Tube Stations: Tower Hill (Circle and District Lines); Aldgate (Circle and Metropolitan Line) **Rail:** Fenchurch Street

History

The original church was dismantled in 1734 as it seems the surrounding ground had been so raised by many burials that it was about to rise above the church itself! As such, a new church was constructed from brick in 1739-40 by James Horne. In a city so full of seemingly beautiful churches it is somewhat refreshing to find his critics labelled it to be too ugly for London and following its final service in 1921 it was demolished in 1926. The proceeds of the sale

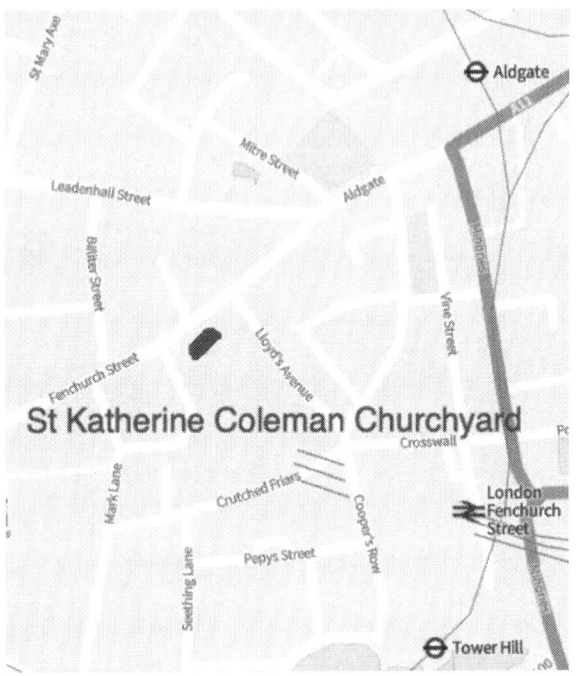

Contains OS data © Crown copyright and database rights 2020

enabled the building of St Katherine Westway over in Hammersmith whilst some of its monuments stayed local and now reside in St Olave Hart Street.

The site of the church was acquired by Lloyd's Register of Shipping, which had been established, and by the end of the 20th century they needed to expand their Fenchurch Street offices and purchased many of the neighbouring plots of land. However as part of the development brief, it was required that the former churchyard be preserved as a small public garden and it was re-landscaped, retaining existing mature trees, with new planting, raised beds, stone and timber seating, and a stainless steel fountain.

If you head east along Fenchurch Street, in around five minutes you will reach Aldgate Square with a number of gardens around, and about or alternatively a minute away southwest is Fenchurch Place.

St Katharine Cree Churchyard

At A Glance: Perhaps the most secret, and in my experience hardest to find, open garden in the City of London. Entirely surrounded by quite tall though nondescript looking buildings and accessed through a blue gate on Mitre Street, which in the five or six years I have been visiting seems to be locked as often as it is open even during its advertised opening hours.

It's well worth the perseverance when one does gain access however, and you'll find the most secluded, quiet and green garden with some headstones and monuments still evident.

Site location: 86 Leadenhall Street/Mitre Street
Postcode: EC3A 3BP
Grid ref: TQ334811
Size in Hectares: 0.043
Type of site: Public Gardens

Date(s): Medieval - 1965

Listed Structures: St Katharine Cree Church and Gateway to churchyard

Site ownership: Diocese of London

Site management: The church and Friends of St Katherine Cree

Open to public?: Yes

Opening times: 10.30am-4pm, Mondays - Fridays (apparently)!

Public transport - Tube Station: Aldgate (Circle and Metropolitan Line) and Liverpool Street (Central, Metropolitan, Circle, Hammersmith & City Lines) **Rail:** Fenchurch Street

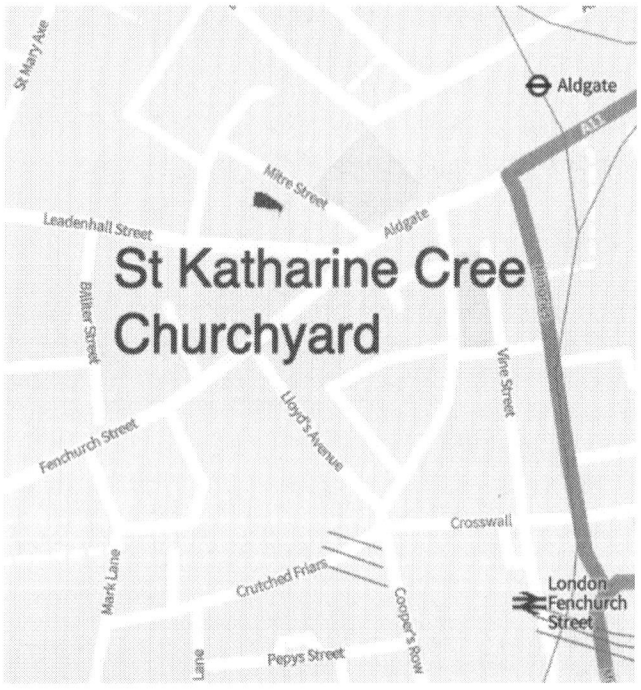

Contains OS data © Crown copyright and database rights 2020

History

A church has been here from at least the early 13th century, with a parish of St Katharine de Christchurch referred to in a will of 1280 AD. Creechurch is actually an abbreviated form of Christchurch and references the Priory of Holy Trinity, Christ Church in Aldgate, that was founded another 172 years earlier!

St Katharine's was built to serve inhabitants of the priory precinct on the site of the priory churchyard and became a separate parish church in 1414 but retained the Christchurch from its association with the Priory, and soon the parish churchyard was a separate entity.

Like with the garden, the church can be hard to find open but it's well worth trying as it is a rare example of a Gothic design with Renaissance detail. The font by Nicholas Stone was presented to Sir John Gayer, Lord Mayor of London in 1641, whose escape from a lion is commemorated!

It is thought that the painter Hans Holbein lies here having died of the plague in 1554, and both Handel and Purcell played the organ here. The present church of St Katharine Cree was built in 1628-31 when the older church was completely demolished with the exception of the lower portions of the steeple that survived the Great Fire, Blitz and numerous other incidents since it was constructed in 1504.

The church has had bells in its tower since the 16th century and they have very recently been restored with access to the church not from Mitre Road but round the corner in Leadenhall Street.

Despite being entirely surrounded by tall buildings, the garden here is surprisingly serene

The churchyard was laid out as a garden in 1965, and there are several interesting features and memorials which make it a fascinating mix of garden and churchyard.

Just across the road from the entrance to the garden you can find Mitre Square with its horrific Jack the Ripper related history and just beyond it Aldgate Square and St Botolph Without Aldgate.

St Laurence Pountney Graveyards

At A Glance: Head off from busy Cannon Street and step back in time to a secluded backwater. Two private gardens lined by wonderful yew hedgerows all under the canopy of mature plane trees.

The locale is also home to some wonderful old houses and architecture including some of the finest original merchant houses in London.

Site location: Laurence Pountney Lane/Laurence Pountney Hill, off Cannon Street
Postcode: EC4N 6EU
Grid ref: TQ327808
Size in Hectares: 0.0534
Type of site: Private Garden
Date(s): Medieval; 1666; 18th, 19th centuries and 2009.
Listed Structures: 1 - 2 Laurence Pountney Hill. Vestry House; retaining wall and railings of churchyard; 5 and 9 Laurence Pountney Lane, 6 Laurence Pountney Hill
Site ownership: Diocese of London
Site management: Private
Open to public?: Very rarely
Opening times: Private but visible from the street
Public transport - Tube Station: Bank (Central, DLR, Northern, Waterloo & City Lines) and Cannon Street (Circle and District Lines)
Rail: Cannon Street

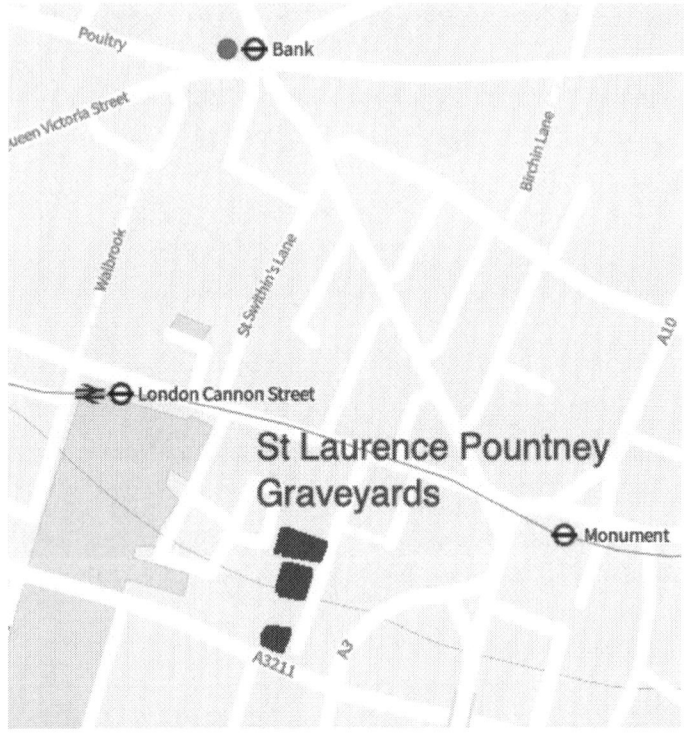

Contains OS data © Crown copyright and database rights 2020

History

St Laurence Pountney is named after Sir John Poultney. In the 1330s he was the Lord Mayor of London and founded Corpus Christi College in the parish of St Lawrence, and the street has had this name ever.

John Stow mentions how the churchyard was used as the place where Flemish weavers gathered to be hired for work in the last decades of the 14th century. Due to a dispute the weavers of Brabant were to gather for the same purpose in the churchyard of St Mary Somerset some quarter of a mile distant.

Both the church and college were destroyed in the Great Fire of 1666 and not rebuilt, with the parish then united with that of St Mary Abchurch. A plaque here illustrates the heritage of the site but what isn't mentioned is a fascinating account of an eyewitness who told the government inquiry into the Great Fire that he "saw the Fire break out from the inside of Lawrence Pountney Steeple, when there was no fire near it", and so implied the possibility of **arson**.

A pedestrian walkway leads to Martin Lane with two raised and railed gardens on each side which were once burial grounds. These days both gardens are private, and contain trees, shrubs and a number of tombs with the walls dating from around 1780 AD.

To the east is St Martin Otgar whereas two minutes further west just off Canon Street is St Swithin's Churchyard.

St Magnus the Martyr Churchyard

At A Glance: Just off Lower Thames Street and two minutes' walk from Monument Station is this mostly paved garden, home to a magnificent clock that travellers would once see crossing London Bridge from Southwark and with stone blocks from various incarnations of the bridge. There is even an oak post which has been dated to Roman times, and which was part of either the Roman embankment or original bridge.

Site location: Lower Thames Street
Postcode: EC3R 6DN
Grid ref: TQ329806
Size in Hectares: 0.0318
Type of site: Public Gardens
Date(s): Medieval and 1671
Listed Structures: St Magnus the Martyr Church
Site ownership: Diocese of London
Site management: City of London Open Spaces Department
Open to public?: Yes
Opening times: 24/7 (Church: Tue-Fri: 10am-4pm, Sun 10am-2pm)
Public transport - Tube Station: Monument (Circle and District Lines) and Bank (Central, DLR, Northern, Waterloo & City Lines)
Rail: Cannon Street

History

St Magnus the Martyr Church has been has been on this site one way or another since at least the 11th century and is the resting place of several Lord Mayors of London. With the Dissolution of the Monasteries the church passed to the Crown before eventually ending up with the Bishop of London by Queen Mary in 1553.

After the Great Fire, rebuilding work commenced in 1668 and was completed by Sir Christopher Wren in 1671-84, though the stone tower with octagonal cupola wasn't completed for another 30 years.

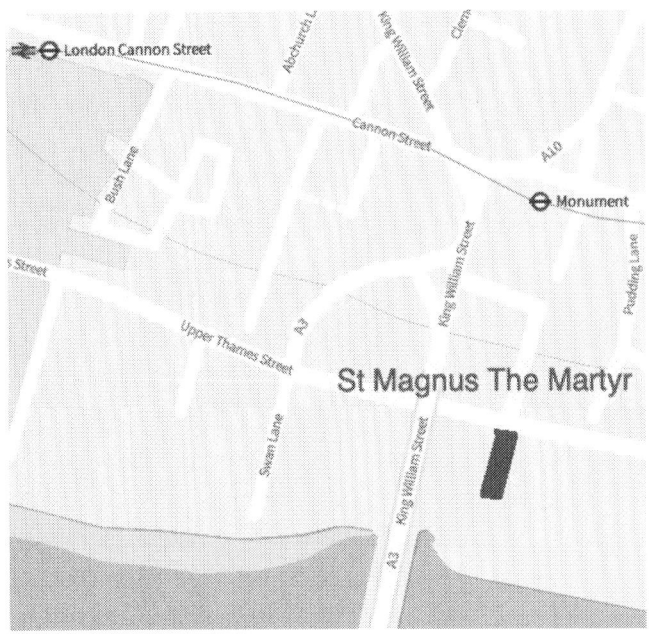

Contains OS data © Crown copyright and database rights 2020

The prominent clock tower was once visible to those walking from Southwark across London Bridge and was gifted to the church by Sir Charles Duncombe. Apparently Sir Charles when a young apprentice boy he couldn't find a public clock and missed his appointment with his master on London Bridge and so he vowed that should he ever have the means to do so, he would rectify the situation so that no one else might suffer the same fate. Missing the meeting obviously didn't do too much harm to his finances as Sir Charles Duncombe also presented the church with the organ in 1712 having become Lord Mayor of London too!

A plaque on the site states that the churchyard previously formed the main road approach to the Old London Bridge between 1176 and 1831. In the 1760s the church was substantially altered following a fire which destroyed the vestry room and much of the church. Subsequently the road onto Old London Bridge was widened and a pedestrian route created by demolishing two of the church's west bays, and the base of the tower became a porch.

A notable segment of not just Church but British history came when one time rector Miles Coverdale published the first English language bible in 1535 and his remains were eventually reinterred here 300 years later. Nearby there were once St Margaret New Fish Street which was destroyed in the Great Fire and is now where the Monument is, as well as St Michael Crooked Lane, which despite or because of its 13th-century origins was pulled down in 1831 when London Bridge road was built.

The churchyard is generally paved though there is some planting at the river end and there are railings fronting onto Lower Thames Street with a raised bed that is home to some planting and two trees. In the churchyard is a large piece of oak that was found in 1931 and thought to be either part of the Roman London Bridge or surrounding embankment.

Where the church steeple now is was once the likely position of the Roman gateway leading from the original bridge to the City of London. Fragments of stone arches from subsequent iterations of London Bridge can also be seen in the garden, recovered when Adelaide House was built adjacent to the church in 1921.

It's well worth going into the church itself as it is richly decorated and has a wonderful organ. There is also a fine model of old London Bridge to be seen.

If you head up to The Monument and turn down Monument Street then on your left you will find the well-named One Tree Park.

St Margaret Lothbury

At A Glance: Sandwiched between large commercial premises and somewhat hidden away from the main Lothbury street are the partial remains of this old churchyard which have been converted into a small garden.

Site location: Lothbury with access through Church Court
Postcode: EC2R 7HH
Grid ref: TQ327812
Size in Hectares: 0.0235
Type of site: Public Gardens
Date(s): 1683-1690
Listed Structures: St Margaret's Church, Overseas Bankers Club at number 7 Lothbury and the former Royal Bank of Canada building at number 6 Lothbury.
Site ownership: Diocese of London
Site management: St Margaret's Church
Open to public?: Yes

Opening times: As with the church 9am-5.15pm Monday-Friday
Public transport - Tube Station: Bank (Central, DLR, Northern, Waterloo & City Lines) and Monument (Circle and District Lines)

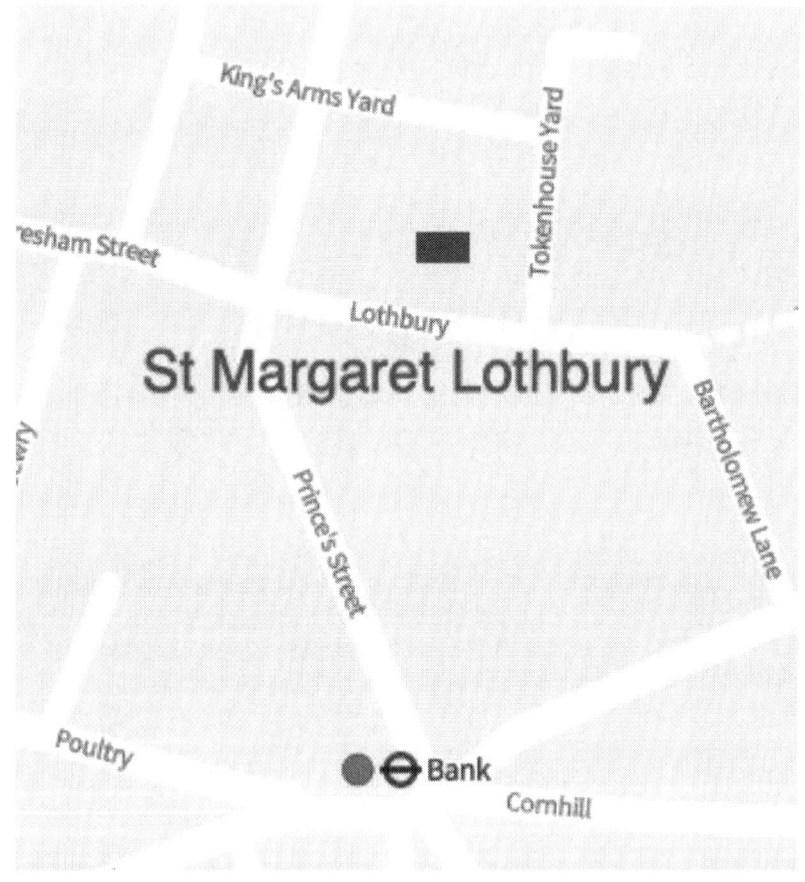

Contains OS data © Crown copyright and database rights 2020

History

The first substantial mentions of St Margaret's Church come towards the end of the 12th century and likely takes its name from a family name, possibly the Lotha family. The medieval church stands over the River Wallbrook. The generosity of then Lord Mayor of London Robert Large allowed the church to be rebuilt and enlarged upon in 1440.

The church was destroyed in the Great Fire of 1666 and the present church of St Margaret's by Sir Christopher Wren dates from 1683-90, with the tower completed slightly later by around 1700.

The early 19th-century church organ was restored in 1984 and nearby on each side of the altar are wooden figures of Moses and Aaron that were originally in St Christopher-le-Stocks church, which was demolished to create space for the Bank of England.

St Margaret's Court is a small courtyard north of the church, largely paved with a wooden bench. There is also a raised bed with shrubs and a small tree.

St Margaret Pattens

At A Glance: There has been a church dedicated to St Margaret of Antioch on this site for almost 900 years. This is likely the fifth church on site. The garden is small consisting of a paved area with a solitary tree that somehow beckons you to the medieval streets beyond.

Site location: Rood Lane/Eastcheap
Postcode: EC3M 1HS
Grid ref: TQ331808
Size in Hectares: 0.0083
Type of site: Public Open Land
Date(s): 1684-7
Listed Structures: St Margaret Pattens Church
Site ownership: Diocese of London
Site management: City of London Corporation Open Spaces Department
Open to public?: Yes
Opening times: 24/7 (Church 10am-4pm Mondays-Fridays)
Public transport - Tube Station: Monument (Circle and District Lines) **Rail:** Cannon Street

History

The previous and fourth church on this site was destroyed in the Great Fire of 1666 and rebuilt by Sir Christopher Wren between 1684 and 1687 with the construction costing in the region of £5,000.

The title 'Pattens' not only distinguishes the church from others of a similar name but is likely related to Pattens that were made nearby and example of which can be found in the excellent little church information area just inside the doorway.

Contains OS data © Crown copyright and database rights 2020

Pattens were a type of under-shoe that had a wooden sole and was fitted with leather straps all mounted on a large metal ring to raise the wearer from the muddy roads. Like the Basketmakers' Company, the Pattenmakers' Company has been associated with the church since the 15th century and an exploration of the church interior will reveal the names of past masters and Prime Wardens of both companies

At one time the church was owned by the great Richard Whittington who then conveyed it to the Corporation of London. After the Great Fire the parish of St Margaret was joined with that of St Gabriel when the latter was destroyed and not rebuilt, its churchyard remaining at Fen Court.

In 1954 the church ceased to be a parish church, becoming one of the City's Guild churches. Sadly damaged in WWII, St Margaret Pattens was restored in 1955-6 and finally in 1998 the tower and spire were restored.

The small paved area to the south of the church features a single tree, but is a very atmospheric welcome to medieval London. The churchyard was once much bigger and actually extended under the adjacent shop.

Not to be missed is a relatively new (at least by London standards) pedestrian street by the name of Plantation Lane which was created in 2005 and leads to Mincing Lane.

Set in the paving is a work of art entitled 'Time and Tide' by artist Simon Patterson. It consists of a glass wall in the form of a light-box with an illuminated image of the surface of moon from Michael Light's book *Full Moon*. In the pavement are inlaid lines of text that list and cover a huge amount of history of the City of London. Mention is made of public buildings, churches, heraldic colours, Livery Companies, the processional route of condemned prisoners, Thames Crossings, invasions and disasters, kings, queens and bishops, Roman deities, and street names.

Wander down St Mary at Hill and you will find the church of the same name on the right with its attached churchyard, while alternatively just a little way away is the wonderful St Dunstan-in-the-East.

St Martin Orgar Churchyard

At A Glance: A small garden on the site of the old church St Martin Orgar which was partly though not completely destroyed by the Great Fire but whose remains fell into disrepair through the subsequent centuries.

Site location: Martin Lane
Postcode: EC4R 0AU
Grid ref: TQ328808
Size in Hectares: 0.0466
Type of site: Private Garden
Date(s): Medieval and 17th century
Listed Structures: Railing, wall and gates to former churchyard
Site ownership: Diocese of London
Site management: Private
Open to public?: No
Opening times: None but visible from the street
Public transport - Tube Station: Monument (Circle and District Lines) **Rail:** Cannon Street

Contains OS data © Crown copyright and database rights 2020

History

Named after its one time owner, and 12th century Deacon Ordgaurs, St Martin Orgar previously stood in Martin Lane and following it being passed to the Dean of St Pauls, garnered a churchyard by the mid-13th century.

The street was quite well known as having a bad reputation from unscrupulous moneylenders before the Great Fire of 1666 swept everything away including the congregation who joined with St Clement Eastcheap. However the church was not entirely destroyed in the Fire, with much of the steeple and nave being repaired and used as a meeting place and chapel for Huguenot Protestants who had fled persecution in France. Early in the 19th century however it was truly falling apart and tall, but the steeple was pulled down.

The tower must have been truly blessed as it was pulled down in 1847 to allow for the widening of Cannon Street but then rebuilt in 1851 complete with the old bell and a clock with the building now used for commercial purposes. It is thought that the bells of St Martin Orgar are those referenced in the nursery rhyme 'Oranges and Lemons': 'You owe me five farthings, Say the bells of St Martins'.

During excavations in 1987, the remains of the medieval church were rediscovered, and the churchyard, and now a private garden whose rich foliage can be glimpsed from the street.

Hidden away just off the start of St Clements Lane is St Clements Eastcheap whilst head west through the lanes and you will reach St Laurence Pountney.

St Martin Outwich Churchyard

At A Glance: A simple raised flowerbed is all that remains of the former churchyard of St Martin Outwich midway between Liverpool Street Station and Aldgate.

Site location: Camomile Street
Postcode: EC3A 6DQ
Grid ref: TQ332813
Size in Hectares: 0.0103

Type of site: Public Garden
Date(s): Medieval and 1538
Listed Structures: None
Site ownership: City of London Corporation
Site management: City of London Corporation Open Spaces Department
Open to public?: Yes
Opening times: 24/7
Public transport - Tube Station: Liverpool Street (Central, Circle, Hammersmith & City and Metropolitan Lines) **Rail:** Liverpool Street

Contains OS data © Crown copyright and database rights 2020

History

The parish of St Martin Outwich dates from around 1196 AD and was constructed in Bishopsgate Street at the expense of the Oteswich family, hence its name.

In 1385 it was vested in the Merchant Taylors' Company and escaped the Great Fire of 1666 but wasn't so fortunate in 1765 when it was destroyed by one of the many other historic fires which the City has witnessed. Though rebuilt in 1796-98 it was demolished in 1874 with the parish uniting with that of St Helen's Bishopsgate in 1872. The churchyard was separate from the church itself which is near St Helen's Bishopsgate.

St Mary Aldermanbury

At A Glance: A lovely little two-level garden including a sunken section with lawn, yew and mature plane trees below the street level, whilst on the upper level is more intricate planting as well as an interesting memorial to Shakespearian actors.

Site location: Love Lane/Aldormanbury
Postcode: EC2V 7HP
Grid ref: TQ323814
Size in Hectares: 0.0979
Type of site: Public Gardens
Date(s): 12th century and 1960s

Listed Structures: Foundations of the former St Mary's Church as well as the monument to Heminge & Condell in former churchyard
Site ownership: City of London Corporation
Site management: City of London Corporation Open Spaces Department
Open to public?: Yes
Opening times: 24/7
Public transport - Tube Station: Moorgate (Circle, Hammersmith & City, Northern and Metropolitan Lines) **Rail:** Moorgate

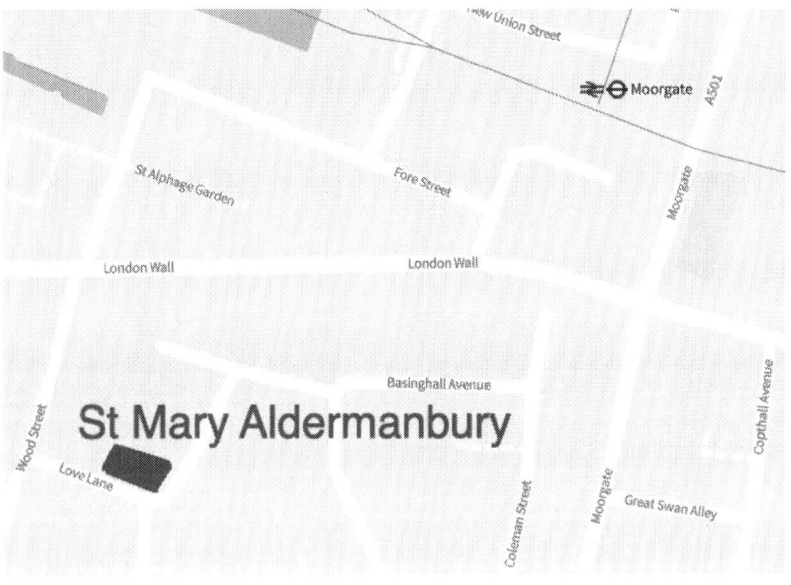

Contains OS data © Crown copyright and database rights 2020

History

Due to the large number of St Mary churches, St Mary Aldermanbury may have come by its name from the nearby Aldermans' Berry or Court Hall, which is where the nearby Guildhall now stands.

The churchyard dates from 1250 AD with the church dating almost a century earlier. It belonged to the Dean and Chapter of St Paul's, until it passed to the Elsing Spital or hospital in 1331, when John Stow mentioned that the Cloisters here was home to an ginormous shank bone which measured 28.5 inches in length though still supposedly that of a man!

To the south of the former churchyard, Love Lane has existed since the 14th century if not earlier. John Milton is known to have married his second wife Katherine Woodcocke here on 12th November 1656.

Aside from the steeple, the church was ravaged by the Great Fire of 1666 and rebuilt by Christopher Wren.

Sir Christopher Wren built his church on the foundations of the 1437 predecessor and these can still be seen in the lawn here. In 1965-9, the remains of the fabric of Wren's building were removed to Westminster College in Fulton, Missouri, USA and restored as a memorial to Winston Churchill. All that remains is a plaque in the garden given by Westminster College which gives the history of the church that once stood here.

There are many big names buried here, none more infamous than the 'hanging judge', Judge Jeffreys and members of his family.

Jeffreys, who often boasted that he had 'hanged more men than all the judges of England since the time of William the Conqueror' died in the Tower following his capture after the Glorious Revolution in 1688 while trying to flee the country dressed as a seaman in the East End. Lucky to escape with his life from an angry lynch mob, he was taken to the Tower of London where he died from illness. Initially he was buried in the Tower but later his remains were brought to St Mary in 1693.

Part of the medieval remains upon which Sir Christopher Wren later built his church

Following WWII bomb damage, the site of the church and its churchyard was acquired by the Corporation of London along with residual land from Wood Street Police Station, and was laid out as public gardens.

Within the gardens are areas of lawn, flower and shrub beds, a variety of trees and an ornamental box hedged knot garden, with seating areas and a raised paved area which is surrounded by hedging. This has a bust of Shakespeare by Charles Allen on a granite plinth, upon which are inscriptions explaining its history. The monument was 'given to the nation' by Charles Clement Walker of Shropshire in 1896 in memory of John Heminge and Henry Condell. They were fellow actors of Shakespeare and they lived in the parish before being buried here. It is due to them that Shakespeare's works have been handed down.

To the southeast you have the expansive Guildhall Yard and Piazza and its innumerable sights. To the north is Aldermanbury Square and at the far end of Love Lane is St Alban's Tower.

St Mary Aldermary Churchyard

At A Glance: Nestled at the southern end of Bow Lane is this old church with a raised paved garden under the shade of a mature tree.

Site location: Queen Victoria Street/ Bow Lane/Watling Street

Postcode: EC4M 9BW

Grid ref: TQ324810

Size in Hectares: 0.0305

Type of site: Public Gardens

Date(s): 11th and 16th Centuries; 1625-9 and 1682

Listed Structures: St Mary Aldermary Church

Site ownership: Diocese of London

Site management: City of London Corporation Open Spaces Department

Open to public?: Yes

Opening times: 24/7 (Church: 11am-3pm Monday and Thursdays)

Public transport - Tube Station: Mansion House (Circle & District Lines)

Rail: Cannon Street

Listed Structures: St Mary Aldermary Church

Site ownership: Diocese of London

Site management: City of London Corporation Open Spaces Department

Open to public?: Yes

Opening times: 24/7 (Church: 11am-3pm Monday and Thursdays)

Public transport - Tube Station: Mansion House (Circle & District Lines)

Rail: Cannon Street

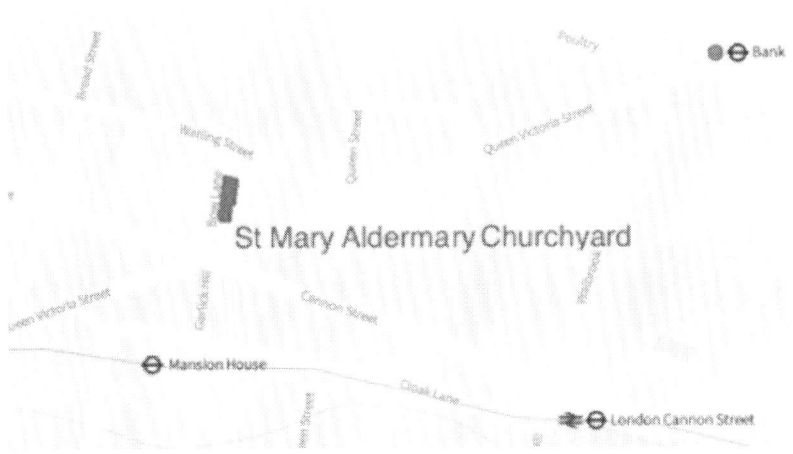

Contains OS data © Crown copyright and database rights 2020

History

Beating off no doubt stiff competition, St Mary's Church was described by John Stow as 'older than any church of St Mary in the Citie'. The name Aldermary may refer to it being the oldest or eldest church so dedicated. When William the Conqueror reigned, the church was within the living of the Priory of Christ Church Canterbury.

Henry Gold who was a rector here was executed in 1534 for his involvement with the 'Holy Maid of Kent', a nun who prophesied against the marriage of King Henry VIII to Anne Boleyn. John Milton married his third wife here in 1662 just before the church was all but destroyed by the Great Fire of 1666, requiring a Wren rebuild in 1679 that cleverly incorporates the lower reaches of the earlier church steeple.

The church has a small garden by the west entrance of the church, with three headstones which are set back against the wall amongst shrubbery and more set into the footpath which leads to the church door, and there are some magnificent cast iron railings to be seen that fit in perfectly with the medieval street.

Turn left at Watling Street and it will bring you out to several gardens including 25 Cannon Street, alternatively two minutes away to the Southwest along Queen Victoria Street you have Cleary Garden and closer than that to the south-east is a small garden in Queen Street.

St Mary-at Hill-Churchyard

At A Glance: Best approached from the infinitely more handsome cobbled Lovat Lane than St Mary at Hill itself, this completely enclosed churchyard provides a welcome relief from the busy nearby streets. However if you do come down St Mary-at-Hill you get a great view of The Shard.

Site location: St Mary-at-Hill/Lovat Lane
Postcode: EC3R 8EE
Grid ref: TQ330807
Size in Hectares: 0.0228
Type of site: Public Gardens
Date(s): 12th century and 1670-6
Listed Structures: St Mary-at-Hill Church

Site ownership: Diocese of London
Site management: City of London Corporation Open Spaces Department
Open to public?: Yes
Opening times: As with the church, 11am-4pm Monday-Friday
Public transport - Tube Station: Monument (Circle and District Lines) and Bank (Central, DLR, Northern, Waterloo & City Lines)
Rail: Cannon Street

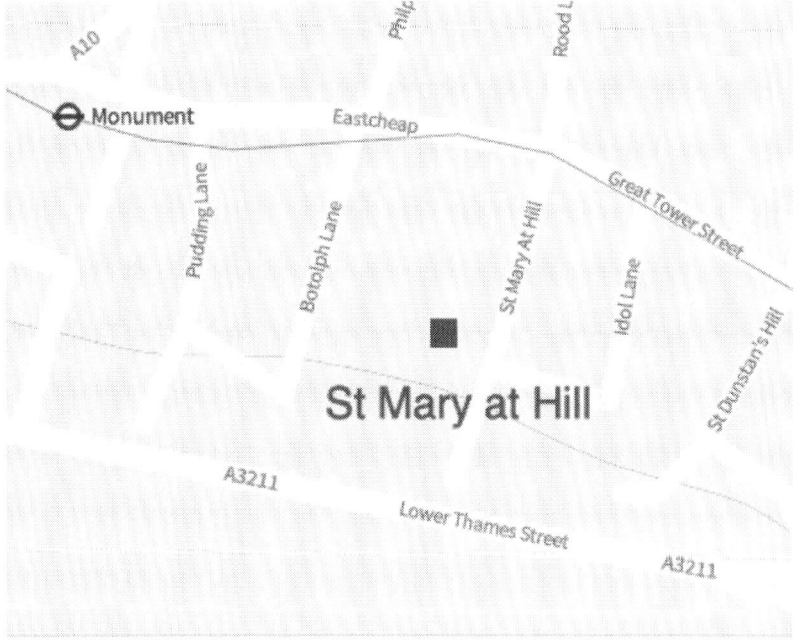

Contains OS data © Crown copyright and database rights 2020

History

The church of St Mary-at-Hill dates to at least the 12th century along with its churchyard; it must have been quite respectable as the Abbots of Waltham Abbey lived next door.

A number of former Lord Mayors of the City are buried here and in the 15th and 16th centuries mention is made of the 'The Great Churchyard' which leads one to think the churchyard here was significantly more expansive than what remains today.

The medieval church was partially destroyed in 1666 and rebuilt by Sir Christopher Wren in 1670-74 reusing the medieval west end and building upon the other surviving walls. Minor alterations came in the early 19th century and that was mostly that until in 1988 the church suffered from a severe fire in the roof, but the damage was repaired.

To enter the old churchyard you have to go down a passageway that leads off the main street. Having not accepted new burials since 1846, the garden now enjoys a simple plan with paving stones and a central flowerbed and a small tree all surrounded by a brick retaining wall. The garden is also home to a lead rainwater butt that is used as a planter despite dating from 1788, with two small seats here also.

Head down St Dunstan's Lane to the magnificent ruins of St Dunstan-in-the-East.

St Mary Staining Churchyard

At A Glance: A wonderful little garden with plenty of seating, lawns, planting and a very mature plane tree and all complemented by a terrific piece of modern architecture next door designed to let the light flow into the garden.

Site location: Oat Lane/St Albans Court
Postcode: EC2V 7EE
Grid ref: TQ322815
Size in Hectares: 0.0358
Type of site: Public Gardens
Date(s): 12th century and 1965
Listed Structures: None
Site ownership: Diocese of London
Site management: City of London Open Spaces Department
Open to public?: Yes
Opening times: 24/7
Public transport - Tube Station: St Paul's (Central Line)

History

The first mention of a church here occurs in 1189 AD when reference is made to an 'Ecclesia de Staningehage'. Staining probably derives from a landowner from Staines and neighbouring Oat Lane is probably descended from the Oats market which existed here during the Tudor period.

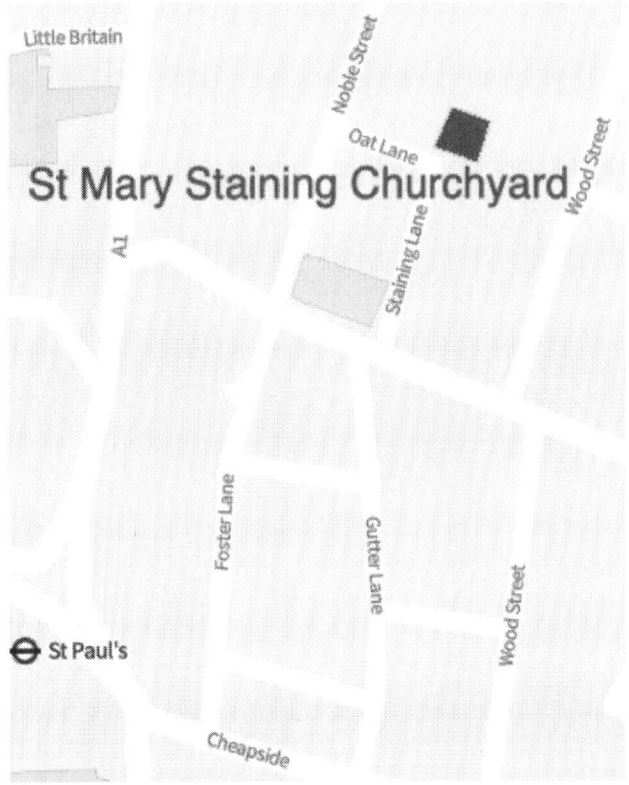

Contains OS data © Crown copyright and database rights 2020

In 1278 AD, accused of robbery, Richard de Codeford fled and took refuge in the church, killing his pursuers with a lance through a hole in the window!

The church was repaired in 1630 but destroyed in the Great Fire of 1666 and not restored. In 1965 the Corporation of London took over the maintenance of the open space created on the site. There is now a raised area of grass with a large plane tree that dominates and contrasts well with the modern adjacent building. A path leads past a lawn with gravestones towards the rear of the garden. There are also some shrubs and raised flowerbeds.

This garden is nestled against a modern office block which has been designed to let light in which is does remarkably well.

Go through St Alban's Court to St Alban's Tower or head to Noble Street Gardens for a peek at the Roman Wall.

St Mary Woolnoth

At A Glance: Not much refuge from modern life can be sought here, situated as it is just feet from Bank Station. A fantastic front gate welcomes you into the tiny paved garden and the Nicholas Hawksmoor-designed church beyond.

Site location: Lombard Street/King William Street
Postcode: EC3V 9AN
Grid ref: TQ327810
Size in Hectares: 0.0089
Type of site: Churchyard
Date(s): 13th century; 1716-27 and 1890 and 1992.
Listed Structures: St Mary Woolnoth Church. Also the gate piers and gates to church
Site ownership: Diocese of London
Site management: The church except for the window boxes which are maintained by the City of London Corporation Open Spaces Department.
Open to public?: Yes
Opening times: As with the church 9.30am-4.30pm Mondays - Fridays.
Public transport - Tube Stations: Bank (Central, DLR, Northern, Waterloo & City Lines) and Monument (Circle & District Lines) Rail" Cannon Street

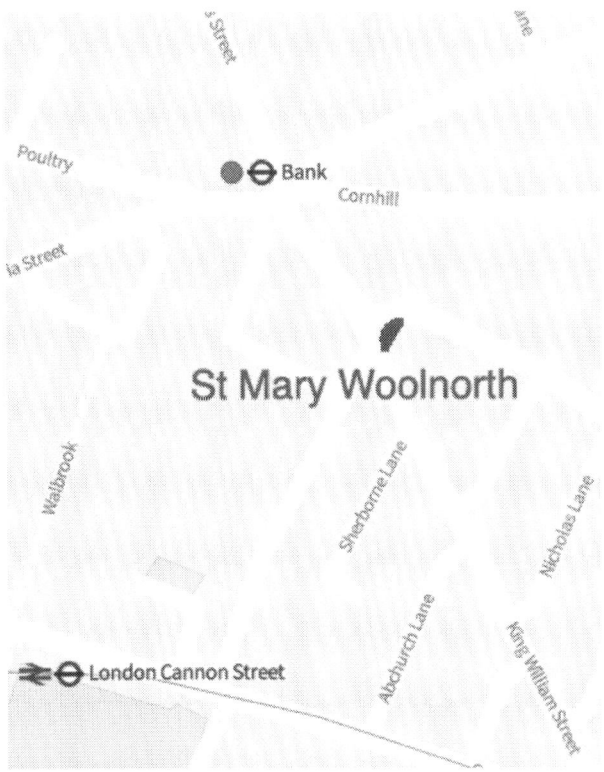

Contains OS data © Crown copyright and database rights 2020

History

The history of this site goes back further than might be thought as fragments of a possible pre-Christian temple were discovered here during one of the church rebuilds in 1716 AD.

Once known as St Mary the Nativity, St Mary Woolnoth is first referred to in 1273-4 when the church belonged to the Priory of St

Helen's Bishopsgate until the Dissolution of the Monasteries. The church was rebuilt in1438 and a charnel chapel was built in 1496 which was used for burials.

Despite being badly damaged in the Great Fire of London, St Mary Woolnoth was only repaired rather than rebuilt by Sir Christopher Wren, which perhaps explains why the church quickly fell into dilapidation and following the Fifty New Churches Act of 1711, it was rebuilt by Nicholas Hawksmoor in 1716-27. The splendid iron railings date from around 1900 and 1992.

An interesting quirk in the history of this church is that the crypt of the church was once used as a booking hall for Bank underground station, which was built alongside the church on King William Street in 1897-8.

An adjacent development in 2004 presented the opportunity to open up a passageway behind the church. However the garden here is very small, simply a semi-circular paved forecourt with some planting and seating, bordered by railings with an elaborate gate.

To the north you can find the Royal Exchange Gardens but if you're brave, explore the lanes to the west and reach St Stephen Walbrook Churchyard.

St Mary-le-Bow Churchyard

At A Glance: An expansive paved garden with plenty of seating just outside one of the most iconic churches in all of London.

Site location: Bow Churchyard, Cheapside
Postcode: EC2V 6AU
Grid ref: TQ323811
Size in Hectares: 0.1048
Type of site: Public Gardens
Date(s): 1670-80; 1963 and 2009.
Designer(s): Burns + Nice landscape consultants 2009.
Listed Structures: St Mary-le-Bow Church and the statue of Captain John Smith
Site ownership: Diocese of London
Site management: City of London Corporation Open Spaces Department
Open to public?: Yes
Opening times: 24/7
Public transport - Tube Station: Mansion House (Circle and District Lines **Rail:** Cannon Street

History

This iconic cockney church was possibly so-called for being built on arches with another theory being that it once had arches on top of its steeple, and was first recorded here around 1,000 years ago with a churchyard present just over a century or so later around 1157 AD.

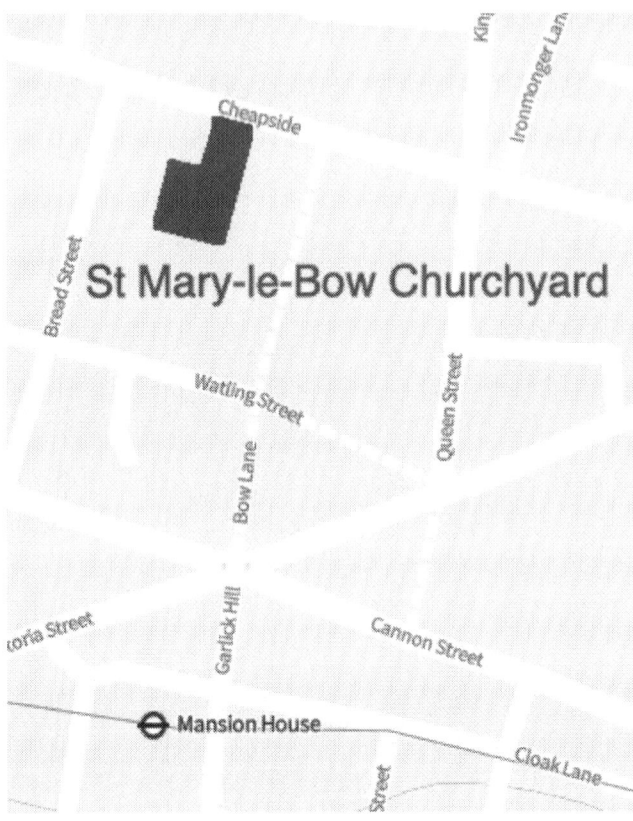

Contains OS data © Crown copyright and database rights 2020

In 1091 the building's roof was blown off in a storm and in 1271 the steeple collapsed; both terrible disasters which killed a large number of people.

The notorious history doesn't end there as in the late 12th century, a rebel by the name of William FitzOsbert also known as Long-beard took refuge in the church steeple, which was eventually set on fire to oust him and his followers. They were all taken to Smithfields and hanged.

In 1284 a draper named Lawrence Duber took refuge here having apparently committed a murder. He was actually hanged within the church by friends of his victims who tried to make it look like a suicide. Eventually the truth came out and the church was interdicted. The friends were put on trial and sixteen men were hung for their part in the extrajudicial killing and a woman was burned to death for her part.

Following its destruction in the Great Fire of 1666, Sir Christopher Wren rebuilt the church during the 1670s and actually based his work on the Temple of Peace in Rome which he no doubt thought fitting as he discovered the building sat atop a Roman causeway, though latterly it is believe this may be a crypt of a Norman church. Despite its near total destruction in the WWII, the church was rebuilt in the 1950s and 60s.

An interesting feature of the church is that of a small balcony over the doorway overlooking Cheapside, which at one time might have been provided as a place to view the processions, tournaments and other entertainments which for so long took place along Cheapside.

Despite all of the above, the church is possibly most famous for its bells (Bow bells) which have a long cultural history in themselves, and hark back to Norman times when they were rung to mark the curfew and then in later centuries they were rung to signal it was time for the local shops to close. It is said that only those born within earshot of Bow bells can claim to be true cockneys. In times past the bells could be heard for many miles though now due to traffic, tall buildings and modern life, the bells can often only be heard in a narrow radius from the church itself.

Captain Smith in midwinter

After WWII the churchyard area was extended and repaved. In 1960 a statue of Captain John Smith was put in place. Captain Smith had been a member of the Cordwainers' Company, and set sail from Blackwall which eventually led to him founding the colony of Virginia in 1606. His statue was located here due to its proximity to the old site of the Cordwainers' Hall. Handily sermons advocating the colonisation of the New World also took place here in the 17th century which makes the location particularly fitting. The intrepid sailor died in 1631 and is actually buried at St Sepulchre Churchyard, a church associated with the Cordwainers' Company since 1631.

Earlier in the 21st century the churchyard seating and lighting were improved upon and, along with the leafy mature plane tree, the statue of Captain Smith very much remains the focus.

From here it is a short walk west along Cheapside to St Peter Cheap on the corner of Wood Street or head off Cheapside to the east up Ironmonger Lane to St Olave's House.

St Michael Cornhill Churchyard

At A Glance: One of those unexpected little gardens that can't be seen from the roadside. Instead it is reached through a series of alleys which makes happening across it all the more delightful.

Set against the imposing church with a lawn, low level planting and the odd tree, this garden also has plenty of benches which is handy as it can be quite a sun trap!

Site location: Cornhill/St Michael's Alley
Postcode: EC3V 9DS
Grid ref: TQ329810
Size in Hectares: 0.0491
Type of site: Public Gardens
Date(s): Medieval; 15th century, 1670-72 and 1857-60
Listed Structures: St Michael Cornhill
Site ownership: Diocese of London
Site management: City of London Corporation Open Spaces Department
Open to public?: Yes
Opening times: As with the church 8.30am-5pm, Mondays - Fridays
Public transport - Tube Station: Bank (Central, DLR, Northern, Waterloo & City Lines) and Monument (Circle and District Lines)

History

St Michael's Church is an ancient church being situated as it is in the heart of old Roman Londinium. In 1055 AD the church was given to the Abbey and Convent of Evesham by a priest called Alnothus or Alnod and then in 1503 the Abbey passed it to the Drapers' Company.

The Sheriff of London in 1429 was a William Rus or Rous, and he was a tremendous supporter of the church. He bequeathed lands and tenements, £100 for an altar in the chancel and £40 towards the new steeple as the previous one had burnt down in 1421. As such he is buried in the chapel of St Mary here.

Contains OS data © Crown copyright and database rights 2020

It's not too hard to imagine where the garden is now once having been the cloisters. Much was destroyed in the Great Fire and rebuilt by Sir Christopher Wren very soon afterwards, except for the steeple which was only repaired but like other such cases soon required a rebuilding with Nicholas Hawksmoor overseeing this in 1721.

Sir George Gilbert Scott designed the vaulted cloister between the churchyard and St Michael's Alley in 1868 having previously modified the church in the 1850s. To the east of the churchyard is the Rectory and Vestry built in 1913-14 by Charles Reilly. A bronze war memorial by the church entrance on Cornhill is by Richard Goulden, dated 1920.

The old churchyard garden has a paved path (with some gravestones set into the pavement) around two sides and areas of open lawn. Flowerbeds, shrubs and trees are around the perimeter on two sides and a row of benches against the church wall, with gravestones set into the paving. There is also a memorial birdbath in one of the flowerbeds.

The neighbouring St Peter Upon Cornhill is just moments away if you can avoid the numerous nice pubs in the area.

St Nicholas Cole Abbey

At A Glance: A quiet spot just a few minutes from St Paul's Cathedral at a happily reopened Wren Church. It is thought the name here comes from St Nicholas of Myra, the patron saint of fishermen.

Site location: Queen Victoria Street/Distaff Lane/Old Fish Street Hill
Postcode: EC4V 4BJ
Grid ref: TQ321809
Size in Hectares: 0.0167; 0.0315 adjacent court
Type of site: Churchyard
Date(s): 12th century; 1672-78 and 1962

Listed Structures: St Nicholas Cole Abbey Church
Site ownership: Diocese of London
Site management: Church of England
Open to public?: Yes
Opening times: 24/7 (Church all days except Saturday**)**
Public transport - Tube Station: Mansion House (Circle and District Lines) and St Paul's (Central Line) **Rail:** Blackfriars

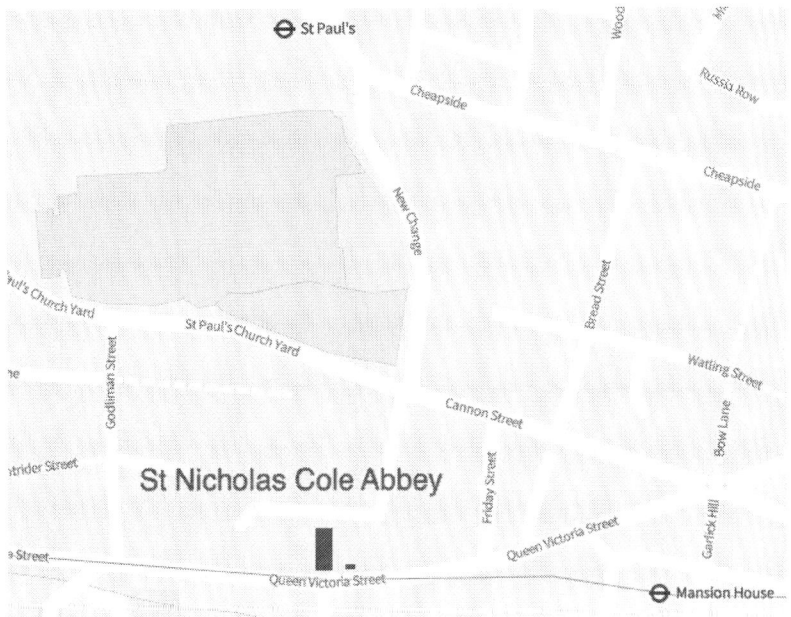

Contains OS data © Crown copyright and database rights 2020

History

The building that stood here before the Great Fire was quite ancient even before the steeple was built in 1377. St Nicholas Cole Abbey had belonged to the Dean and Chapter of St Martin-le-Grand until Henry VII granted it to the Abbot and Convent of Westminster; until its dissolution.

The gardens to the west of the church with Distaff Lane Gardens just visible to the rear

The building was destroyed in the Great Fire of 1666 but speedily rebuilt by 1677. At that time the parish joined with that of St Nicholas Olave. There was 90 years of general upheaval from 1874 due to enforced modifications due to the newly laid out Queen Victoria Street, early 20th-century restorations and then WWII bombings, and things looked bleak when the Free Church of Scotland closed here in 2003.

In 2006 the Church of England announced that it was to be converted as a National Centre for Religious Education. Following a period of quiet, in the last decade Sunday and midweek services have returned to St Nick and for those who aren't of a religious persuasion, the café inside is well rated with of course sumptuous surroundings.

The area to the west side of church was laid out as a public open space with paving, a raised bed along the wall abutting the church and seating; a number of trees have been planted and it provides excellent views of St Paul's Cathedral. Though Queen Victoria Street is often busy during the week, Distaff Lane is normally quiet so when the planters are in bloom and the trees in leaf it can make for quite a nice spot to visit.

For those wondering about where the name came from, John Stow was a 16th-century historian who believed that 'Cole' was a corruption of 'Cold Bay', it being sat on an exposed bank of the Thames or alternatively 'Cold Harbour' which would have offered travellers shelter.

Just to the north of here is the brand new Distaff Lane Garden.

St Olave Hart Street Churchyard

At A Glance: A really beautiful small garden in delightful surroundings that is in one of the quieter spots of the City and a favourite of Charles Dickens.

Site location: 8 Hart Street/Seething Lane **Postcode:** EC3R 7NB
Grid ref: TQ333808   **Size in Hectares:** 0.0358   **Type of site:** Public Gardens
Date(s): 11th and 15th Centuries; 1731-2, 19th century and 1920s
Listed Structures: St Olave's Church; Entrance gateway, wall and C18th railings
Site ownership: Diocese of London
Site management: City of London Corporation Open Spaces Department
Open to public?: Yes
Opening times: As with the church 10am-5pm Monday - Friday
Public transport - Tube Station: Tower Hill (Circle, District Lines)
Rail: Fenchurch Street

History
First recorded in the late 12th century, St Olave is the smallest intact medieval church in the City of London. King Olaf fought with Æthelred the Unready against the Danes in the Battle of London Bridge in 1014 AD. He was canonised following his death in 1025 and this led to a spate of churches being dedicated to him; a reminder of how these islands once tilted towards Scandinavia rather than continental Europe.

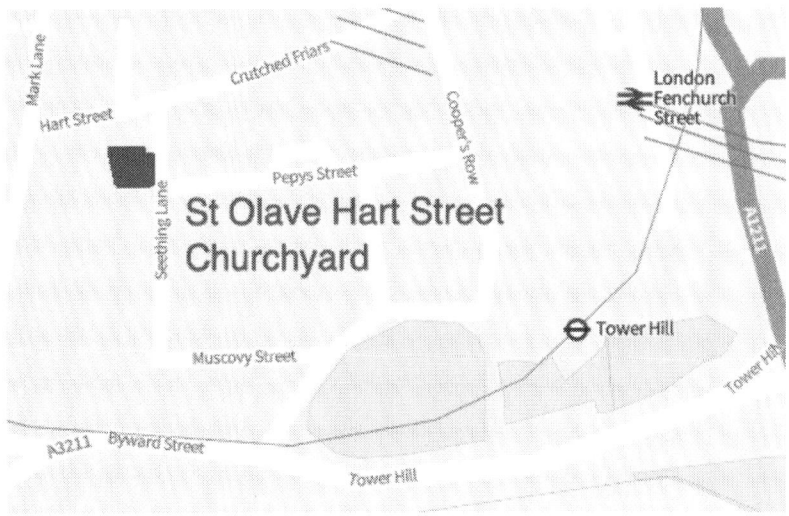

Contains OS data © Crown copyright and database rights 2020

A new church was built in the 13th century and though parts of this remain in the crypt, most of the church is from the 15th century.

There has been a churchyard here since at least 1345 and the burial registers from 1563 onwards are well-preserved and include a record of Mother Goose being buried here on 14 September 1586, though who she might have been is something of a mystery.

The church has strong associations with Samuel Pepys, who was buried here, and the nearby Navy Office at Seething Gardens; Pepys referred to it as 'Our own Church'.

Unusually the church survived the Great Fire, in part due to the fact that Pepys took matters into his own hands and had many of the wooden structures surrounding it removed. On the south aisle wall of the church was a doorway leading to the gallery for use by the Navy Office. It was constructed in 1660 at the behest of Pepys in order to get to the church from the Navy Office and his home in Seething Lane without getting wet!

Don't let the foreboding skulls put you off from entering what was the favourite churchyard of Charles Dickens, rich in medicinal herbs.

Fittingly, Samuel Pepys was buried in the crypt and a monument to him and his wife is in the church together with a memorial plaque.

Many victims of the infamous 1665 plague were buried here. Records indicate the first such victim was on 24 July 1665 for 'Mary, daughter of William Ramsay, one of the Drapers' Almsmen'. In fact tradition has it that the first appearance of the plague was in the Drapers' Almshouses in Cooper's Row, just a few minutes' walk down present day Pepys Street.

The churchyard has a gateway dating back to 1658 from Seething Lane which is most notable for its pediment featuring a carved skull and crossbones after a design by Hendrik de Keyser. The churchyard also has strong connections with Charles Dickens who wrote of it "My best beloved churchyard, the churchyard of St Ghastly Grim".

The church was badly damaged in 1941 and rebuilt from 1951. The churchyard still had many tombs until around WWI when it was redesigned to how we find it now with a path from the street entrance to the south door of the church. There are shrubs in the corners of the garden and a small path round a central bed, with some gravestones set against the walls and some wonderful 18th-century railings.

Many of the plants in the garden were used to offer traditional herbal remedies and are clearly labelled.

As the church has large south-facing windows that, rather unusually for London, are not blocked due to the presence of the garden, the interior is often wonderfully lit by sunlight making it easy to spend time enjoying the wonderful building.

St Olave Silver Street

At A Glance: This small garden is pinned up between London Wall and an overbearing glass and steel tower, and comes across as slightly unloved and forlorn. On the plus side there are some benches, a mature oak tree and some smaller shrubs and lawn and a connection to Shakespeare too.

Site location: London Wall/Noble Street
Postcode: EC2V 7EE
Grid ref: TQ322815
Size in Hectares: 0.0647
Type of site: Public Gardens
Date(s): 12th century
Listed Structures: None
Site ownership: Diocese of London (former churchyard); garden extension City of London Corporation
Site management: City of London Corporation Open Spaces Department
Open to public?: Yes
Opening times: 24/7
Public transport - Tube Station: St Paul's (Central Line); Barbican (Circle, Hammersmith & City, Metropolitan Lines) **Rail:** Moorgate

Contains OS data © Crown copyright and database rights 2020

History

Another church and garden dedicated to King Olaf giving some illustration of the importance of Scandinavia in British history which is now often overlooked. The first reference to a church here is to St Olave de Mukewelle-Strate in around 1200; it is dedicated to King Olaf the first Christian King of Norway who fought in England alongside Æthelred against the Danes.

The church was both rebuilt and enlarged at the start of the 17th century but only enjoyed a short life before being destroyed in the

Great Fire when it was decided it would not be rebuilt with the parish amalgamating with St Alban, Wood Street. John Stow described it as 'a small thing and without any noteworthy monuments' which may be still a suitable summation of the garden today, though actually the garden is perfectly lovely considering the soulless building that overshadows it.

'A small thing without any redeeming monuments'… true then and now.

Silver Street is one of the few places in London where we can know with certainty that William Shakespeare once lived. In 1604 Shakespeare spent a number of years lodging with a French family called the Mountjoys on Silver Street, Cripplegate. We know this owing to legal evidence that survives from May 1612, when Shakespeare gave evidence in a lawsuit about a marriage dowry of £60. The evidence confirms his presence as a lodger at a house on Silver Street in the Jacobean period.

The garden which was once the churchyard is on two levels surrounded by very established shrubs and bushes. On the London Wall side there are evergreens such as laurel whereas there are roses and trees near the entrance and the odd tomb.

Up a small flight of steps is a grand birdbath made out of granite, and on each side of the steps are small antiquated information plaques, and a small number of gravestones remain within the raised lawn.
Just across the street you have the Noble Street Gardens whilst across London Wall you have the Barber Surgeons with its garden and Roman Fort Gate.

St Olave's House

At A Glance: St Olave's House is the steeple of the church of St Olave Jewry with the former churchyard now a wonderfully secluded garden off the usually quiet Ironmonger Lane.

The garden has been open to the public since the 1890s, and St Olave's House is leased as offices to solicitors.

Site location: Ironmonger Lane/St Olave's Court

Postcode: EC2V 8EY

Grid ref: TQ325812

Size in Hectares: 0.039

Type of site: Private Garden

Date(s): Medieval; 1671-79 and the 1890s.

Listed Structures: Tower of St Olave Jewry

Site ownership: London Diocesan Fund, leased to Winter Scott Solicitors

Site management: Winter Scott Solicitors

Open to public?: Yes

Opening times: Front garden publicly accessible, with garden area to north private.

Public transport - Tube Station: Bank (Central, DLR, Northern, Waterloo & City Lines) and Monument (Circle, District Lines)

History

Old Jewry was the neighbourhood where Jews first lived after their arrival with William the Conqueror and they remained here until their expulsion by Edward I. Upon their return, they settled upon a new district with this area becoming known as Old Jewry.

The antiquated medieval church was replaced after the Great Fire by a new church by Sir Christopher Wren in 1671-79. St Olave's Church found itself largely redundant and surplus to requirements so was pulled down except for the west tower, west wall and part of the north-west wall, which were converted as the rectory for St Margaret Lothbury.

Contains OS data © Crown copyright and database rights 2020

The churchyard here dates back to at least the mid-14th century but all known human remains were removed from the churchyard in 1888-9 and it became a garden, though interestingly both this Victorian and recent excavations unveiled previous foundations dating from the 9th century and also Roman brickwork.

An alleyway runs alongside the garden from Ironmonger Lane to Old Jewry named St Olave's Court. The garden has fine railings and a cobbled pathway to the actual house with there being some shrubs and seating under the canopy of mature trees,

The impressive Guildhall Yard and Piazza is to the north that leads to many other gardens. Alternatively, just off the other side of Cheapside you have St Pancras Churchyard.

St Pancras Churchyard

At A Glance: Not to be confused with the similarly named churches in Camden, this was the site of the medieval church of St Pancras Soper Lane. When it was destroyed in the Great Fire of 1666, the parishioners then went to St Mary-Le-Bow. The churchyard though was used as a place of burial from around 1370 to the 19th century before finally being converted into a garden after WWII.

Aside from an information plaque on the wall there would be no evidence of its former use but as the garden has been recently renovated in the last few years it is well worth visiting if only for its characterful benches.

Site location: Pancras Lane
Postcode: EC4
Grid ref: TQ324810
Size in Hectares: 0.021
Type of site: Public Garden

Date(s): Medieval
Designer(s): Studio Weave (2010)
Listed Structures: The remains of St Pancras Church
Site ownership: City of London Corporation
Site management: City of London Corporation Open Spaces Department
Open to public?: Yes
Opening times: 24/7
Public transport - Tube Station: Bank (Central, DLR, Northern, Waterloo & City Lines)/Monument (Circle and District Lines)

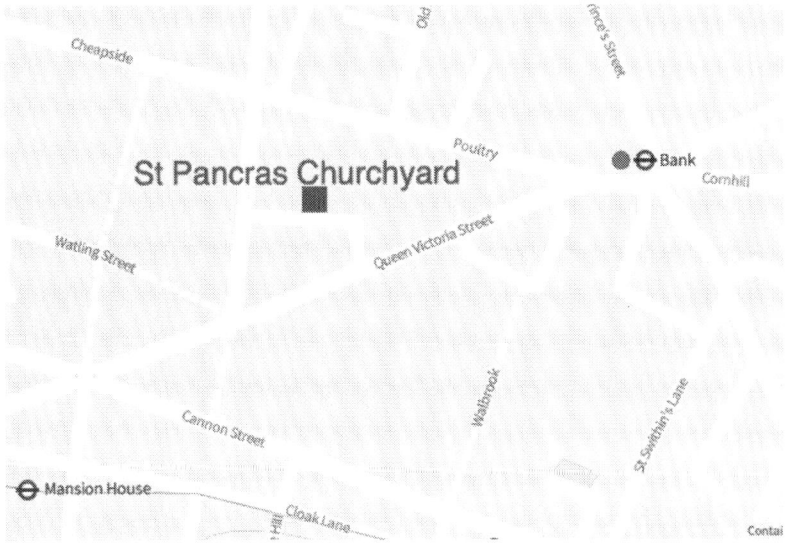

Contains OS data © Crown copyright and database rights 2020

History

The 1963 excavations of the site revealed the medieval church had a 12th-century chancel and 6 metre wide nave.

At the turn of the Millennium the garden was firmly behind a wall and small iron gate. In 2010 the City of London acquired the leasehold of the site in order to turn it into a public garden. A design competition was held and the winning design was submitted by Studio Weave.

The finished garden is said to represent the Romanesque architecture of the church sprouting afresh from the earth, following the Great Fire. The benches were individually carved by students of the City & Guilds of London Art School, which has long associations with the City. The students based their carving on historically referenced Romanesque church carvings.

There are likely more benches here than any other City of London garden, foot for foot. A number of flowerbeds are set about the new paving, with three mature trees reducing the impact of the surrounding buildings.

A few minutes to the west along Cheapside you will find the historic St Mary-le-Bow Churchyard whilst two minutes to the east is St Stephen Walbrook Churchyard, and along the way you will see the Bloomberg Building with its reinstated extension of Watling Street and an artistic interpretation of the old waterways in these parts.

The new look both improves access and appearance

St Paul's Cathedral Churchyard

At A Glance: It is hard to be brief about anything relating to St Paul's on a site that may well go back before Roman times. The first cathedral was erected in 604 AD and the present cathedral by Sir Christopher Wren is the fifth on the site. His third design was accepted in 1675 and construction took 35 years. The completion is marked by the statue of Queen Anne erected in 1712.

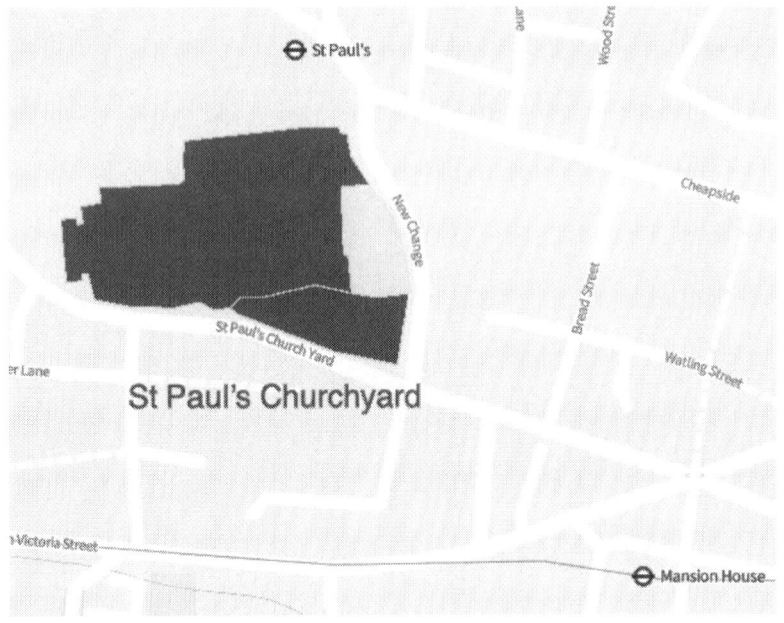

St Paul's Churchyard

Contains OS data © Crown copyright and database rights 2020

There are London plane, gingko, maple, lime, ash, mulberry and eucalyptus south of the nave whilst to the north are some of the oldest plane trees in the City as well as a giant fir tree. A beautiful rose garden is to the south.

Site location: St Paul's Churchyard
Postcode: EC4M 9AB
Grid ref: TQ320811
Size in Hectares: 0.91
Type of site: Public Gardens
Date(s): 604, C12, C13, 1675-1711; 1879; 1966 and 2020

Listed Structures: St Paul's Cathedral; railings to St Paul's Churchyard; Tower of former St Augustine's Church. Chapter House, footings of destroyed cloister and chapter house. Paul's Cross; statue of Queen Anne and the 40 stone boundary posts in cathedral forecourt

Site ownership: Diocese of London

Site management: City of London Open Spaces Department

Open to public?: Yes

Opening times: Partly unrestricted; part open 6am - 4pm winter and until 8pm in the summer

Public transport - Tube Station: St Paul's (Central Line) and Mansion House (Circle and District Lines)

History

It is entirely possible that ancient Britons had a site on this hill, it being a rare high point in what would have been a very marshy and flat area. The Romans built a temple of Diana here as well as Roman baths. The first Christian king in England, St Ethelbert who ruled Kent, was behind the construction of the first cathedral here in 604 AD.

There had been a law school here within the Cathedral precincts but in the 13th century it was closed by King Henry III who forbade law to be taught within the City in order to benefit the law schools which he had founded in Oxford. In 1285 to keep out robbers and ne'er-do-wells, the precincts were surrounded by large brick walls and the area was quite vast encompassing everywhere within Creed Lane, Ave Maria Lane, Paternoster Row, Old Change and Carter Lane.

There was the wooden St Paul's Cross where people would assemble including many famous preachers and from where many prestigious announcements and proclamations were issued. In 1527 William Tyndale's English language bible was set ablaze here as were works by Luther. No wonder with such tumultuous history the cross was destroyed in 1643, though rebuilt in 1913 by Sir Reginald Blomfield exactly on the original spot which had thoughtfully been marked by an elm tree.

Fascinatingly Sir Christopher Wren had already been asked to renovate the old cathedral and his designs were accepted just 6 days before the Great Fire of London in 1666 which obviously required a total rebuild, and it wasn't until 1675 that his third design was accepted. The 1712 statue depicting Queen Anne in front of the building was erected to mark the 35 years it took for the mammoth project to come to fruition.

The remains of Chapter House cloister can still be seen in the gardens to the south side of the cathedral nave. The churchyard was closed for burial, and negotiations to create recreational open space began in 1874 with the City of London Corporation soon being tasked with managing the gardens.

The garden was extended when the eastern side of the churchyard was closed in 1916 and later enlarged on the south-east side in 1966 as a legacy of war damage when St Paul's Choir School was built.

The tower of St Augustine Watling Street, an 11th-century church though twice rebuilt even before WWII, was restored and incorporated into the Choir School.

A statue of John Wesley was erected in the paved courtyard garden on the north side in 1988 commemorating his connections with this place. There is also a 1870s sculpture of Thomas a-Becket.

Looking through the gardens to St Paul's Cathedral

In 1999 a memorial to the Londoners killed in WWII bombardments by sculptor Richard Kindersley was installed by the north portico of the Cathedral and unveiled by HM The Queen Mother on 11th May 1999.

The gardens are known for their importance in nature conservation and are replete with all manner of mature trees including plane, gingko, maple, lime, ash, mulberry and eucalyptus. Nature was further prioritised with the replanting in 2011 of the eastern shrub border. Nectar-rich flowers for insects and plants with berries providing year-round food for birds and others specifically to create habitat for ground nesting birds can now be found as part of the ongoing mission to improve biodiversity.

The second half of June will see the part of the garden around the statue of John Wesley reopening following works to improve wheelchair access to the Cathedral.

If you want to see St Paul's with a new perspective then why not go to One New Change.

St Peter Cheap

At A Glance: Due to its location this sheltered garden can be surprisingly busy. Located on the site of the medieval church of St Peter Cheap though often known as West Cheap, the church was lost in the Great Fire of 1666 and subsequently not rebuilt.

Site location: The junction of Wood Street/Cheapside

Postcode: EC2V 6BT
Grid ref: TQ322812
Size in Hectares: 0.0155
Type of site: Public Gardens
Date(s): Medieval and 19th century
Listed Structures: None
Site ownership: Diocese of London
Site management: City of London Corporation Open Spaces Dept. (small portion of site maintained by church)
Open to public?: Yes
Opening times: 24/7
Public transport - Tube Station: St Paul's (Central Line) and Mansion House (Circle and District Lines)

Contains OS data © Crown copyright and database rights 2020

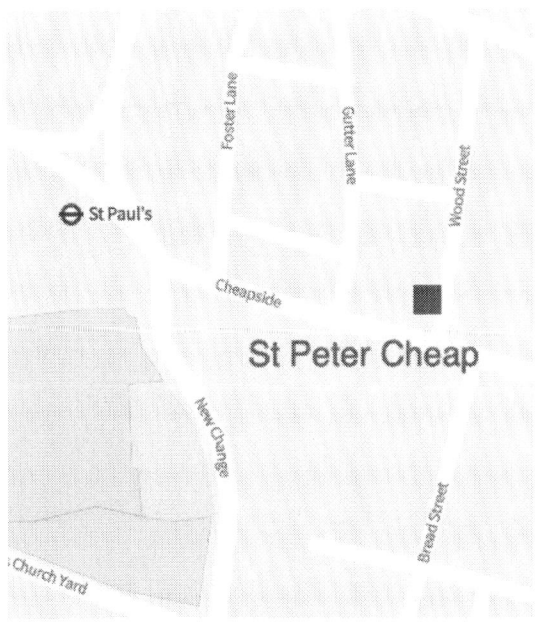

History

The word 'cheap' is the Anglo-Saxon word for market and for centuries the street names indicated what produce was for sale in each street, and thus Wood Street must have been the go-to place for timber before 1066. One of Edward I's Queen Eleanor Crosses was erected here centuries later and it became something of a shrine until it was removed by the Puritans.

The churchyard is now laid out as a garden and is predominantly paved but with seats. There is a large plane tree which is mentioned in *The Reverie of Poor Susan*, a poem by William Wordsworth. The tree itself is thought by some to be the oldest in the City of London whilst the tree ferns are more recent additions to the garden.

There are three gravestones surviving including a stone tablet of 1687 set into remnants of the wall, originally 17th century but since refaced. The original railings from 1712 remain, however, and do look out for the plaque of St Peter with his keys looking out to Wood Street.

St Mary-le-Bow is almost across the road in Cheapside but if you venture north hopefully you will find the Guildhall Yard and Piazza with a cluster of nearby gardens to enjoy.

St Peter's Cornhill

At A Glance: Just a short distance from St Michael Cornhill is the other well-hidden garden just off Cornhill. This one has more mature planting and perhaps more to take in with some mature plane trees offering delightful shade in mid-summer.

Site location: Cornhill/Gracechurch Street/St Peter's Alley
Postcode: EC3V 3PD
Grid ref: TQ329811
Size in Hectares: 0.0367
Type of site: Public Gardens
Date(s): 11th century; 1677-81, 1872, 1997
Listed Structures: None
Site ownership: Diocese of London
Site management: City of London Corporation Open Spaces Department
Open to public?: Yes
Opening times: 24/7 (Church generally not open except with prior arrangement through St Helen's Bishopsgate)
Public transport - Tube Station: Bank (Central, DLR, Northern, Waterloo & City Lines)/Monument (Circle and District Lines)

History
If legend is to be believed then the church was founded here in 179 AD by Lucius, and indeed a Roman wall is known to pass under the north-east corner of the church.

Contains OS data © Crown copyright and database rights 2020

The earliest reliable reference to St Peter Cornhill is in 1040 AD. There was a churchyard by 1231 and this was mentioned by Charles Dickens in *Our Mutual Friend*, who described the graves as 'conveniently and healthfully elevated above the living'.

The old church being lost in the Great Fire, the present church was built by Wren in 1677-84 and the garden offers good views of it.

The churchyard is now laid out as public gardens with a raised area of grass, mature trees and shrubbery on either side of the path from the entrance on St Peter's Alley. A small figure of St Peter can be seen on the Victorian iron gates. The garden was re-landscaped in 1997 and there is nowhere more restful in this busy part of the city with several benches on offer to enjoy the two plane trees.

If you head down Leadenhall Street then on your left you will soon find St Helen's Square and St Andrew Undershaft Churchyard.

St Sepulchre without Newgate Churchyard

At A Glance: Situated on a street corner opposite the highly regarded Viaduct Tavern pub, and originally dedicated to St Edmund, a church has said to have been here since 1137 AD though much of the building is post the Great Fire.

The first mentions of the churchyard can be found in 1240 AD and much of it is now a public garden and includes a Garden of Remembrance to soldiers of the Royal Fusiliers City of London Regiment, which has a centuries-long connection with the church. An area of former churchyard to the north is private and not accessible to members of the general public.

Site location: Holborn Viaduct/Giltspur Street
Postcode: EC1A 2DQ
Grid ref: TQ317814

Size in Hectares: 0.1073

Type of site: Public Gardens

Date(s): 12th century, 1670 and 1962

Listed Structures: St Sepulchre Church. Also the railings & walls of the churchyard on Holborn Viaduct

Site ownership: Diocese of London

Site management: City of London Corporation Open Spaces Department

Open to public?: Yes

Opening times: 24/7 (not the area of north of the church which is closed off) Church open Tuesdays and Thursdays 12-2pm and Wednesdays 11am-3pm

Public transport - Tube Station: St Paul's (Central Line) **Rail:** City Thameslink

Contains OS data © Crown copyright and database rights 2020

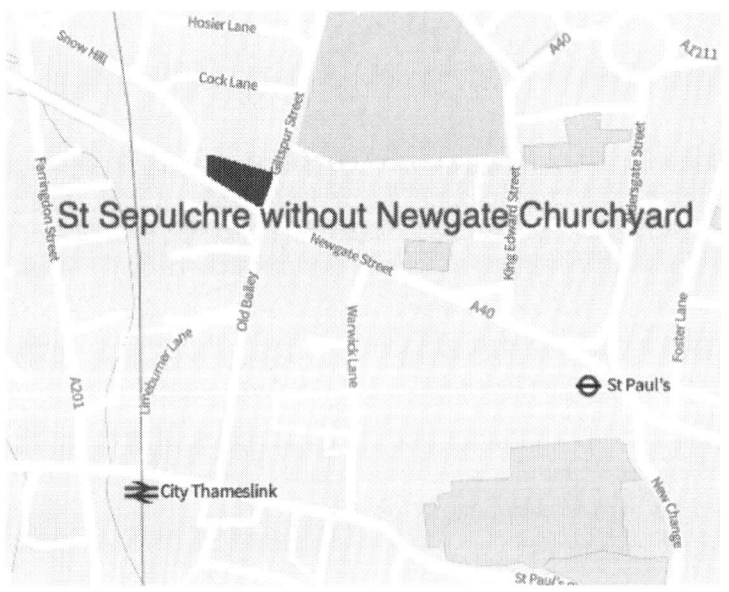

History

Following the Dissolution of the Monasteries the church remained in possession of the Crown until 1610. The church bell here is said to have summoned prisoners at Newgate Prison to the gallows after Robert Dowe had left an endowment to the parish in his will of 1605 on condition that a hand-bell which he also left should give '12 solemn tolls with double strokes, and then, after a proper pause, deliver a solemn exhortation' and that the 'great bell of the church should toll on the morning, and that, as the criminals passed the wall, the bellman or sexton should look over it and say 'All good people pray heartily unto God for these poor sinners, who are now going to their death'!'

A little way down Giltspur Street and you can see the old Watch-House which was built in 1791 to protect the churchyard from body snatchers. It was destroyed during the Blitz but rebuilt in 1962.

Captain John Smith, Governor of Virginia, who died in 1631, is buried here; he had an eventful life fighting Ottoman Turks and leading the colonisation of the New World. A section of the churchyard was lost, however, in 1871 with the road widening associated with the construction of the Holborn Viaduct.

The remains of the former churchyard area are behind railings to the south and east of the church and consist of lawns, mature trees and a number of seats with a tomb to check out too.

This area is rich in gardens with Christchurch Greyfriars further up Newgate Street towards St Paul's and St Bartholomew-the-Great amongst others down the end of Giltspur Street.

St Stephen Walbrook Churchyard

At A Glance: Situated as it is next door to Mansion House, St Stephen Walbrook is the parish church of the Lord Mayor of London. There has been a church here since the Saxons built one here in the 7th century and that was likely built upon the remains of the Roman Temple of Mithras which has recently opened to the public in the Bloomberg building.

St Stephen's was originally on the west side of the River Walbrook but in 1428 the Lord Mayor purchased land from the Grocers' Company on the east side to build a new, larger church. Sir Christopher Wren rebuilt it after the Great Fire of London and it's one of his larger churches.

Having suffered during the Blitz, the church was repaired in the 1950s complete with a garden behind the church which was once a graveyard. It is largely paved but still home to considerable bedding, a number of trees and considerable seating.

Site location: 39 Walbrook/St Stephen's Row
Postcode: EC4N 8BN

Grid ref: TQ326810

Size in Hectares: 0.0297

Type of site: Private Garden

Date(s): Medieval; 1672-9 and 19th century

Listed Structures: St Stephen's Church and the Gate Piers to churchyard on St Stephen's Row

Site ownership: Diocese of London

Site management: Church of England

Open to public?: Yes

Opening times: 10am - 4pm Mondays - Fridays.

Public transport - Tube Station: Bank (Central, DLR, Northern, Waterloo & City Lines); Cannon Street (Circle and District Lines) and Mansion House (Circle and District Lines) **Rail:** Cannon Street

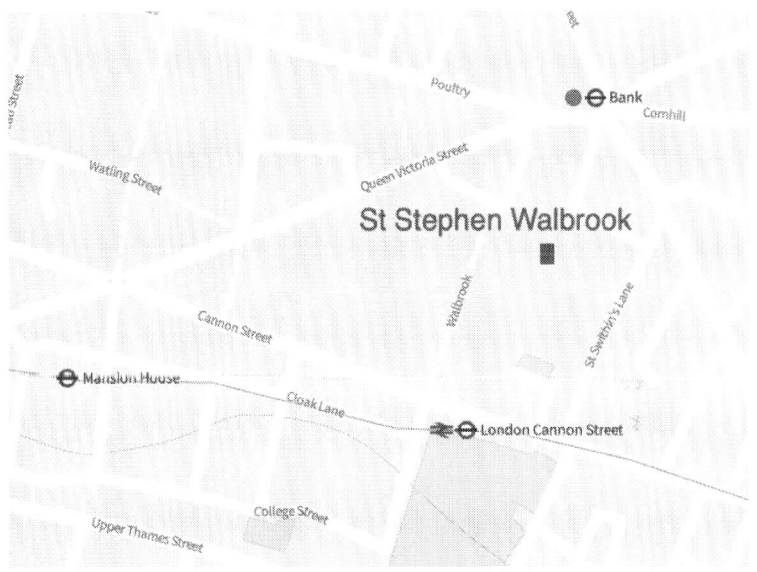

Contains OS data © Crown copyright and database rights 2020

History

Despite there being a church in this area for centuries earlier, St Stephen's church was first mentioned only in 1096 AD, and in 1100 AD it was given to the monastery of St John at Colchester. The Lord Mayor of London purchased land from the Grocers' Company on the east side of the Walbrook in 1428 in order to build a new, larger church which was completed in 1439 and survived until the Great Fire, later being rebuilt by Sir Christopher Wren.

St Stephen Walbrook is one of Wren's largest parish churches and has a wonderful dome, perhaps an early prototype for the even grander one to the west. A later addition to the building is the spire which was added to the square tower in 1713-15.

Wren's church was badly damaged in 1941 but reconstructed, and in 1954 a rededication took place. It was further restored in the 1980s. Interestingly it was here in 1953 that The Samaritans was founded by a member of staff and one telephone.

Behind St Stephen's Church is the largely paved raised churchyard with access from St Stephen's Row through an ornamental gate and steps to the garden.

For what seemed like the best part of a decade the garden gates have been locked but seemingly this clean and simple garden is accessible once more. Today the churchyard has seats and modern sculpture with a few trees scattered around to add structure but mostly it is low level planting.

A few graves remain and are incorporated into the pathways.

A secluded garden in the very heart of the City.

Not too far away to the west is Cleary Garden and to the north is the Royal Exchange Gardens. However if snug and secluded gardens are your thing, then you can't beat St Swithin's Church Garden which is a few minutes south and just off Cannon Street.

St Swithin's Church Garden

At A Glance: A truly hidden and unexpectedly beautiful garden hidden away from Cannon Street which used to belong to St Swithin's Church, the then patron saint of Winchester. The legend goes that if it rains on this day, there will be 40 days of rain, and if it stays fair there will be 40 days of fair weather.

Despite it being engulfed by a very modern office development whose sloping roof somehow lets more light in than should otherwise be the case, it is hard to find a more peaceful place to sit in the heart of the City.

Site location: Oxford Court off Cannon Street
Postcode: EC4N 8AL
Grid ref: TQ326809
Size in Hectares: 0.0233
Type of site: Public Gardens
Date(s): Medieval; 1677-87; 1960s
Listed Structures: None, though the London Stone is just around the corner in Cannon Street
Site ownership: City of London Corporation
Site management: City of London Corporation Open Spaces Department
Open to public?: Yes
Opening times: Generally daytime hours
Public transport - Tube Station: Cannon Street (Circle and District Lines) **Rail:** Cannon Street

History

There was a St Swithin's Church on this site by the 11th century and a churchyard by 1285. The steeple that was built here in 1420 was one of the first built for the purpose of hanging bells.

Contains OS data © Crown copyright and database rights 2020

Destroyed in the Great Fire, St Swithin's Church was rebuilt by Sir Christopher Wren in 1677-86 only for it to be so badly damaged in WWII that it was demolished, leaving us only the churchyard today that survives as a striking garden.

Many of the great and the good of the city are buried here but before most of them, St Swithin's was the burial ground of Catrin Glyndwr, daughter of Welsh hero, Owain Glyndwr, as well as her two children. She was captured in 1409 and taken with her children and mother to the Tower of London to await their fate. Owain's revolt failed and their burial here is remembered with the memorial to Catrin Glyndwr but also to the suffering of all women and children in wars generally.

The beautiful St Swithin's Garden

The garden has several modern benches with many trees and shrubs which give it a fantastically lush feeling particularly in the summer when the hydrangeas flower in white. The soil is covered in dark grey slate which not only matches the modern office building but no doubt harks back to Catrin Glyndwr with North Wales being an historic slate producing region.

At one time the church was known as St Swithin, London Stone and this is due to the location of the famous London Stone outside the south wall of the church which been here or across the road since Roman times. Having been stored in the London Museum for a few years whilst 111 Cannon Street was redeveloped, it is now back on display in the street for all to see.

St Laurence Pountney Graveyard is a few minutes away east on the other side of Cannon Street whilst in the other direction at the corner of Cloak Lane is the small memorial garden which is the publicly accessible part of Tallow Chandlers' Hall Courtyard.

St Vedast alias Foster Churchyard

At A Glance: A gorgeous little garden just a few minutes from St Paul's but entirely overlooked by the countless visitors there. Named after the 6th-century St Vedast who was Bishop of Arras.

Now a tranquil courtyard garden with some interesting memorials on the wall and a section of Roman road.

Site location: Foster Lane/Cheapside
Postcode: EC2V 6HH
Grid ref: TQ322812
Size in Hectares: 0.0095
Type of site: Public Gardens

Date(s): 12th century onwards
Listed Structures: St Vedast's Church and St Vedast's Rectory
Site ownership: Diocese of London
Site management: Church of England
Open to public?: Yes
Opening times: As with the church 8am-6pm, Mondays - Fridays
Public transport - Tube Station: St Paul's (Central Line)

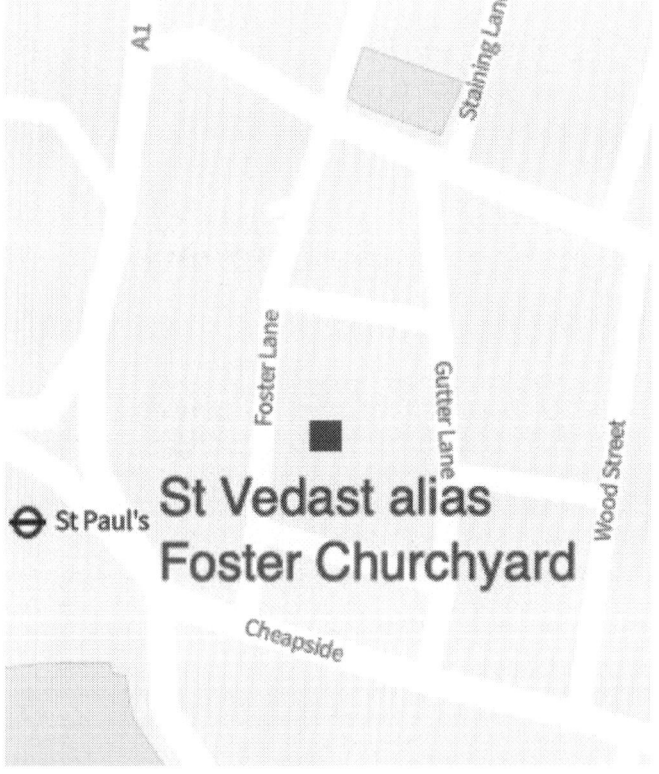

Contains OS data © Crown copyright and database rights 2020

History

It is thought a church has been here for 900 years with a replacement constructed early in the 17th century, that was itself damaged in the Great Fire of 1666 and was quickly rebuilt twice in the years that followed; firstly by the parish in 1672 and in the 1690s by Sir Christopher Wren himself.

A little tricky to find but well worth the effort.

St Vedast was all but destroyed during the Blitz and the post-war restoration was undertaken by Stephen Dykes Bower who cleverly remained true to Wren's original design whilst also gathering and using fittings from other Wren churches to add even further authenticity.

With burials long since ended in the churchyard just to the north of the church and down a short passage, there is now a small tranquil courtyard garden with a paved area and an ornamental tree in the centre. There is ample seating and some interesting plaques to see as well as some Roman history that is set into the church wall.

If you want to get away from the crowds near St Paul's then walk up Fosters Lane to the delightful sunken garden that is St John Zachary Garden.

Staple Inn Garden and Courtyard

At A Glance: Behind one of only four original Elizabethan timbered buildings in the city. A really unspoilt and beautiful courtyard and garden almost opposite Chancery Lane Tube station that has survived plagues, fires, Great and otherwise, bombs and even a V2 rocket. A good place for a quiet wander.

Site location: Southampton Buildings, High Holborn
Postcode: WC1V 7QJ
Grid ref: TQ311815
Size in Hectares: 0.1299
Type of site: Private Garden

Date(s): 14th century
Listed Structures: Nos. 4-6 Staple Inn, with courtyard pump attached to No.6. Staple Inn Buildings North and South. Lamp post and cobbled setts in Staple Inn Court
Site ownership: Tongate, leased to the Institute of Actuaries
Site management: Keneth Peters Asset Management Limited
Open to public?: Yes
Opening times: Generally week days during office hours
Public transport - Tube Station: Chancery Lane (Central Line)

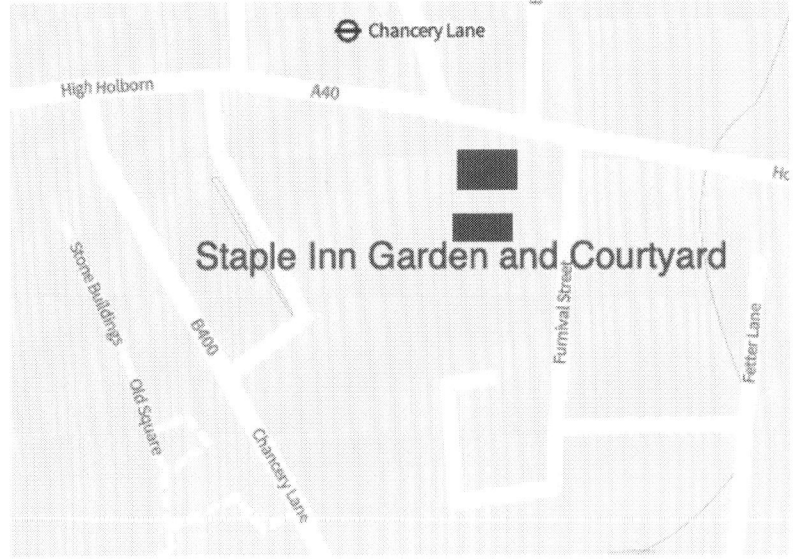

Contains OS data © Crown copyright and database rights 2020

History

'Le Stapled Halle' in Holborn dates from at least the 13th century. Its interesting name derives from a 'Staple', which was a 13th-century tax on wool and for a century it was used for the trading of wool and other commodities but when in 1415 the Society of Staple Inn was established it soon became the largest of the Inns of Chancery.

A fine hall was built in a manner of style and grandiosity similar to the great buildings of Oxford and Cambridge. Fortunately Staple Inn escaped the Great Fire of London although sections were partially damaged and rebuilt in a subsequent fire and only saved from Victorian demolition teams after a public outcry. The building and courtyard were struck by explosive and incendiary bombs during WWII and a V2 rocket landed near the fishpond south of the hall.

Thankfully the hall is still with us and was restored after the wall was again refurbished in 1996. As for the gardens, look out for a plaque in the pavement where the old well and pump in the courtyard provided the Inn with notably pure water from underground springs, reportedly having medicinal qualities until it was capped in 1922.

The formal ornamental garden is slightly sunken from the ground level of the adjoining pavement and separated by fine railings and gates, but a lovely place for a wander and to take in the lawn, fountain and planting including a circular-shaped bed of roses.

There are plenty of flowerbeds as well as bushes and trees along the perimeter, and some lovely cobbled footpaths leading hither and thither giving the impression that little has changed.

Unlike many historic courtyard spaces, it remains car free. Perhaps it wasn't always as tranquil as an old notice is visible that warns 'The

PORTER Has Orders To Prevent Old Clothes Men & Others From Calling Articles For Sale. And Rude Children Playing. No Horses Allowed Within This Inn.'

A beautiful retreat just seconds from busy Holborn

Just outside the City you have Lincoln's Inn to the west and Gray's Inn to the north but for City purists a few minutes east along the A40 will bring you to St Andrew Holborn Church Garden and across the road the St Andrew Street Garden.

Stationers' Hall Garden

At A Glance: A short walk from the steps of St Paul's are the gardens of Stationers' Hall. The outer courtyard can be easily accessed and doesn't have too much to recommend it other than what you can see externally of Stationers' Hall itself.

Through a gated archway is the inner garden which though it has much more to offer is sadly closed to the public except via appointment to the Clerk.

Site location: Stationers' Hall Court off Ludgate Hill/Ave Maria Lane
Postcode: EC4M 7DD
Grid ref: TQ318811
Size in Hectares: 0.0496
Type of site: Private Garden
Date(s): 17th century to 1930s
Listed Structures: Stationers' Hall
Site ownership: Worshipful Company of Stationers & Newspaper Makers
Site management: Worshipful Company of Stationers & Newspaper Makers
Open to public?: By appointment only
Opening times: By appointment only
Public transport - Tube Station: St Paul's (Central Line) **Rail:** City Thameslink

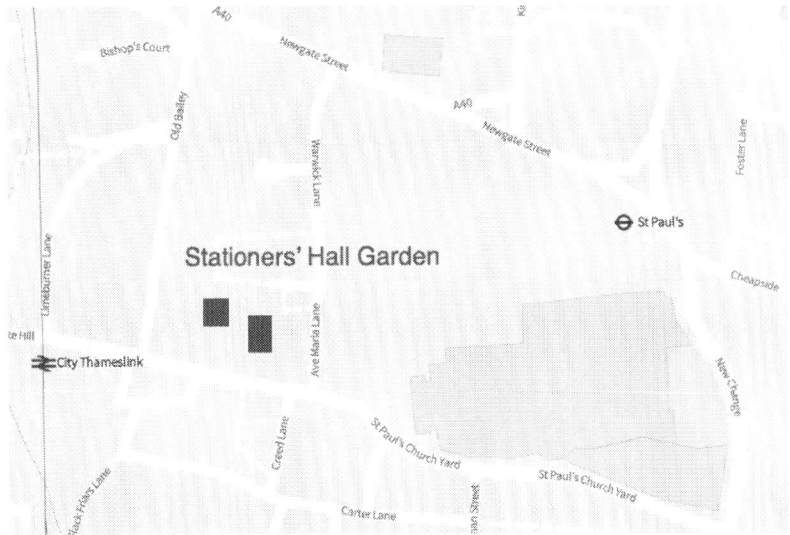

Contains OS data © Crown copyright and database rights 2020

History

Stationers' Hall Garden actually finds itself on the burial site of St Martin-within-Ludgate. Ludgate Hill, which was called Ludgate Street until 1865, was originally a Roman route through the Romans' west cemetery. In fact a gravestone of a Roman soldier of the Second Augustan Legion in a tunic and cloak was found near St Martin's and now resides in the Museum of London.

Robert of Gloucester asserted that St Martin's church was founded in the 7th century by an English prince called Cadwallo or Cadwallader who was also buried here; this, however, is unverified by modern research.

In 1322 AD Robert de Sancto Albano is recorded as rector and in 1437 land was leased by the Lord Mayor of London to build a steeple so the church was either expanded upon or founded at this time.

Prior to its rebuilding after the Great Fire of London, St Martin's Church had been situated just outside the city walls adjacent to the former Lud Gate which was the western gate to the City and constructed in 69 BC. It might have been so named after the legendary King Lud, a possible founder of London who was also allegedly buried here. Ludgate itself was removed around 1760 as it was an impediment to traffic, and only one possible remaining stone lies nearby.

The Worshipful Company of Stationers started in 1403 AD and the word 'Stationer' actually originates from traders who would sell their services as writers or illuminators from fixed or stationary stalls outside the nearby St Paul's.

Modern printing came to England in the late 15th century, and the guild embraced this with printers playing an increasingly important role, and is conveniently located for the famous Fleet Street printing presses and newspapers.

After its destruction in the Great Fire of 1666, Sir Christopher Wren rebuilt the present church of St Martin in 1677-86 albeit on a footprint slightly to the west. The western wall of the church actually includes a section of the old Roman Wall.

Happily St Martin's Ludgate had the least damage of any City church in WWII. Its former churchyard now forms the private garden of the Stationers' Hall.

A passageway leads off Stationers' Hall Court to the secluded inner garden, the layout of which was finalised almost 100 years ago with a mixture of paving, flowerbeds and now mature trees.

Just a minute north is Amen Court and just beyond that is Warwick Square. Neither of these will likely detain you too long, so afterwards carry on up Warwick Lane to Christchurch Greyfriars Churchyard or alternatively take one of the side streets on the other side of Warwick Lane and you should find your way to Paternoster Square.

Tallow Chandlers' Hall Courtyard

At A Glance: The Worshipful Company of Tallow Chandlers purchased this site in 1476 though it suffered the obligatory rebuilding work following the Great Fire.

It's not generally possible to view the private courtyard garden but in 1970 a small raised garden was created at the corner of Dowgate Hill and Cloak Lane by Past Master and Mrs Deverell Stone in memory of their son Mark.

Site location: 4 Dowgate Hill
Postcode: EC4R 2SH

Grid ref: TQ325808
Size in Hectares: 0.0136
Type of site: Private Garden
Date(s): 1476; 1671-73 and 1978
Listed Structures: Tallow Chandlers' Hall
Site ownership: The Worshipful Company of Tallow Chandlers
Site management: The Worshipful Company of Tallow Chandlers
Open to public?: Occasionally
Opening times: Private but open to the public on special open days and through organised tours.
Public transport - Tube Station: Cannon Street (Circle and District Lines) **Rail:** Cannon Street

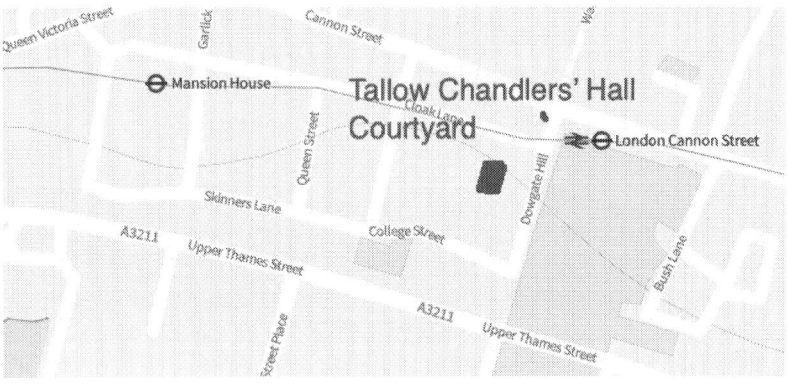

Contains OS data © Crown copyright and database rights 2020

History

The Worshipful Company of Tallow Chandlers was created in 1300 when 'oynters' or tallow melters formed a fraternity to regulate the quality of materials used in tallow candle-making and related industries.

Tallow Candles were used to light the streets of the City of London since at least the 15th century and the Tallow Chandlers' Company was tasked to supply men to the city watch to ensure this was done every night.

The present Hall was built in 1671 after the original was destroyed in the Great Fire of 1666. It is thought that both were built upon the walls of the palace of the Roman governor of London.

Although some refurbishment has taken place over the years and some parts were damaged in WWII bombing, generally the old hall remains the same as when it was built.

A small but well cared for external garden was created on the corner of Dowgate Hill and Cloak Lane by Past Master and Mrs Deverell Stone in memory of their son Mark, in 1978.

Just to the south down College Street you'll find Whittington Garden.

The Garden at 120

At A Glance: Standing at 15 storeys, a new and free-to-access roof garden offering great views of the City and many other parts of London from beyond Parliament in the west, Crystal Palace in the south, Greenwich in the south-east and a fascinating view up Whitechapel High Street to Stratford and beyond on the horizon.

Site location: 120 Fenchurch Street

Postcode: EC3M 5BA

Grid ref: TQ332809

Size in Hectares: 0.22

Type of site: Public Roof Garden

Date(s): 2019

Designer(s): Building by Eric Parry Architects, garden by Latz & Partners

Listed Structures: None

Site ownership: Saxon Land

Site management: Saxon Land

Open to public?: Yes

Opening times: Weekdays 10am - 6.30pm (10pm in summer months) and some weekends in the summer too.

Public transport - Tube Station: Monument and Tower Hill (Circle and District Lines), Aldgate (Circle and Metropolitan Lines) **Rail:** Fenchurch Street   Contains OS data © Crown copyright and database rights 2020

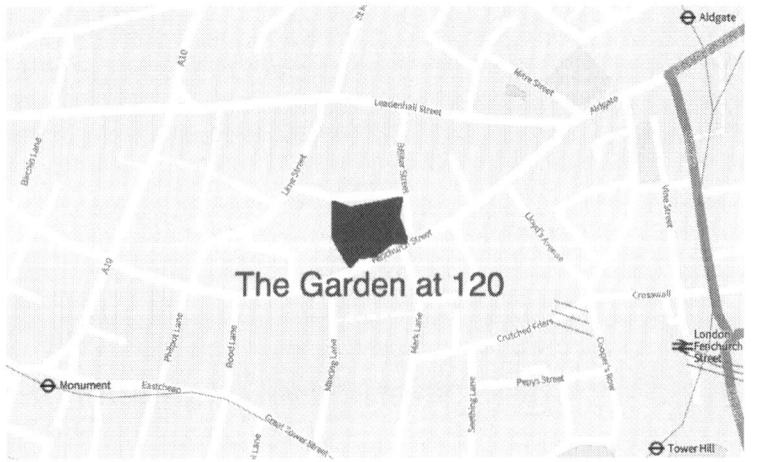

History

The Garden at 120 sits fifteen storeys up atop One Fen Court, the new HQ for Italian insurance company Generali, and has been somewhat grandiosely described as the building with 100 views.

If you've ever been around the City of London then you might have realised how obviously preoccupied with finance and big business it is, with relatively few attractions for Londoners or tourists.

This roof garden was created due to a new and substantial push to bring more to the City rather than leave the area from St Paul's to the Tower of London as something of a wasteland.
It is now the condition of construction of many modern towers that they have to maximise public access in order to be given permission for them to be constructed at all. There are several more elevated roof gardens in London but they either have to be booked ahead or have a quite hefty entrance fee.

The fun begins before you even reach the garden; while walking through the ancient though gleaming Hogarth Court, be sure to look up to see fantastic digital art installations by Vong Phaophanit and Claire Oboussier on the ceiling.

There is a limit of around 200 people in the roof garden at any one time so it is technically possible that on a very busy hot day there may a brief wait to go through the security process (please don't bring any items that you would not take on an aeroplane).

The free roof garden with the best views in London

On your first visit here it's easy to be struck by just how large and open it is with the crystalline shapes of the garden reflect the language of the architecture. The forms are taken up in the arrangement of the planting beds, surfacing, water feature and the pergola structure. Even the floor is folded to create a landscape on the roof that varies in height, solving the surface water drainage and creating different levels.

The Yorkstone used as paving takes up the materiality of the footways on ground floor level to underline the garden being a public open space.

A steel pergola structure crowns the building on the 15th floor giving height and structure in place of trees that would likely not do well up here. The supports are designed for the wisteria trunks of this green canopy that surrounds the visitors in summer with lush green, giving shade and framing extraordinary views of the London skyline.

The walls enclosing the roof facilities have been integrated into the garden design and amended to spatially improve the situation. The enclosures are turned into attractive greened walls that create protected seating opportunities amongst boxed hedging and other well-tended shrubs.

A water basin structures the space spatially into a terrace and a seating zone. The calm surface reflects the sky, brings in cooling and conveys an intimate garden atmosphere along with the lush planting.

On a cold or windy day it can be a bit testing up here but there is nowhere quite like it on a warm sunny day. You can find your own favourite view of London and while the day away but whilst you're here do check out Fen Court which you can see from the west side of the roof garden, though it and the incredibly moving memorial to the slave trade are much better experienced close up.

The Master's Garden

At A Glance: A quiet, hidden gem of a garden is a real treasure in a very historic part of the City of London and can be found on the north side of the Temple complex, a short distance from Fleet Street.

The L-shaped garden, which has been planted with a mix of herbaceous plants, shrubs and trees, runs between Temple Church and the Master's House which was the residence of the Master of the Temple at the Temple Church. The main garden is an elevated plateau, built above 17th-century catacombs that were created to provide more burial space for Temple Church.

Site location: Church Court, Inner Temple, access via Temple Lane/ Tudor Street
Postcode: EC4Y 7DE
Grid ref: TQ312810
Size in Hectares:
Type of site: Private Garden
Date(s): 1667
Listed Structures: The Master's House
Site ownership: Jointly between the two Inns of Middle Temple and Inner Temple
Site management: Jointly between the two Inns of Middle Temple and Inner Temple
Open to public?: Occasionally
Opening times: Opens for special events such as the Open Gardens.

Public transport - Tube Station: Blackfriars and Temple Stations (Circle and District Lines) **Rail:** Blackfriars and City Thameslink

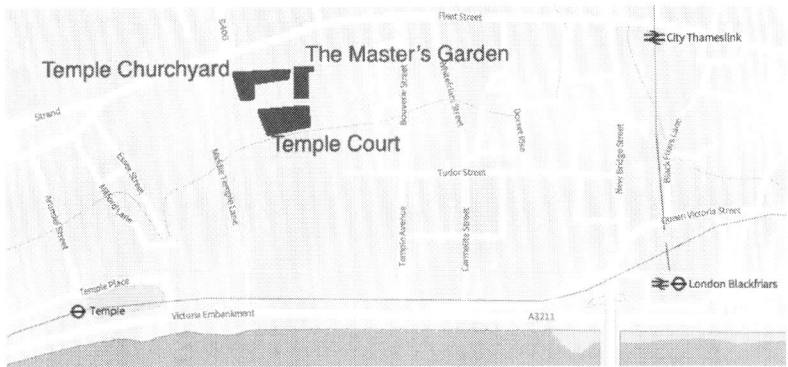

Contains OS data © Crown copyright and database rights 2020

History

Built in the 12th century, St Mary's Church in the Temple was built by the Knights Templar to serve both Inner and Middle Temple following the relocation of the Templars from Holborn.

Heavily influenced by what the Knights had observed in the Holy Lands, the church was consecrated in 1185 by none other than the Patriarch Heraclius of Jerusalem himself. Enlargement works were carried out in the following century including the effigies of Knights which can still be seen in the nave.

Famously, the Knights Templar were dissolved by the Pope in 1312 and a few decades later the Knights of St John who had inherited the property gave it to students who were studying English Common Law and hence set in motion the creation of the Inner and the Middle Temple.

Though Temple Church escaped the Great Fire of 1666, Sir Christopher Wren obviously didn't have enough to do and refurbished the church anyway in 1682. The original Master's House from 1667 was destroyed in the Blitz and has been replaced by a building with a duplicate façade.

There is a lot to see around here so why not move on to the Temple Churchyard.

The Temple Churchyard

At A Glance: Set in the heart of a gorgeous legal area of London, Temple Church because most famous for *The Da Vinci Code* a few years.

First consecrated in 1185 AD, there may not be a great amount of biodiversity here as compared to nearby Temple gardens but the air of history is unmistakable.

Site location:
The Temple, access via Temple Lane/Tudor Street
Postcode: EC4Y 7BB
Grid ref: TQ312810
Size in Hectares: 0.0628

Type of site: Churchyard

Date(s): 12th century onwards

Listed Structures: Temple Church and also the statue of John Hiccocks.

Site ownership: Temple Church

Site management: Temple Church

Open to public?: Yes

Opening times: Churchyard garden and Church Court unrestricted.

Church: The church is open daily but check the website for details as it can close for special events.

Public transport - Tube Station: Blackfriars and Temple Stations

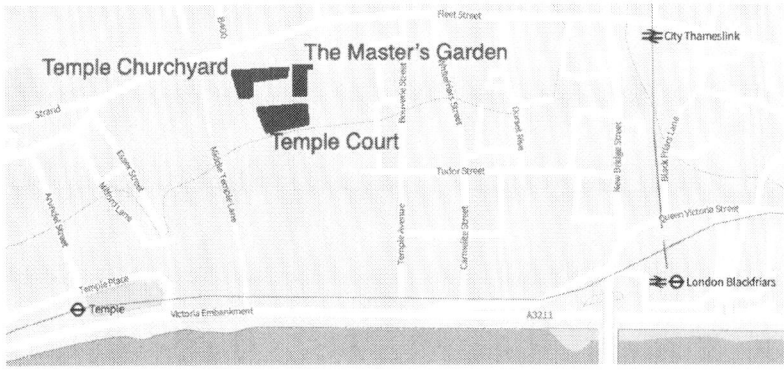

(Circle and District Lines) **Rail:** Blackfriars and City Thameslink
Contains OS data © Crown copyright and database rights 2020

History

Built by the Knights Templar in the late 12th century, St Mary's Church in the Temple serves the Inner and Middle Temple.

For a full history of this area, see the preceding notes on The Master's Garden.

North of the Temple Church is a paved area of churchyard with a number of tombs, bounded to the north by a wall and railings. Beyond these is a raised area of former churchyard laid out as small garden with one tree.

The famous Temple Church

A handful of tombs remain visible including a 1726 memorial to Iohannes Hiccocks.

After looking round Temple Court to the south of the church, it is only a few minutes to the fabulous Inner Temple and Middle Temple.

Tower Hill Gardens

At A Glance: One of those rarest of things in the City of London, a small park with a children's play area!

Site location: Tower Hill
Postcode: EC3N 4DR
Grid ref: TQ336807
Size in Hectares: 0.2219
Type of site: Public Gardens
Date(s): 20th century and 2010
Listed Structures: Roman London Wall
Site ownership: City of London Corporation
Site management: City of London Corporation Open Spaces Department
Open to public?: Yes
Opening times: 24/7
Public transport - Tube Station: Tower Hill (Circle and District Lines) **Rail:** Fenchurch Street **DLR:** Tower Gateway

Contains OS data © Crown copyright and database rights 2020

History

Tower Hill Gardens is a garden that is right up against one of the best preserved sections of the Roman London city wall, all 68 metres of it!

During the 20th century the area was a simply landscaped garden with grass and a few trees and flowerbeds but was remodelled in 2010 as part of the Corporation's City Play Partnership with the only other similar park in the City being at the relatively nearby King George's Field.

There are several very mature trees here and some hedging to block out the roadside and give shelter to the play areas, lawns and various mounds and other natural features for children to enjoy a bit of rough and tumble.

Though not in the City of London you might want to find the old Mulberry Bush in the gardens on the other side of the busy road or a few minutes to the west is All Hallows-by-the-Tower and above that, Seething Lane Gardens.

Tower of All Hallows Staining

At A Glance: All that remains of All Hallows Staining is the restored medieval tower in this largely paved garden in a seemingly forgotten part of the City.

Site location: Mark Lane
Postcode: EC3R 7BB
Grid ref: TQ332808
Size in Hectares: 0.0661
Type of site: Public Gardens
Date(s): 13th and 20th Centuries
Listed Structures: Tower of All Hallows Staining and Lambe's Chapel Crypt
Site ownership: City of London Corporation
Site management: City of London Corporation Open Spaces Department
Open to public?: Yes

Opening times: Weekdays during office hours
Public transport - Tube Station: Aldgate (Metropolitan Line) and Tower Hill (Circle and District Lines) **Rail:** Fenchurch Street

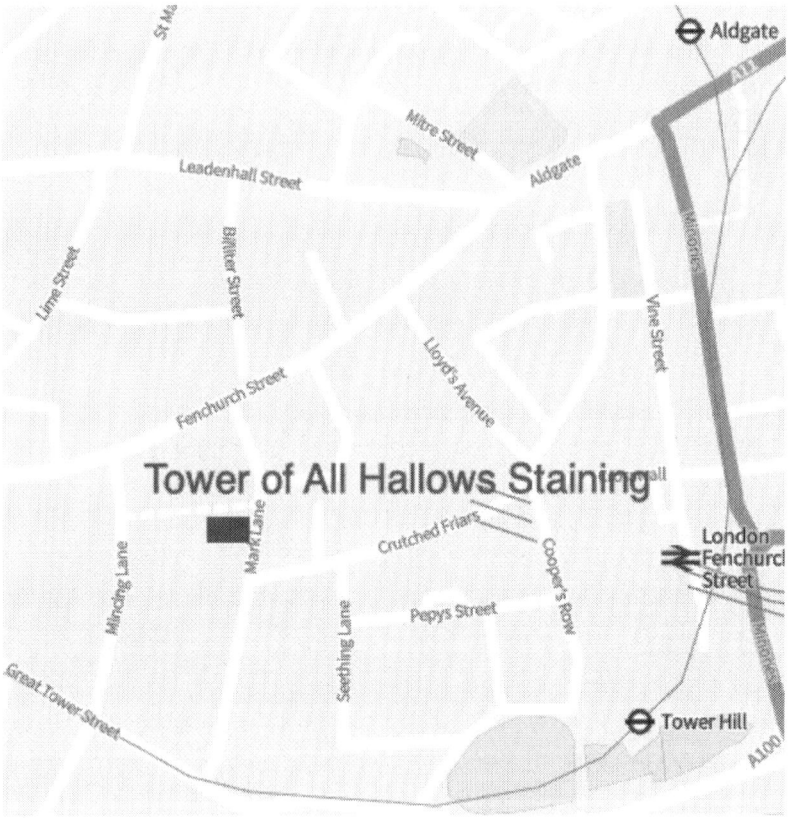

Contains OS data © Crown copyright and database rights 2020

History

The medieval tower of All Hallows Staining dates from 1320 AD though the church that once stood here was 100 years older still.

Enlarged in 1615, the church survived the Great Fire in 1666, before partially collapsing in 1671. Horrifically this was likely due to the foundations of the building being weakened due to the large number of burials here, most likely from the Plague!

The rest of the church collapsed following mass burials from the Plague!

The church was rebuilt in 1674 but in 1870 it was demolished and the parish united with that of St Olave Hart Street all of 60 seconds' walk away. The site was sold to the Clothworkers' Company, whose Hall was adjacent to the church, on condition that the medieval steeple was preserved in good order.

Following the widespread war damage, between 1948 and 1954 the Tower of All Hallows Staining formed the chancel of a prefabricated church known as St Olave Mark Street that housed the congregation of St Olave Hart Street for the duration of the repairs to that church.

Now all that remains is the old steeple which can be found within this small paved public garden along with some shrubs and tombstones. However, recently it has been announced that the adjacent Clothworkers' Hall site is likely to be completely transformed into a futuristic glass and steel tower complex and so the nature of this peaceful place may soon change forever.

Two minutes away is the beautifully updated Seething Lane Gardens to the south-east but on the other side of Fenchurch Street it is well worth visiting Fen Court and the adjacent The Garden at 120.

Tower of St Mary Somerset Church

At A Glance: The 12th-century St Mary Somerset church was largely demolished in the 19th century, leaving this rather elaborate tower set amongst recently refurbished gardens. A very welcome splash of green next to the eternally busy Upper Thames Street.

Site location: Upper Thames Street/Castle Baynard Street/Lambeth Hill
Postcode: EC4V 4GG

Grid ref: TQ321808
Size in Hectares: 0.0166
Type of site: Public Gardens
Date(s): 12th century onwards
Listed Structures: Tower of former church of St Mary Somerset
Site ownership: Diocese of London (former churchyard) and the rest comes under the City of London Corporation
Site management: City of London Corporation Open Spaces Department
Open to public?: Yes
Opening times: 24/7
Public transport - Tube Station: Mansion House (Circle and District Lines)

Contains OS data © Crown copyright and database rights 2020

History

John Stow recorded how in 1370 AD weavers from Brabant congregated where this garden now is to be hired for jobs. Back then it was in the churchyard of St Mary Somerset and though rebuilt after the Great Fire, remained here until Queen Victoria Street required the majority of the church to be torn down and much of the cemetery to be built over as a roadway.

The church was demolished in 1869 and the site fell under the ownership of the Corporation of London in September 1872. All would have been lost but thankfully the square stone tower was saved by an Act of Parliament.

In the early years of this millennium the garden was largely closed due to sewerage works. Though one of the mature trees was damaged in the works, the re-landscaped garden is now open, and it looks really smart. There are several blocks of shaped hedging, with trees and benches on the east side of the tower. It is similar on the west side except here is paved terracing as the garden climbs steeply up to Lambeth Hill.

Don't spend too much time looking for the castle in Castle Barnard Street. Though there was a time when London had two or three castles, Castle Barnard was mostly lost several centuries ago and its final vestiges were removed from the riverside and built over around the time this garden was established.

Two minutes to the east is the multi-levelled Cleary Garden but if you can make it up the slope, cross over Queen Victoria Street for St

Nicholas Cole Abbey and other gardens such as the new Distaff Lane Garden that form a chain up to St Paul's.

Much of the church and churchyard was levelled to create the Victorian road network

Tower Place

At A Glance: A relatively modern open space that was created in 1962-66 to the southwest of All Hallows-by-the-Tower Church and designed to set off the modern office blocks to the south by the river.

Site location: Lower Thames Street/Byward Street

Postcode: EC3

Grid ref: TQ333806

Type of site: Square

Date(s): 1962-6 and 1992-2002

Listed Structures: None

Site ownership: City of London Corporation

Site management: City of London Corporation Open Spaces Department

Open to public?: Yes

Opening times: 24/7

Public transport - Tube Station: Tower Hill (Circle and District Lines) **Rail:** Fenchurch Street

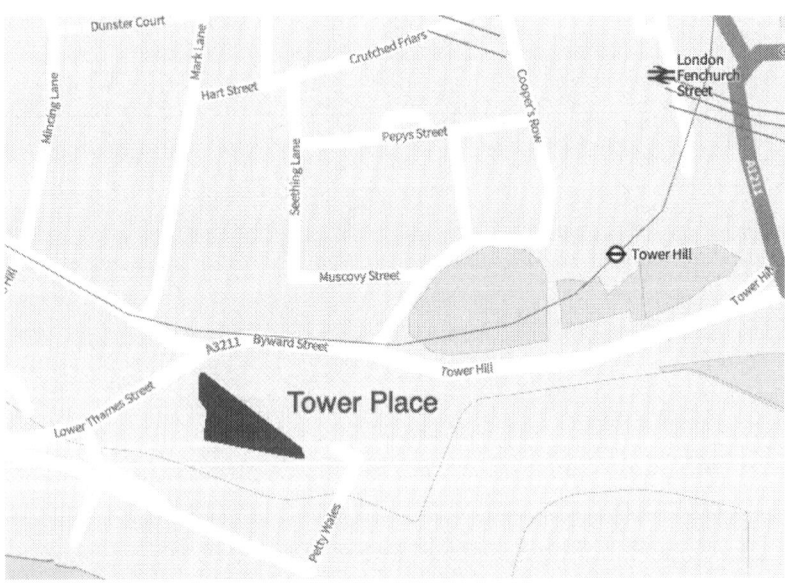

Contains OS data © Crown copyright and database rights 2020

History

Centuries ago where the modern glass offices are there used to be a Royal Navy armoury. It literally blew sky high and took out much of All Hallows-By-The-Tower church when it did so, as can be seen by looking at the brickwork of the building facing the square.

In the post-war reconstruction effort a 1960s office block was erected along with two courtyards which included markers to indicate the outline of the old church burial ground, but with the construction of new glass buildings, this was all redeveloped in the years between 1992 and 2002.

The development sought to create a new public plaza with trees and water in front of All Hallows Church as well as open up traditional views of the church and nearby Tower of London.

For one of the most picturesque ruins anywhere and perhaps the most beautiful garden in the City, why not next visit St Dunstan-in-the-East.

Wardrobe Place

At A Glance: A hidden square with lots of character. Generally paved with four mature trees all surrounded by period housing.

Wardrobe Place was named after the King's Great Wardrobe that housed the Crown's storage of clothing and arms. Being the Ward (an administrative division) of London where the robes were kept, it no doubt gave us the name for this item of furniture.

Site location: Wardrobe Place off St Andrew's Hill/Carter Lane
Postcode: EC4
Grid ref: TQ318810
Size in Hectares: 0.0399
Type of site: Square
Date(s): 18th century onwards
Listed Structures: 1, 2, 3, 4, 5, 5A, 5B Wardrobe Place and adjoining archway
Site ownership: City of London Corporation
Site management: City of London Corporation Open Spaces Department
Open to public?: Yes
Opening times: 24/7
Public transport - Tube Station: St Paul's (Central Line); Blackfriars (Circle and District Lines)

History

The Wardrobe was moved to Lombard Street in 1311 AD having originally been housed in The Tower of London before coming here in the 1360s but like so many other places, the Wardrobe was destroyed in the Great Fire of 1666, as can be seen by an on-site plaque.

In 1720 Strype noted that 'the Garden of the King's Wardrobe is converted into a large and square court, with good houses'. In the fullness of time this became Wardrobe Place and the houses and court remain good to this day.

Contains OS data © Crown copyright and database rights 2020

Just to the south of Wardrobe Place you have St Andrew-by-the-Wardrobe.

Warwick Square

At A Glance: Despite its close proximity to St Paul's Cathedral. Warwick Square is a simple and in many ways unremarkable square, little visited by anyone but those trying to gain a bit of a peek towards an old Victorian place of execution.

Site location: Off Warwick Lane
Postcode: EC4M 7BP   **Grid ref:** TQ318812
Type of site: Public Gardens
Date(s): 1966-1972   **Listed Structures:** None
Site ownership: City of London Corporation
Site management: City of London Corporation Open Spaces Department
Open to public?: Yes   **Opening times:** 24/7
Public transport - Tube Station: St Paul's (Central Line)

Contains OS data © Crown copyright and database rights 2020

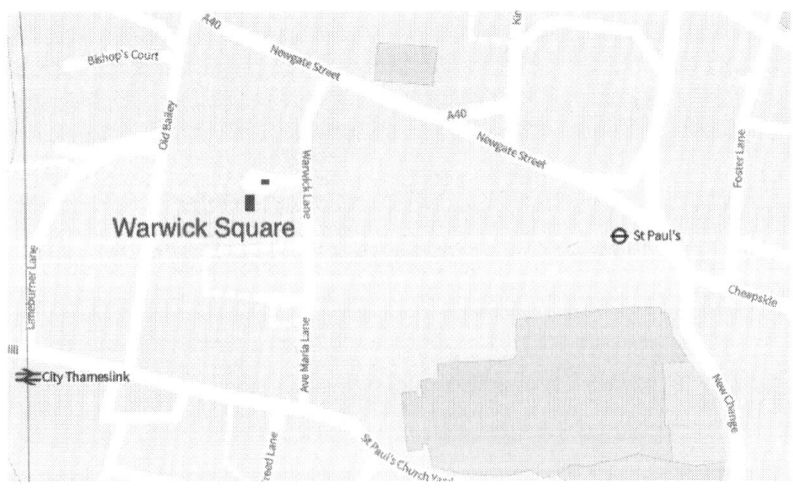

History

The origins of the name here come from the Earls of Warwick whose mansion was in Warwick Lane in the 14th century.

The square today opens out from Warwick Lane and is against rather grim mid-20th-century buildings erected to extend the Central Criminal Court that had been erected on the former site of notorious Newgate Prison.

Deathly quiet as usual, which is handy as people were hanged just feet behind here

Landscaping in the square is a simple affair and consists of a traffic island that is home to two trees and at the far end to the west behind railings, a paved area with bedding plants, a birdbath and some seating.

Across Warwick Lane you will find the large open space of Paternoster Square but northwards you will find Christchurch Greyfriars Churchyard and Christchurch Greyfriars Church Garden.

West Smithfield Garden

At A Glance: Originally Smoothfield lay just outside the city walls. There is an incredible amount of history within a few feet of this little garden and it's well worth spending some time exploring every nook and cranny.

Aside from some mature trees there is a bronze statue of 'Peace' and some recent seating so you can take the weight off your feet.

Site location: West Smithfield
Postcode: EC1A 9BD
Grid ref: TQ318816
Size in Hectares: 0.1441
Type of site: Public Gardens
Date(s): 1872
Listed Structures: 'Peace' Drinking Fountain
Site ownership: City of London Corporation

Site management: City of London Corporation Open Spaces Department
Open to public?: Yes
Opening times: Generally daylight hours, locked at dusk.
Public transport - Tube Station: St Paul's (Central Line); Barbican and Farringdon (Circle, Hammersmith & City and Metropolitan Lines).
Rail: Farringdon

Contains OS data © Crown copyright and database rights 2019

History

Historic Smithfield, once 'Smoothfield' lay just outside the city walls. It was a rather grotty part of town and home to jousting and countless executions as well as markets.

Many a famous figure met their demise here at Smithfield and nearby you will find memorials to some of them including the Scottish hero William Wallace, who was hanged, drawn and quartered in 1305. Wat Tyler, who led the Peasants' Revolt, is another important though often overlooked figure and he was beheaded in 1381, after he had sought assistance at St Bartholomew's Church following his betrayal and stabbing by the Mayor of London.

Executions carried on for centuries and in the 1550 over 200 Protestants were burnt at the stake and some of these are remembered here too.

A livestock market was recorded here in the 17th and 18th centuries and St Bartholomew's Fair was held here annually until 1855 following which it was closed due to it being a 'nuisance', no doubt public revelry getting out of hand as it is often wont to do.

Where the garden is now became waste ground when Smithfield Market first opened in 1868 but under the Metropolitan Meat and Poultry Market Act of 1860 it was 'for ever reserved and appropriated as an open public space'.

In the centre of the gardens is a drinking fountain with a bronze figure of Peace. It was completed in 1873 by sculptor John Birnie

Philip, though the Gothic stone canopy that once covered it has long since gone.

The gardens are tranquil by day but at night Smithfield is incredibly busy with the meat trade

In Victorian times Smithfield meat market became notorious as an area when men would swap their wives given that divorce was complex and expensive. This gave us the term 'meat market' when people go to clubs to meet prospective partners. It is said that the sculptor of the 'Peace' statue was so horrified by these events that wanting to make sure 'Peace' was of unquestionable moral fibre, the designer returned and welded a wedding ring to her finger.

The underground ramp that all but surrounds the garden used to lead to a tube station for the Metropolitan Line.

On the 6th December 2006 a new stone seat was unveiled in the garden and inscribed with text giving the history of the area.

It has recently been announced that Smithfield meat market may soon be moving out to be replaced by the Museum of London. It may be worth visiting this garden soon before it gets swamped by tourists because as it is at the moment, it is relatively empty and peaceful. One day the only reminder of the meat industry here may be the cattle trough outside the gardens.

To the east is the historic St Bartholomew-The-Great whilst to the south is St Bartholomew's Hospital and the gardens contained within. Do have a look at the various memorials on the hospital boundary wall abutting West Smithfields and the old WWI Zeppelin bombshell marks on the wall for a more unexpected side of local history.

Whittington Garden

At A Glance: A really well maintained and shady small garden named after the legendary Lord Mayor of London, Richard (Dick) Whittington. There are small flowerbeds and lawns and plenty of seats and trees to shelter under. The noise of the fountain does a lot to hide the nearby traffic on Upper Thames Street.

Site location: Upper Thames Street/Colleague Street
Postcode: EC4R 2RL   **Grid ref:** TQ324808
Size in Hectares: 0.0208   **Type of site:** Public Gardens
Date(s): 13th and 17th Centuries and 1960
Listed Structures: St Michael Paternoster Royal Church
Site ownership: Diocese of London for area adjacent to church. The majority however falls under the City of London Corporation
Site management: City of London Corporation Open Spaces Department
Open to public?: Yes
Opening times: 24/7 (Church is 9am-5pm Mondays - Fridays)
Public transport - Tube Station: Cannon Street (Circle and District Lines) **Rail:** Cannon Street

Contains OS data © Crown copyright and database rights 2019

History

The Whittington Garden is named after perhaps the most famous Lord Mayor of London, Richard Whittington, who was buried in St Michael Paternoster Royal Church in 1429. This was just one of several churches and establishments which he financed, this one on top of an earlier church.

This church was destroyed in the Great Fire of London and rebuilt by Sir Christopher Wren. It's hard to believe but in Roman times the site of the gardens was on the riverbank and until the Blitz necessitated their clearances, this area was more recently home to buildings associated with the fur trade.

The paved segment of the garden with the small fountain

Whittington Garden has two parts and for its size is delightful. One part is grassy with hedging and the other has paving with seats, shrubs and a fountain. Over the years since WWII, there has been some additional planting outside the church too which now looks altogether more established than it once did.

A minute away you have the small garden towards the top of Queen Street or along Skinners Lane you might find St James Garlickhythe Church Garden. Alternatively up Dowgate Hill you have Tallow Handlers' Hall Courtyard with St Stephen Walbrook Churchyard to the north and St Swithin's Church Garden to the east just off Cannon Street.

About the author

I have been writing a range of fiction and non-fiction books for 20 years as well as magazine articles relating to the environment. My books are available from book shops and in various online formats such as Kindle, iBooks and many others including *Lest We Forget: A Concise Companion to the First World War* by Lume Books of London, *101 Most Horrible Tortures in History and Straight From The Horse's Mouth - 100 Idioms, their Meanings and Origins.*

I have a popular blog which regularly attracts over 100,000 readers with history, culture and travel related posts along with my own aimless musings and through all of this have fleeting appearances on various BBC radio stations and international television networks.

Most of my time since 2013 has been spent creating, running and expanding Ye Olde England Tours. I was the first to offer private and totally bespoke door-to-door tours in London. 99% of them were original when I created them, it's easy to check that out too. I've never wanted a Blue Badge, I have multiple degrees in history and love showing people around as if they were family. Many of my tourists comment that they are glad they are on our tours and not with those self-important staid blue badge guides who are very particular over how long their tours last and where and what they will cover. Indeed during the Coronavirus I've been receiving lots of food parcels and donations from around the world from my new family!

These days there are various people who have tried to copy my ideas but they can't replicate the passion, good humour and knowledge or the dedication.... I've worked every single day from autumn 2013 to March 2020. Ye Olde England Tours has hundreds of 5-star reviews on all the big and little sites. Bizarrely, I'm not at all money orientated which is maybe why I've become successful and I've worked with the Commonwealth War Graves on war related projects, BBC Comic Relief with our original and much imitated Sherlock Tour as well as television producers, celebrities, international and national leaders and best of all the general public from 0-94 years of age so far. Check out our website at www.yeoldeenglandtours.co.uk or visit our listings on Trip Advisor, Viator, Get Your Guide, Musement, Expedia and others.

Ye Olde England Tours and our Secret, Sacred Gardens of London Tour.

If you enjoyed this book you might like to come on our Secret, Sacred Gardens of London Tour. It has been rated by Tripadvisor as being the number one off-beat and local experience in the whole of London! We don't visit all the gardens mentioned in this book but most of what I think is the best and you'll get to see parts of London that even Londoners know next to nothing about as well as learning 2,000 years of history and the odd funny tale too. We might not even see a single tourist! All our walking tours naturally practise social distancing but none more so than our Secret, Sacred Gardens of London Tour.

Printed in Great Britain
by Amazon

17371764R00217